Walk East Until I Die

Mike Pinnock, a retired engineer, began walking long distance paths in 1982 and has completed 16 in the UK. His lone trek to Istanbul continues each year; in April 2017, at the age of 71, he reached Bonn in Germany.

He lives with his partner Polly in both Spain and the UK. This is his second book.

Cover photograph – Dursey Island, County Cork – looking towards cable car and the mainland.

Walk East Until I Die

A Trek through Irish History and Beyond

Mike Pinnock

Published in 2018 by Taberno publications

© Mike Pinnock 2018

ISBN 978-1-9998385-0-8

Designed by John Hawkins, www.jhbd.co.uk

Printed in Great Britian by Clays Ltd, St Ives Plc

ACKNOWLEDGEMENTS

I would like to thank my partner Polly for her
help and support and for Helen Baggott for
her thorough proof reading. I am also indebted
to, and would like to thank: Éamon Browne of
Killarney library, Patsy Fitzgerald of the Carrick-
on-Suir Heritage Centre, David Flynn and Owen
Doyle of the Graiguenamanagh Historical Society
and author Jim Rees.

Contents

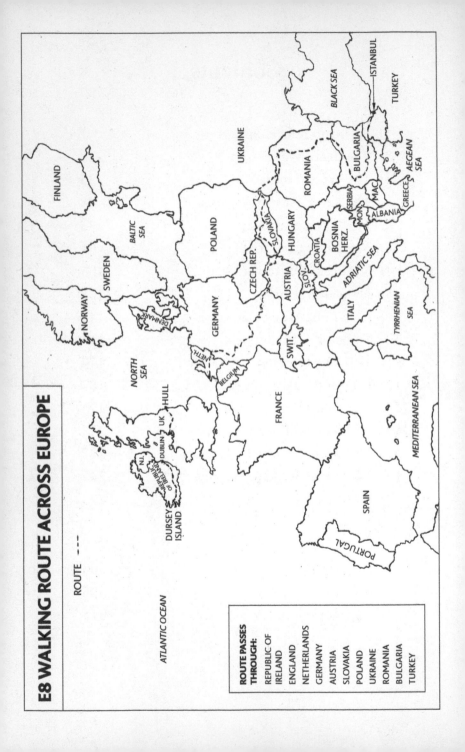

E8 WALKING ROUTE ACROSS EUROPE

ROUTE - - -

ROUTE PASSES THROUGH:
REPUBLIC OF IRELAND
ENGLAND
NETHERLANDS
GERMANY
AUSTRIA
SLOVAKIA
POLAND
UKRAINE
ROMANIA
BULGARIA
TURKEY

One

A Dream not yet Spiked

Two years ago – before all this started
I woke up from this really strange dream about Spike Milligan walking backwards for Christmas across the Irish Sea. What the hell could that possibly mean? I switched on the bedside light and scribbled on a Post-it note so that I stood a chance of getting back to sleep. But I knew it wouldn't happen. It was four o'clock in the morning and this stupid, comic 1956 UK hit by the Goons just kept churning around and around in my brain. So I gave up, got up and tapped into the computer *I'm walking Backwards for Christmas*.

It turns out that it's a sad song of unrequited love that the singer has for an Irish colleen. He dreams he is comforted by an angel and she suggests to him that the only way he can possibly prove his love is to perform the miracle of walking on water; across the Irish Sea no less. And to make it even more impossible it has to be backwards.

So I interpreted *my* dream experience like this: Here I was at the age of 67 with, I felt, something still to prove to the world – and, more to the point, to myself. I'd read somewhere that if you get less than six hours sleep a night there's a 12% greater chance of dying prematurely. My usual was four hours and the average life expectancy for a man in the UK is around 77.6 years, which meant I probably didn't have much time left.

But what could I do? Everything of significance had already been done it seemed, and even the downright obscure stuff had been done and taken to the limit. *The Guinness Book of Records* is full of the sort of thing I wasn't about to attempt. You wouldn't catch me being rolled in a barrel or fired from a cannon – not that I'm the right calibre. And I didn't have the faintest inclination to practice such potty pursuits as throwing gum boots, hurling haggis or spitting tobacco over ridiculously long lengths. There wasn't even much hope of becoming the world's oldest bridegroom – I'd have to survive to the age of 121. To make any sort of an impression upon the world at my age it seems I'd have to do something as impossible as walking backwards across the Irish Sea with Spike.

Meriden, England – May 2013

From the Queen's Head pub the Way goes up steps, crosses a main road, passes through a gate and heads uphill. Many spirits had passed this way; Thomas Pennant, a Welsh-born travel writer was drawn through the sloughs here by horses in 1780 on his way from Chester to London and commented on the apt derivation of the 16th century name given to the place: Myre-den meaning dirt-bottom. Today it claims to be the centre of England and is known as Meriden; although the true geographical centre of the country is actually a disused airfield 11 miles away.

The going is grassy clay. The ascent draws beads of perspiration this bright May morning; the start of my fourth day of walking. The spirits are with me on this modest climb, as they are everywhere in this world; spirits from 800 years before Pennant's arrival in these parts. The original settlement here was known as Alspath, described in the Domesday Book of 1086. It's claimed that Lady Godiva of Coventry nakedness-horseback fame founded the originally thatched Norman church of St Laurence in 1147.

There are muddy gateways but no stiles as I climb. A rabbit darts from trees and scampers away. The field track is part of the Heart of England Way that runs for 100 miles south from Cannock Chase in Staffordshire to Bourton-on-the-Water in the Cotswolds. Some inquisitive cows follow me up towards St Laurence churchyard. The ground is smothered in bluebells at this time of the year and the more recent graves are tidy and decorated with flowers. I leave the churchyard through another gate and by a stone wall, read a plaque giving details of the Way and some information about Meriden. The Way is part of a much longer European route: the E2. Had anybody walked its entire length? Perhaps I could after all do what has never been done?

I check on the Internet; there are 11 European walking routes, with a twelfth planned. It's proposed that the E2 will run from Galway in Ireland to Nice in France, but the Galway section, where I think of starting, doesn't yet exist and on the website it's suggested there's some doubt that it will *ever* open. In practice it currently starts in Carlisle, which from a recent survey is supposed to be Europe's most promiscuous city. But for me, despite this accolade, it's an uninspiring start point – sorry, Carlislians.

Of the 10 remaining routes, the one that grabs me most is the E8. Firstly it begins in Ireland, a country with which I've always felt a close affinity, even though, apart from my Christian name (and I've had the Michael taken out of me a lot in my lifetime) there are no associations or family ties. I was, however, sent to a Catholic infant school, not because my family were Catholic, but simply because it was the closest school to where we lived. I was bullied there by a boy called Duffy; undoubtedly of Irish extract and the inventor, I thought then, of the phrase 'to be duffed up'.

The E8's second attraction is that it passes (or will eventually pass) through 11countries, six of which I've not yet visited. Thirdly, my dad had been posted to Turkey during the Chanak crisis of 1922 at the age of 18. I still have some postcards that he bought there – views of Istanbul (then Constantinople), where it's proposed the E8 will finish. I'd like to take these with me to see how the modern city has changed. It'd be a fitting end to the achievement – if I make it.

The E8 starts (or finishes) at Dursey Head on Dursey Island, facing the Atlantic, in the south-west corner of the Republic of Ireland. It has been largely generated by linking a series of previously defined long-distance trails. It runs through England, Holland, Germany, Austria, Slovakia, Poland, Ukraine, Rumania, and Bulgaria to Turkey. Well, that's not quite true, it will do someday, but for now the first 4,131 kilometres are identified and, hopefully, waymarked as far as the Beskid Pass at the Ukraine border. Except for 400km through Bulgaria, the route through the latter four countries has yet to be created. If I can walk as far as the Beskid pass, I reason that by the time I reach there the remaining sections will probably be open.

Would I be the first to do this? Maybe not, but I reckon I'd be the oldest.

Others who'd made similar treks had camped rough, with rucksacks crammed with everything they might need; bloody heavy loads. I'd done that in the past and got the tee shirt – although I since can't remember where I left it. An alternative is to stay in bed and breakfasts or hotels, but it's a relatively expensive way to travel.

Then I remember that I own a camper van and push-bike. The camper is a 19-year-old Peugeot Talbot Compass Drifter bought six years ago and little used since except for one significant continental trip and as a temporary residence whilst moving house. The bike was a very cheap purchase and so has little sophistication; only half the gears currently work, the chain frequently comes off for no apparent reason and the brakes sometimes bind up. But I can't afford (or in truth am perhaps too parsimonious) to buy a new one – it'll have to do.

My plan evolves: it's to deliver the bike to the end of each daily leg, drive the camper to the start of that leg, walk the walk, then cycle back to collect the camper. Alternatively I can first do the bike ride to the start of each leg. I'll use campsites where I can replenish my water, shower and do my washing, but otherwise the idea is to wild-camp. The only problem I can foresee is parking the six-metre-long camper close to the E8 path.

So how long will it take me to complete the walk? A single trip would be very complicated, and anyway there are too many other things going on in my life. I reckon I could average 25km a day comfortably and therefore should be able to do the whole 4,131km in 165 days. At that rate it would take me 12 years to complete the walk and if I make it to Istanbul I'll be an ancient 80-year-old. But then I realise that the as yet undefined sections of the route through Ukraine, Romania, Bulgaria and Turkey have not been included in this figure. So this means the final distance is likely to be at least 6,000km – and I'll more likely be aged 84 *if*, or (very optimistically) *when*, I reach Istanbul.

My aging body will undoubtedly be a factor as to whether I make it – even If I don't manage to die beforehand. But I think that this crazy thing I'm about to embark upon will become my *raison d'être* that might just keep me going to reach that age.

I decide to use a rationale of self-imposed rules: I will always start from exactly the same point on the path the next day as I finish the previous day - this will be my first rule. My second rule is to walk every step of the way, even where there is no defined route. Thirdly I determine that if by accident I miss a sign, there is no point in backtracking westward in order to regain the designated easterly trail.

So I've made some basic decisions. What's left is to purchase a touring map of Southern Ireland, gather information from the Internet, buy *The Irish Coast to Coast Walk* by Paddy Dillon together with the Discovery series of maps he recommends and then book a ferry from Holyhead to Dublin.

But as well as the challenge of the walk, I want to learn something about the history of the countries I'm walking through. First up is the adventure of Ireland.

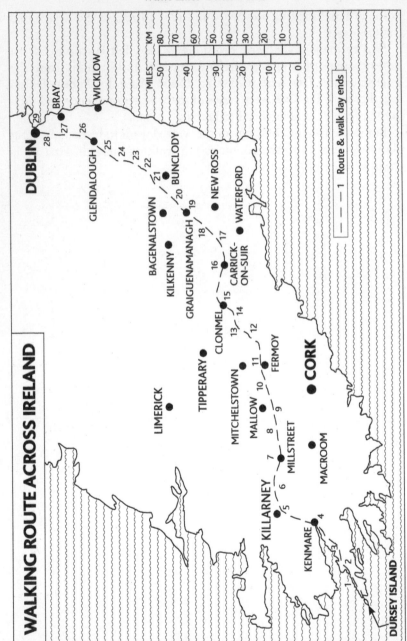

Two
The Beara Way

'Summer of youth in which we have been
I spent with its autumn;
winter of age which overwhelms everyone,
its first months have come to me.'
From: *The Lament of the Old Woman of Beare* – Anonymous

Sunday 16th June 2013 – Dursey Island to Allihies
I should have known what to expect. The previous day, having not
understood that the most direct route from Killarney to Kenmare
is not always the best, I'd driven the camper precariously around
the lane-width bends of the N71 coast road, negotiated with some
difficulty tourist-packed coaches coming in the opposite direction
and steered around overhanging cliff faces. I should have taken (as
directed by signposts that I ignored as being illogical) the less direct
but less bendy N22.

The R571 from Kenmare to Dursey, located at the western end of
the Beara peninsula, snakes just like the N71 around the coastline, its
width reduces and the severity of its bends increases the closer I get to
Dursey. A hare darts in front of the camper van, out for his very early
morning stroll and forage. It causes me to brake sharply before I then
chase him for some distance along the road. Luckily he's all I come
across as I sound the horn nervously at every blind bend.

The Beara peninsula in Irish folklore received its name from Beara,
daughter of the King of Castille whom Owen Mór, the King of
Ireland had married after sailing to Spain following a battle he'd
lost. On his return he's said to have landed on what is now Bere
Island, taken his wife to the highest hill, looked out across the water
and named the whole peninsula within his view 'Beara'.

Myths and legends mingle and crossover to folklore in Ireland.
The island was first inhabited around 6000 BC and its history

until the 11th century, drawn from pagan myths, was compiled by an anonymous scholar and recorded in *The Book of Invasions* or *Lebor Gabála Érenn*. It's purported to be a true record of the successive invasions and settlement of the Celtic people in Ireland up to that time.

The Firbolgs were one of the earliest of such settlers who were then defeated in battle by the peoples of the Goddess Danu (Tuatha De Danann) who, it's claimed, arrived in ships on the coast of what's now Connemara. Not having come across any bridges yet, they apparently burnt their ships instead so that they wouldn't be tempted to return home in them – foolish perhaps, or maybe they were just so taken by the beauty of the landscape. Tuatha De Danann, mythology has it, were in turn finally defeated by the Milesians who probably sailed from Galicia in Spain and landed in County Kerry; they were the first Celts to arrive in Ireland. It's said that it was the wife of one of the defeated kings of the Tuatha De Danann – Eriu – who caused the island to be named Eire after her.

I of course learn all this stuff later, but now my camper is perched in a small parking area high above Ballydonegan just west of Allihies. I stuff my walking gear and lunch into a rucksack, don a cycle helmet, fluorescent jacket and bike clip, sling the rucksack on my back and cycle off; it's a procedure I'll soon repeat many times.

On the way to the cable car that straddles Dursey Sound it begins to spatter with rain. Then whilst I bag the cycling gear, put on my walking boots and lock my bike to a noticeboard, a few black clouds begin to drift in ominously below the blanket of white. A quote I'd read from *The Irish Times* crosses my mind: 'There will be early morning showers becoming heavier and more persistent as the day progresses. This is now the twenty-second consecutive day of this forecast.' The first part of this erstwhile forecast looks likely to become true for today and I'm just praying that this isn't the start of another 22 such days. The rain is accompanied by a gathering wind and I fret that the cable car might not be running. At the ticket office I disclose my scepticism to the man in the kiosk.

'No problem,' he says.

'But will I get back?' I ask. He assures me with a reassuring smile (or is it a mischievous grin?) that all will be well.

A 4x4 had passed me on the road to the cable car and a middle-aged German couple are preparing to go over too, so I wait for them. It's a silent journey across because the man speaks no English, the lady just a few words, and I have no German. But anyway we're all too tense to converse, sitting rigid still and making sure we stay well away from the dubiously secure sliding door that gave us access to this tiny cab.

The cable car is Ireland's solitary one and is in fact the only one in Europe that goes over sea water; it came into operation in 1969, before which the island would very often be cut off from the mainland for weeks on end by gale force winds. It looks likely to me that one such wind is again on its way; the cabin sways and creaks nervously which makes *me* (especially as I'm a retired engineer) also very nervous, an emotion which heightens as the car bumps noisily over the central support structure. But we make it across.

On the island the drizzly rain becomes heavier and I put on waterproofs which, as *The Irish Times* forecast predicted, will remain on for the rest of the day.

To begin the trek east to Istanbul I have first to walk west to Dursey Head 6.5km away. The choice is to use the southern boreen or the northern track that climbs to the central spine of the island. I decide to do the climb first and take the boreen back. I steam up and, looking back down after five minutes, see that the German couple are sheltering behind the cable-car building, perhaps thinking about getting back to the mainland before the strengthening winds trap them on the island. Oh shit! I suddenly realise I'll be the only non-islander here – and together with the residents there will be all of 11 of us on the island.

The track drops down then climbs again to the Martello signal tower at which point I think I'm not too far from the start point of the walk proper at the head. I can see the Calf Rock a distance off alone in the gunmetal sea; a dark triangular shape surrounded by foaming white surf, a redundant old lighthouse at its summit pointing like an index finger skyward.

I'm wrong in my assessment; it's much further than I think to Dursey Head; the track rises and falls yet again before I reach a rectangular stone ruin perched on the end of the land (which I'm later told was once a coastguard station). I frighten a family of sheep who've made the station their home, then skirt around the ruin to face the Atlantic and the Calf Rock. Here I sit on my rucksack, so as not to get a wet bum, looking down on the angry, white-horse sea, and eat my sandwiches. It's 12.30 and after a very quick lunch I'm about to set out for Istanbul.

As I take my first few steps to the east, very conscious these first steps are a momentous moment, I say aloud to myself in the wind:

'Here I go then to Istanbul.'

The ram of the family of sheep, a majestic creature with amazing curled horns, poses for me in a stance of defiance on the broken-down wall of the ruin. I'm invading his home and maybe he thinks I'm also threatening his family. I pull out the camera to try and capture him but he probably thinks I'm about to shoot him and rapidly retreats within the walls of the ruin where the rest of his family, a ewe and two lambs, are already hiding. I look down, pick up a tuft of wool which I hope is from him and stuff it into the side pocket of the rucksack, deciding then to carry it with me for good luck every step of the way to Istanbul – if of course I eventually make it.

After I've progressed the first 500 metres east, up and down two hills in a gale force wind that almost takes me off my feet, I realise I'm missing something. I'd taken out my denture to eat lunch and suddenly realise I've left the thing on the ground somewhere high above the sea at the back of the ruin. This is my second senior moment in two days; the first was hearing the microwave crash to the floor of the camper as it flew off a shelf because I'd driven away up a hill and forgotten to secure it. But this latest lapse has potentially far more serious repercussions; without the denture, and thus my false front tooth, I look either comical or frightening dependent upon how you might feel at the time. There's no way I'm going to walk back to the cable car without it, let alone across Ireland.

So now in a crazy panic I throw off the rucksack and dash back 500 metres west (sadly away from Istanbul), up and down two hills again and in a gale force wind that almost takes me off my feet. Will the denture be there or has the defiant ram trampled it into the ground or worse, scuffed it down the cliffs into the Atlantic Ocean? I scoot around the back of the ruin and frantically scour the grass where I thought I'd sat. Where the hell is the thing? All kinds of wild contingency plans flash through my brain – where the hell is it? Shit

16

where is it? There it is! But it wasn't where I'd expected it to be. No matter. I say a little prayer of thanks to the tooth fairy.

'Mr Coastguard ram' emerges again before I set off for a second time towards Istanbul, weighing me up with his marble-crazed eyes, tantalisingly posing on the walls of his ruin. I try to snap him but again he darts off, leaving only his rear end to become digitised.

I complete the Dursey loop by way of the boreen, passing Ballynacallagh and the foundation remains of the castle that was once the small garrison of Donal Cam O'Sullivan Beare, head of the O'Sullivan clan whose name originated from the Celtic King Milesius of Spain. The castle was destroyed by English soldiers led by John Bostock in December 1602. Philip O'Sullivan claimed that the soldiers massacred 300 Catholic Irish, mainly old men, women and children, throwing them onto the rocks below. They were the members of the O'Sullivan clan who'd been put there for safekeeping whilst the men were off fighting the English. Those men left by O'Sullivan to guard the innocents who survived the attack were taken 20km east to Castletownbere and hanged.

I don't dally at the castle site because I'm worried the increasing high winds will soon stop the cable car operation and I'll be trapped on the island (perhaps for days). Back at the cable car station I anxiously ask a lady sitting in a car if it's still running:

'It's on its way,' she says, and so it is. It turns out the lady is the owner of a house I'd just passed that had a sign up offering complimentary teas. It seems she's waiting to collect some visitors to escort there. Maybe she's hoping the wind speed will increase to storm or hurricane and they'll be lucratively trapped there for days.

I'm alone in the cabin on the return trip and only then do I spot a notice declaring that in just over a week's time the cable car will be out of operation for mechanical, structural and operational inspection. Now I feel even more nervous than I had on the outward journey. Less than 18 months ago Cork County Council had banned the carrying of cows, calves and sheep in the cabin due to concerns about overloading. The practice had been undertaken for many years by those farming on the island and it was a decision that greatly upset them.

Back on the mainland, the walk along the Beara Way towards Allihies is strenuous, involving a scramble – climbing in places, particularly in the ascent from the cable car. It takes me about three hours, during which time it rains and blows continuously to varying degrees – not quite hurricane force, but close.

At Ballydonegan beach near Allihies I decide to stop for the day; a rusty steel pole sunk into the sand between tufts of marram grass will be a good locking point for my bike before I start tomorrow morning's walk. Also, it's a convenient point from which to walk inland and pick up the R575 back to the camper.

In the camper I strip off wet clothes, drape them out to dry, stuff the walking boots with newspaper and sort out clothes for the evening. Then I phone my partner Polly. We keep in touch daily, phoning on alternative nights so that she at least knows where I am. My daughter Susie also has my daily planned schedule and Hope, my eldest granddaughter is tracking my progress on a map of Ireland that Susie has pinned on their noticeboard.

Because I'm wild-camping that night I decide to splash out on a meal. Luckily I choose the famous O'Neill's bar in Allihies. It's a Sunday night and there's Irish music and the place is packed. A group plays on concertina, guitar, bodhrán, fiddle, whistle, mandolin and accordion. It's wonderful. It rounds off not a bad day at all – apart from the weather of course.

Monday 17th June – Allihies to Eyeries

I'm wild-camping in what passes for a lay-by (it's actually just a slightly wider piece of road) on the R571. Very few cars pass, so I'm hopeful of a good night's sleep. But there are always concerns about wild-camping because of the horror stories circulated amongst motor-homers about break-ins and attacks and, having not camped in Ireland before, I'm not sure what to expect, especially given Anglo-Irish history and my prominent GB sticker.

At around midnight I'm sitting in the cab of the van when a car pulls over and stops on the other side of the road. It stays for about 15 minutes with its indicator flashing. Is someone planning to break into the van, thinking I'm asleep? I still feel uneasy even when it leaves after half an hour. So the night is one of fitful sleep with a knife close by my side and at six the next morning I'm up like a shot when Irish voices sound outside. Later I reflect on both situations and dispel my paranoia with some logic; the motorist had probably stopped to take a phone call and the voices were probably two touring cyclists chatting as they rode past.

As planned, I drive to Eyeries and park. Then I discover that the previous day I must have had a third senior moment; when I'd unlocked the bike from the noticeboard at the cable car I'd apparently left its cable-lock on the ground – because I don't have it now. I try to buy one at O'Sullivan's food store; they sell just about everything else, including a good packed lunch, but not a suitable bike-lock. Then I remember I'd damaged the roof-ladder of the camper backing into a wall last year and had secured it with a lock and chain. So now I purloin this for another use and rope up the ladder.

The 11-mile bike ride back to the beach at Ballydonegan is tough and I soon realise why a cycle is sometimes called a pushbike; there is a lot of pushing up the hills, of which there are too many, especially as I'm encumbered by a heavy rucksack crammed with walking boots, other clobber and packed lunch.

I chain my bike to the rusty steel pole and follow the fingerposts (each carved with a stooped yellow man with his rucksack and cane) that eventually head past some caravans and out to Allihies Point. The path first skirts the cliffs on a terrace, then turns inland and backtracks on the R575 a little way towards Allihies before I begin a steep and craggy climb up towards the abandoned 19th century copper mine high above the village. I somehow loose the signs after a scramble, with two possible ways ahead. If in doubt it always seems best to choose the route that continues the climb and it pays off now as I reach a tarn from where I catch sight of the chimney of the mine's engine house. Eventually I make it up to a stoned miners' track and head off towards Eyeries.

The most challenging part of the day's walk is over as I stay on the track, and then a footpath high above Coulagh Bay for most of the remaining 10-mile walk. The coastal views are stunning and it's a beautiful day. Everything is perfect – except for my feet. Yesterday they got wet and today there are blisters which are still painful, even though they are coddled now in two pairs of dry socks. At around 5.30pm O'Sullivan's food store again reappears as I emerge hobbling out onto the main street of Eyeries.

The camper is parked almost outside of O'Shea's pub and as I take off my walking gear I see a man and a pint at a table outside drinking in the last of the day's sun – as well as the pint. It seems like a good idea, and so I join him. His name is Richard. He's lived around these parts all his life and was for years a fisherman until the European Union (EU) regulations made life too complicated.

'It was the licences and paperwork that finished me,' he complains.

He explains that in the 1980s there were only five EU fishing regulations, but in the 1990s a further 10 were added and by the end of 2012 there were 89, designed to protect fish stocks and ensure that catches are shared fairly between member states – still, I can see where he was. Richard is my junior by five years, but looks much younger than his years. He has views on most subjects and expresses them unreservedly. He rues the Dublin government's decisions that got the country into huge debt, as he sees it, with Germany. Not realising the potential ferocity of the 'Celtic Tiger', the Germans set Irish interest rates too low.

'I don't like the politics,' Richard says. He reckons that the UK is still very strong – a view perhaps currently not shared by many of its inhabitants – and adds that although Britain and Ireland have had their differences in the past, he feels that the bonds between the two are still very close. I'm cheered by this and his empathy touches me. We drain our glasses and he shakes my hand warmly. I hope Richard's reconciliatory views are ubiquitous within the land but I'm still surprised, given the interwoven history of our two lands that began way back in the early 12th century with the arrival of the Normans.

At that time the present counties of Kerry and Cork through which I'm now walking were still within the Kingdom of Munster. This remained so until 1118, when the Treaty of Glanmire split Munster into the kingdoms of Thomod in the north and Desmond in the south.

According to Mogeoghagan's book (a translation from a lost Irish chronicle) the Normans arrived following a dispute between Tiernan O'Rourke, the King of Breifne and Dairmait the King of Leinster over the affections of a lady. This caused the latter to be exiled to France where (perhaps unfortunately for Ireland), he met King Henry II of England and asked for his help. This request resulted in Anglo-Norman and Flemish mercenaries coming over to Ireland to aid Dairmait regain Leinster.

A notable character amongst these was the Earl of Stiguil, nicknamed Strongbow, of Saxon descent (who knew nothing at that time about apples and the production of a certain drink). Worried that Strongbow's rising influence in Ireland would encourage him to attack England, Henry decided, in 1171, to attack first, and landed a large force in Ireland, encouraged as he was by the Pope's desire to reinforce papal authority over the Irish Church.

Henry's Normans resided in much of the land, including the northern part of the Kingdom of Desmond in the south-west. Desmond was then effectively split following the Battle of Caisglin in 1261 near Kenmare, when the Norman FitzGeralds were prevented from encroaching further south by the combined forces of three Gaelic clans. The Fitzgeralds were thereafter confined to north County Kerry whilst the lands of south County Kerry and west County Cork were retained by the Gaelic clans. Principle amongst Gaelic clans was the MacCarthy and O'Sullivan clans, the latter of which held large areas of land in south County Kerry, west County Cork and the Beara Peninsula.

Heading back west down the Peninsula I give a toot and wave to Richard as I drive past. Back at Ballydonegan beach, I rescue the bike from the rusty steel pole and eat out again at O'Neill's bar in Allihies. No music tonight, but instead the biggest plate of fish and chips I've ever been presented with. There are *so* many chips that for the first time ever I have to leave some.

A beautiful sunset, the sun sinking slowly below some cottages and caravans across the bay from where I'm wild-camping, leaves me with a peaceful feeling – and I have tonight an undisturbed sleep with the phone alarm set for 6am.

Tuesday 18th June – Eyeries to Lauragh

Driving by 7am, I'm back along that crazy, lane-width, winding road before there's a chance of anything emerging abruptly in the opposite direction. I drive through Eyeries. Lauragh is over 13 miles away by road, but it's a 16½-mile walk. I'm not feeling confident that I can make it in a day considering what I know to be a long hilly pre-walk

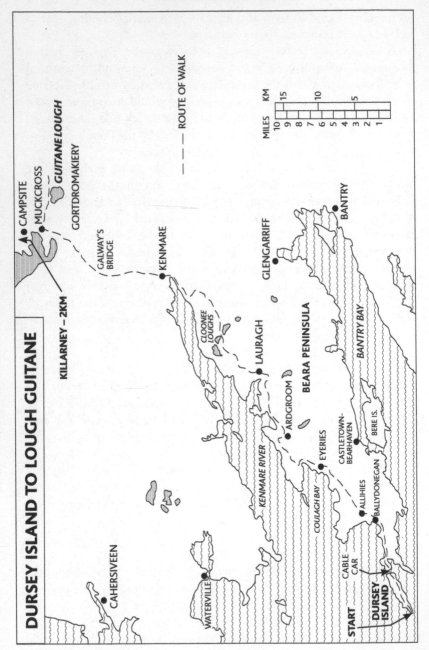

DURSEY ISLAND TO LOUGH GUITANE

KILLARNEY – 2KM

CAMPSITE
MUCKCROSS
GUITANE LOUGH
GORTDROMAKIERY
GALWAY'S BRIDGE
KENMARE
CLOONEE LOUGHS
LAURAGH
ARDGROOM
BEARA PENINSULA
GLENGARRIFF
BANTRY
EYERIES
CASTLETOWN-BEARHAVEN
KENMARE RIVER
BERE IS.
BANTRY BAY
COULAGH BAY
ALLIHIES
BALLYDONEGAN
CABLE CAR
START
DURSEY ISLAND
WATERVILLE
CAHERSIVEEN

– – – – ROUTE OF WALK

MILES | KM
10 9 8 7 6 5 4 3 2 1 | 15 10 5

bike ride, so to hedge my bets I decide to park up around halfway at Ardgroom. It's still a hard ride back to Eyeries.

Chaining the bike to a gate opposite O'Sullivan's food store I repeat yesterday's purchase of a packed lunch and start the walk. Mornings are for me the best. My feet got wet again yesterday but I treated them last night and am wearing two pairs of dry socks this morning, so they feel good. There's also no ache yet from my right shoulder, which came on late in the walk yesterday, even though I tried many adjustments of the rucksack straps but eventually walked with one hand behind my back to take the weight. This must be just old age because I've carried much heavier packs in the past.

I obviously miss some signposts because after half an hour I'm still road-walking when, according to the Discovery map, the Beara Way skirts the coastline on a footpath. The weather is again grand so it doesn't seem to matter much. But, when I catch sight of a fingerpost I reckon a little time can be afforded and I can't resist walking back west to see what's been missed. (I don't really consider this to be breaking my rule three of not backtracking because, well, I only take a peek at the sea and the path that snakes interestingly around the jagged coast.) Continuing back east, I pick up the minor road again on which the route stays for most of the way to Ardgroom. There's almost no traffic and only a farmer with three dogs at his heels and some photogenic donkeys punctuate the walk. Occasionally there are glimpses of the sea and the mountainous Iveragh Peninsula across the water where Irish is still the predominant language. There's a rocky descent into Ardgroom which I make in good time by 1.30pm.

I decide to press on with the second leg of the walk. I drive back to Eyeries, strap the bike onto the camper and motor through Ardgroom to Lauragh from where I bike back to Ardgroom, again finding a friendly locking post. I'm walking again by 3pm.

The terrain soon becomes rutted, boggy moorland with no discernible path. There's some difficulty picking out the fingerposts and sometimes even the green and yellow metal ladder stiles. It's impossible to keep dry feet, even though I try to stick to the tussock highs.

Then suddenly I stumble and am in the bog with my lower right leg at a different angle to my upper leg – twisted at the knee, with an accompanying intense pain. I'm frightened to move in case I can't. I'm in the middle of nowhere, have seen nobody since leaving

Ardgroom and have only a mobile phone (which probably won't get a signal here) as a means of communication.

All sorts of things have been found in Irish peat bogs many years later: swords, butter in oak barrels, skulls with holes drilled in them, bodies (usually murdered) – and now a lone walker stranded with a fractured patellar will be added to the list. These fears flash through my brain, but after a minute I haul myself up and try a test step; it seems I may just have twisted something, but the pain from my knee overrides the pain from the blisters and of the aching right shoulder. I'm in a sorry state as I hobble out onto the R571 road.

I walk for a while easterly on this same road that an hour or so ago I'd struggled along westerly on the bike. I pass a house where a man engages me in questioning conversation and tells me that I'll soon be turning off the road to wilder parts that border Drung Hill. As I climb the track ahead a very large backpack, with a pair of legs in rolled up trousers protruding below it, is creeping upwards. The legs I soon discover belong to Sebastian, a young bearded Frenchman from Brittany who also sports a banded ponytail. We get into conversation as we plod along together. I ask him about his walk.

'I have everything I need,' he says. He is indeed carrying everything he needs for sleeping and eating on the trail; he tells me in good English that he's been camping in the hills and that he's walked from Cork. I don't ask, but deduce he's followed the coast west via Skibbereen and Bantry, before picking up the Beara Way at Glengarriff. He mentions Castletownbere which I'd seen signposted, so I assume that he's done the south coast of the Beara Peninsula down to Dursey Island then like me has walked east following the northern coastline. I am, he says, the first walker he's seen since leaving Cork. He's on his way to Dingle where he has some friends, then plans to get back to Cork where he has some house-building work lined up for July.

At a stream Sebastian asks me if I can pull a water bottle from a side pocket of his rucksack to save him taking it off. He fills the bottle and I'm concerned about bacteria as he uses no purification tablets.

'Always I check there are no houses higher up,' he says. He has had no health problems up to now he tells me.

We walk together across deserted moorland. He takes it very slow because of his load, measuring each stride – but with my aches and pains I don't mind this pace. In places planks have been placed across the bog land and here Sebastian takes it even more cautiously.

'One thing I have learnt in Ireland is that you cannot keep dry feet,' he says, confirming my thoughts as I slip a boot into the bog.

After a while I check our progress; we have averaged only one mile an hour for the past two hours; the day is wearing on and I'm getting worried that it'll be very late by the time I reach Lauragh, so when Sebastian takes another rest break I explain my concern. He understands of course, and I walk on alone.

I spot a deer that on seeing me, leaps over a fence and peers out cautiously from between bushes. Most creatures are afraid of humans it seems; something inborn maybe from centuries of being shot at or otherwise enslaved. Lambs, I'd noticed today, always ran to their mothers to suckle with waggling tails, frightened for sure, as I approached.

The path leaves the moorland and zigzags down through a spinney to reach a lane and cross the Croinseach River. The 17th century priest and poet Geoffrey Keating recorded in his *History of Ireland* that Croinseach was the daughter of Aeodh Fionn, King of Osruighe who lived around AD 600.

At about that time a mission was sent to Anglo-Saxon Britain by Pope Gregory the Great of Rome to convert them from their Germanic paganism to Christianity. The Irish, according to Keating, had already been converted 169 years before this by the 61-year-old St Patrick, who'd been sent by Pope Coelestinus. Patrick was actually the Pope's substitute choice; his first being Paladius who arrived one year before Patrick and landed in Leinster. Here Paladius blessed three churches, but was then banished to Scotland by Nathi, the son of the lord of Leinster, where he promptly died. Nathi of course never realised what he was to bestow upon posterity; had Paladius been left alone to continue his mission he would have died in Ireland, which would have meant that anyone with the remotest of Irish connections all over the world would not be getting blown away on the 17th March and wearing those stupid green hats, but would instead be celebrating St Paladius's Day on whatever date he would eventually have snuffed it. Instead there is of course St Patrick's Day.

St Patrick was an interesting character. He was born in Britain and was captured by a group of Irish pirates at the age of 16; he was then taken to Ireland where he worked as a slave shepherd. Being with the sheep all day afforded him some time to pray, which assisted in his conversion to Christianity. Then, after escaping back to Britain, he again returned to Ireland, this time by choice. Legend has it that he conveyed the concept of the Holy Trinity by showing the Irish the shamrock. He's also supposed to have banished snakes from the land by driving them into the sea – although Ireland had always been a snake free country anyway. The snake story is part of Irish folklore which includes historically based legends as well as fairy tales that together make up Irish culture. The diminutive mischief-making leprechaun is the subject of such fairy tales – and I reckon it was he who made up the snake story.

The Irish escaped occupation by the Romans, so when St Patrick converted the Irish Celts to Christianity they, unlike the English, had seen no other recent invaders. This was soon to change. In the *Chronicle of Ireland*, written between 432 and 911, are records of the Viking invaders who *did* make it to Ireland. Raids were made from 795 to 914. They targeted monasteries, much to the distress of the monks. There was for instance a Viking settlement in Cork – and the Vikings frequently interbred with the natives, penetrated (so to speak), deep into the Kingdom of Munster. They were sometimes even converted to St Patrick's Christianity.

I photograph the placid turquoise Croanshagh River with its mountainous backdrop and continue along the Beara Way, turning left onto another lane that heads on into Lauragh where I've parked. It's 6pm.

It takes me another hour to collect my bike and get to the campsite. The lady tries to charge me six euros more for the same pitch than she did three days ago! We compromise on three.

'If you park on the grass you'll be staying there,' she reminds me helpfully.

Wednesday 19th June – Lauragh to Kenmare
I'm in Kenmare before 9am. There's absolutely nowhere to park the camper; the car park that I'd researched on the Internet is fitted with

height restricting barriers. I'm forced to drive on out of town and park at a shopping complex. It means that today I'll have to make an even longer bike ride of about 16 miles, with a walk to follow of the same distance.

The ride is tougher than I envisage, and again there's a lot of pushing and sweating. It feels like it's all uphill until I round Knockatee Mountain, but then the last two miles are a wonderful freewheel cruise down into Lauragh.

I chain the bike to some railings by a closed-up, derelict pub near Lauragh Bridge. Then I take a few steps back to where I turned off yesterday, – so that every step of the Way is covered. It's 10.45 and already I feel knackered, but it's a beautiful clear day with little wind and I'm wearing shorts for the first time.

After three quarters of an hour of walking I catch sight of Sebastian emerging from some bushes onto the track– he's only just broken camp. We walk together initially along lanes, and then at a house I wait whilst he asks for his water bottle to be filled. He somehow sweet-talks his way inside and is gone for a while. I think that maybe he's been cheeky enough to ask for a bath, which he's told me he's sometimes done, but after about 10 minutes he returns and apologises. It seems that he'd got into a long conversation which may well have involved the request for a bath, as he says:

'They told me there is a lough a little further on where I might bathe.'

I check the map – it's about a two-mile walk.

'It'll be just about right to stop for lunch too,' I say.

Sebastian stops to admire an oak tree. My knowledge of trees is abysmal, so I'm impressed that not only does he recognise it, but knows its name in English. He also tells me that he's very interested in early Celtic history as Brittany and Ireland are both of Celtic origin. He says that we're currently walking the route taken in 1602 by Donal Cam O'Sullivan Beare head of the O'Sullivan clan. I remembered then that I'd come across the remains of his clan's castle on Dursey Island.

The O'Sullivan clan held land in the area all through the Norman occupation, but at Bosworth Field, Leicestershire in 1485 the Norman King Richard III was defeated by Henry, who became King

Henry VII of England, heralding the rule of the Tudors who were soon to change things.

In 1509 Henry's son Henry came to the throne and became the eighth Henry to rule England. Things were pretty uneventful early on. Oh! Apart from a couple of small matters like the invasion of France and Henry having a bit of an affair with his wife's lady-in-waiting – and then upsetting the Pope by asking for a divorce so he could marry her sister Anne Boleyn, which he did in 1533.

A year later Thomas FitzGerald, the 10th Earl of Kildare renounced allegiance to Henry and led a Catholic crusade in Ireland with the aim of getting rid of the English and becoming the sole ruler of Ireland. But his timing wasn't too good; Henry was a bit fed up by now; first the Pope had excommunicated him, and then Anne Boleyn had deliberately given birth to a girl before having the gall to miscarry at the next childbirth attempt. So he got a tad upset by FitzGerald's rebellious nature. His response was to rein-in the unruly Irish Earl by radically reforming Ireland's administration. Consequently by 1540 most of the country was controlled by the King's Dublin cronies.

Now, Henry VIII decided that what Ireland really needed was an official leader – that is to say... him. So in 1542 he introduced the Crown of Ireland Act which proclaimed him King of Ireland. It signalled the start of the Tudor conquest of the land and officially broke its papal ownership. The new Protestant Kingdom was of course not recognized by the Catholic monarchies in Europe. To stamp Protestant authority upon the country a policy of surrender and re-grant was then pursued, making way for the plantation of English and Scottish settlers. What this basically meant, if you were Catholic, was that they took the land from you – then asked you for a rent, so that you could keep it. By the way, you were then expected to renounce Catholicism and convert to Henry's new Anglican Church as well.

When Queen Elizabeth, the daughter of Henry VIII, came to the English throne in 1558; her big fear was that the Gaelic Irish would rise again and provide Spain with a base from which England could be attacked. To counter this threat she divided the whole land into shires to be ruled by sheriffs and also granted land to her courtiers.

The native Irish in many districts were a wild bunch not used or prepared to accept any rule other than that of their tribal chief; they dwelt in mud huts, generally wore no shoes, just a rough kilt and long hair. Tribal war and plundering were a way of life to them, and they didn't much like the English confiscating their land.

Sir Humphrey Gilbert, a Devonian, was appointed governor of Munster and given a remit to expel the rebels and introduce English colonists. Resistance came from James FitzMaurice, the captain-general of the Earldom of Desmond in a conflict named the First Desmond Rebellion. Gilbert was ruthless, massacring all those he came across including women and children, beheading them and laying their heads in rows to terrorise others. FitzMaurice hid out in the Kerry Mountains and resorted to guerrilla tactics to continue the fight before finally submitting in 1573.

But FitzMaurice wasn't finished. Somehow he negotiated a pardon, sailed to France and travelled through Europe to finally arrive in Rome. Here he appealed to the court of the Pope, who supplied him with money together with Spanish and Italian troops. In 1579 they sailed to Ireland to begin the Second Desmond Rebellion. A year later it seemed that this rebellion had been quelled, when yet another rebellion broke out in Leinster.

This time Queen Elizabeth appointed Grey as Lord Deputy of Ireland and sent him with 6,000 troops to sort things out. Grey was nothing if not ruthless, killing and beheaded those he defeated. The civilian population also suffered greatly; losing home, livestock and crops before being struck by famine and epidemics. Approximately 30,000 people in Munster were reported to have died. Even Elizabeth was shocked by Grey's brutality and removed him from office. The rebellion finally came to an end in 1583 when their leader was killed in a skirmish, and by 1600 the Gaelic clans had lost over 4,000km^2 of land to English settlers.

At Upper Cloonee Lough I take off my socks and test the water. I think it's cold and tell Sebastian so, but he's unperturbed, strips down to his underpants and wades in up to his neck and effectively has a bath – except that he has no soap. There is of course nobody in sight and probably nobody for some miles in any direction. If I'd not been there I know he'd have gone in starkers.

I unpack my lunch and am almost finished by the time Sebastian joins me. He produces a hunk of bread and some cheese and meagre though it is he offers me some, which I of course refuse, but then feel bad that I'd not offered him some of mine.

He tells me he's aged 21, that his mother has divorced and married again, and that he has a half-brother. He trained as a cabinetmaker but says he's no idea now what he wants to do with the rest of his life. I can't quite understand this, except I suppose there are so many possibilities at 21 that you might not ever want to make the choice that might then preclude other possible choices.

Sebastian finishes his lunch and stretches out on his back in the sun.

'I always sleep a while after lunch,' he says, and does so. This is the French way, I think, or maybe it's just Sebastian's way. I'm aware that there's still a long way to go to Kenmare but have decided that I'll walk for most of the day with Sebastian; it seems rude not to. So I lie down too, close my eyes and feel the sun warming my cheeks and eyelids. It's a real effort to get going again.

Donal Cam O'Sullivan (remember him?) somehow managed to keep out of the Desmond Rebellions, but eventually joined other Gaelic chieftains to oppose the English. The English themselves had been busy fighting the Spanish, many of whose Armada ships sent by Philip II in 1588 had finished up on the rocky coast of Ireland as a result of a severe hurricane that Queen Elizabeth had luckily prayed for.

In 1601 the chieftains managed to get help from Philip III of Spain, who hadn't learned any lessons from his father about the weather in Ireland. Two-thirds of the force he sent had to turn back because it was somewhat choppy, whilst the remaining third *did* manage to land and take the port town of Kinsale. The Spanish, led by General Frey Juan Del Águila y Arellano (or Don Juan to his friends), were subjected to artillery fire from land whilst simultaneously being harassed from the sea by the English fleet.

Hugh O'Neill, a Gaelic chieftain from Ulster, made the long march south in a cold winter to go to the aid of the Spanish. His force was joined near Kinsale by Donal Cam O'Sullivan's men. They surrounded the English force, led by the competent Mountjoy, Lord Deputy of Ireland, and first held them siege before finally staging an attack. It appears that, for payment of a bottle of whisky (no-doubt

Jameson's) a traitor had tipped off the English who were thus well prepared for the attack and gained the upper hand. O'Neill's forces retreated into the bogs (of the peat variety) where they hoped that the cavalry's horses would not like the soft going, but the cavalry charged through O'Neill's poorly trained infantry, using their lances to great effect. No Irish were spared; the wounded were put to death and any prisoners taken were hanged.

O'Sullivan's men meanwhile had somehow escaped back to Dunboy Castle near Castletownbere and prepared its defence before the advancing English could arrive. The English attacked with a force of 4,000 men against a garrison of 143. (O'Sullivan himself was not there; he was at a post-Kinsale defeat strategy meeting with O'Neill.) The garrison was bombarded for two days by cannon before the defenders surrendered. They were all hanged the next day.

O'Sullivan by now realised that the fight in Munster was lost and so began, together with 1,000 of his clan, including women and children, an epic and now famous winter march of around 300 miles to Leitrim in the north of Ireland. His intent was to combine forces with those of his friend Owen O'Rourke. O'Sullivan's clan experienced famine along the way and hostility from the English and from local Irish leaders. After 14 days only 35 of O'Sullivan's original complement remained by the time he arrived at O'Rourke's castle some had settled on the way, and a few mercenaries had returned to Connaught – but most had just perished.

So Sebastian and I are walking in ancient and historical footsteps. The Beara Breinfne Greenway Trail, created as a tribute to Donal Cam O'Sullivan's march was conceived in 1990 and, about now in 2013, it should be just about finished. If we were both planning to continue north we might even be the first to complete it. As it is, Sebastian will go on it as far as Killarney before turning west to Dingle, whilst I'll stay on it, walking east as far as Millstreet, before I leave it as the trail swings off north.

At about 5pm I start to get a trifle concerned by our slow progress and how far off Kenmare still seems. So I drop my rucksack and wait for Sebastian to catch up so I can say goodbye to him properly before pressing on alone. He tells me he'll probably spend the night on this spot. Before we shake hands I ask if I can see how heavy his pack is. It's a monster – I can hardly lift it; it must be around 30kg – no wonder he's walking so slowly. I walk on, cross a stile a hundred metres further on and take a last glance back at Sebastian, who I think is about to take another nap.

There is a long haul into Kenmare, much of it on roads. Then it's a real slog, with still a painful knee and aching right shoulder, before I reach the shopping complex and the camper. It's late now and I'm very tired.

Sod it I think – I'll leave the bike overnight at Lauragh Bridge. So I drive the camper back again on the road I've both biked and walked already today, then pull in at Beara Camping.

I've completed the Beara Way leg of the E8 in four days.

Last night I cooked-in by gas with great difficulty as, firstly I'm no cook at the best of times, and secondly I'd of course wrecked the microwave. Tonight I walk (again along the R571) from the campsite half a mile up the road to The Lake House pub by Cloonee Lakes. There is, I'm told by the man at Beara Camping, both good food and Irish folk music to be had. He's right.

Three
The White House

'As I leave behind Neidin
It's like purple splashed on green,
My soul is strangely led
To the winding hills ahead.'
From: *As I Leave Behind Neidin* by Jimmy McCarthy

Thursday 20th June – Kenmare
I collect my bike from Lauragh, drive back to the shopping complex in Kenmare, park, and walk into town. At the post office I get directions to the library and find it easily. Breeda the librarian is very helpful.

I know already some of Kenmare's history but want to discover the events that took place between O'Sullivan's march to Leitrim in 1602 and a pivotal time in Kenmare's history of around 1670 when a colony was formed.

In 1605 in England things were about to blow up – well, almost. James I had come to the English throne in 1603 but he hadn't made changes favourable to some Catholics quickly enough. So they proposed to accelerate things a wee bit by blowing him up, along with his Parliament. Unfortunately for them they were betrayed by an anonymous note and the Gunpowder Plot failed. The attempt, however, hardened Protestant opinion against the Catholics. It also shook up James to the extent that three months after the plot, he appointed Sir Arthur Chichester, a staunch anti-Catholic, as Lord Deputy of Ireland.

Ireland at the time was controlled by Gaelic clan chiefs who under Brehon Law each administered their own areas. Chichester did everything he could to make life difficult for the chiefs, who'd ironically all recently been made earls by James. Such was the intensity Chichester's pressure that on 14th September 1607 the

33

chiefs sailed away from Ireland into exile, an event that became known famously as 'The Flight of the Earls'. They never returned.

The Earls left a land devastated by war; most of the cattle were dead and most of the crops had been burnt. The lands once owned by the Earls were confiscated and Chichester set about the 'pacification and civilisation' of Ulster by planting there English and Scottish settlers who swore never to re-sell these lands to the Irish. Other parts of the country had still not recovered from the effects of recent rebellions; the land west of Cork was almost uninhabited and wolves roamed the wastelands of Munster.

The place where Kenmare now sits was once known as Neidin, meaning little nest – it was accessed in the early part of the 17th century with some difficulty. Ownership of the land thereabouts and of the Beara Peninsula did not much change; O'Sullivan Beare's clan remained prominent around Kenmare even though he himself had fled to Spain in 1603 following the Treaty of Mellifont and was murdered by a Dublin Irishman in 1618 whilst leaving Mass in Madrid.

James I died in 1625 and was succeeded by Charles I but things weren't about to get much better for the Irish. Charles was skint and obsessed with gathering monies from wherever; the English people, like the Irish, suffered from his compulsive financial and land tyranny. He appointed Thomas Wentworth, later to become the first Earl of Stafford, as Lord Deputy of Ireland, where he arrived in 1633.

Wentworth *did* manage, it's said, to rid the island of pirates, but then he engaged in similar roguishness himself by collecting monies for his king by every possible means he could think of; in the next five years Customs duties rose by around 125% and he suppressed the Irish trade in woollen cloth because it was in competition with that produced in England. Wentworth eventually slipped up and made a fatal mistake in acquiring an enemy of Richard Boyle, the Earl of Cork. He'd forced Boyle to surrender the college of Youghal because of alleged misappropriation of funds. Boyle held the grudge, but also held political influence which enabled him to eventually get his own back; the English Parliament feared Wentworth was going to use the Irish army against it and John Pym, leader of The Long Parliament, finally managed to get King Charles to sign Wentworth's death warrant. Richard Boyle was a key witness at Wentworth's trial – he was executed in May 1641.

Back in Ireland two puritan lord justices effectively took over control. But rebellion was in the wind – it was time for change.

I need a bit of a change too, and for lunch I stroll down Main Street, Kenmare to find PF McCarthy's. With my meal I order a pint of Guinness.

'First pint of Guinness I've tried for about 50 years,' I say to the barmaid as she scrapes the froth from the top of the glass.

'Hope you like it this time,' she replies.

'I didn't then,' I say. 'I found it too bitter.'

'Your taste buds will likely have changed now,' she speculates.

This time I enjoy the pint, so perhaps she's right – or maybe the Guinness was off or a slightly different brew 50 years ago. Perhaps I've missed out all this time.

I fetch out my research papers from the rucksack, but I already know much of the history of Kenmare; now my interest is in the events that took place between 1641 and the siege that happened at the White House in 1689. I'll have to be focused; the library will close in just over two hours. Tomorrow I'll search for the White House.

The Rebellion began in October 1641 with a betrayed plot to seize Dublin Castle. It, however, spurred a general rising in Ulster and the formation of a Catholic army that culminated the following year in the Confederate Oath of Association being sworn at Kilkenny. The insurrection spread around the country; Protestant farms and settlements were attacked and people were, if not killed, robbed and turned out of their houses. In Munster, the Confederates were commanded by Lord Mountgarret who attacked and took fortresses in Kilkenny, Waterford and Tipperary. By February 1642 almost all the areas of Ireland were held by the Catholics.

In April an army arrived from Scotland; they'd made a covenant with the English and were led by General Robert Munro. Their remit was to put down the rebels who, it had been reported, had massacred Scottish settlers.

Protestants and Catholics subsequently carried out atrocities, and thousands of innocents on both sides of the conflict were killed.

This was a time of great turmoil not only in Scotland and Ireland but also in England. King Charles had fled London and raised his royal standard in Nottingham in August 1642 which was the signal for the kick off of the English Civil War. Until its end in 1646, the Confederates unofficially ruled much of Ireland, proclaiming their loyalty to Charles and fighting against the Scottish Covenanters and the English Parliamentarians led by Oliver Cromwell.

In January 1649 King Charles was found guilty of high treason and executed near the Palace of Whitehall, but the Civil War rumbled on until September 1651; Cromwell, however, pre-empted its outcome by landing in Dublin in August 1649, as General-in-Chief of the Commonwealth armies. His unopposed landing was assisted by previous Parliamentarian victories.

You can't mention Cromwell in Ireland in the same way that you can't mention Joseph Stalin in Ukraine or Margaret Thatcher in Argentina without upsetting someone. He is hated in Ireland – and for good reason. He was instrumental in propagating genocide and land grabbing on a mass scale and he didn't waste much time in starting his conquest. In September he ruthlessly took Drogheda by blasting holes in the town's walls. Wexford too soon befell to the same fate, but it was almost three years before the last towns of Galway and Cavan fell.

The war and Cromwell's exploits in Ireland had made him and the English Parliamentarians penniless. He couldn't pay back the 'Adventurers', a group of businessmen who'd put up the money to finance the war in the first place, and who'd been hankering after houses owned by the Irish in Cork, Kinsale and Youghal and for lands in Munster. Cromwell also couldn't pay the money owed to his officers and soldiers who'd fought in the war. What did he do? A good idea soon sprung to mind. He'd take the lands from anyone who'd been remotely involved with the Confederates, carve it up and apportion it to those good and 'adventurous' people in lieu of payment. The lowly Catholics would not of course be affected by any of this. But Cromwell nonetheless had a role for them; they'd be used to dig the land and wait-on at the tables of his troops.

'What about those people whose lands you've taken?' someone may cautiously have asked of Cromwell. But he'd thought of that too. They'd be transplanted west of the River Shannon to County Clare and to Connacht.

The Act of Settlement was passed in August 1652; it reduced the land held by Catholics from 60% to a mere 8%. It was a brilliant solution for Cromwell, except that it left the nitty-gritty process of detailed land apportionment. It was at this point that Sir William Petty stepped into the frame.

I step back into the reality of the day in Kenmare. I have to find a shop that sells a microwave to replace my smashed-up model. I don't have much time before the shops close. It's a close call. But McSwiney & Sons in the square has the goods. The trouble is that I have to lug the thing back in my arms to the camper – a mile distant. But that night I feast 'luxuriously' on a chilli con carne ready-meal.

Friday 21st June – Morning – Kenmare
I arrive in the town square just as the tourist information centre is opening. It shares the same building as the heritage centre, which traces a potted history of the town via a series of information boards. They confirm what I already know: that Sir William Petty formed a colony here in 1670. The board tells me it comprised English, Welsh and Cornish Protestants (the Cornish not considering themselves English of course). What I didn't know then was that the colony was originally called Neideen but was later renamed Kenmare by Petty's descendent, the First Marquis of Lansdowne, in 1775, in honour of his friend Lord Kenmare of Killarney.

Petty was a man of many talents and a great thinker. When he died in 1581 at the age of 58, he left to posterity 53 chests of writings. He was competent in Latin, Greek and French, as well as having acquired 'the whole body of common arithmetic'. He was a member of the Philosophical Society and wrote an essay on educational reform that recommended education for all in literacy and the introduction of trade schools and a teaching hospital. He tried his hand at a spot of inventing too; a writing machine that would later be known as a pantograph and the catamaran are both attributed to him. If he'd been born a little later in Switzerland he'd undoubtedly have come up with the thing that gets boy scouts out of horse's hooves. He also qualified, after less than four years of study, as a doctor of 'physick' (this being the archaic term for either a laxative, or the practice of medicine).

One of Petty's acquaintances was John Graunt, a protégé of Cromwell, and a statistician, notably in the branch of demography, which interested him. It was Graunt's influence that secured Petty a professorship at Gresham College in London where he put forward his plans for the enhancement of music. It was also Graunt who secured him his next position as physician to Cromwell's army, and in September 1652, at the age of just 29, he arrived in Waterford, Ireland.

Dr Petty soon analysed the medical condition of the troops and quickly organised an improvement in the availability of pharmaceuticals containing the essential ingredients of alcohol and opium; just the job to improve the health of the troops. It also saved the army a lot of dosh which certainly impressed General Charles Fleetwood, the Commander in Chief.

Fleetwood was also impressed by Petty's observations of an old acquaintance of Petty's, a Dr Benjamin Worsley, who'd not long been appointed Surveyor General of Ireland. This was a challenging position designed to solve Cromwell's problem of detailed land apportionment that would enable him to pay off the adventurers, officers and troops. But Worsley was making a fist of the job which Petty duly reported to Fleetwood. So Petty got the job and soon initiated what became known as the Down Survey.

Petty's Down Survey was completed in 13 months, using foot soldiers to collect the details. Petty of course made sure that he profited from the exercise; not only did he purchase debentures from soldiers desperate for money, but also he was 'coincidentally' most fortunate to lead a committee for the distribution of the lands surveyed and so cherry-picked and acquired juicy lands for himself.

When the monarchy was restored to both England and Ireland in the spring of 1660 the revenue from Petty's estates was abundant. He was doing OK thanks. He was also well received in London by the new king – Charles II, who made him a knight and appointed him as one of the commissioners of the Court of Claims, following the second Act of Settlement. Charles also affirmed that all the lands possessed by him in 1659 should remain his forever.

Using the information gained from the Down Survey, Petty had been shrewd in selecting land erroneously thought to be unprofitable.

He chose well; there were woodlands under which might be found marble, iron, copper and maybe precious metals; rivers and streams that could be harnessed; pasture land for cattle, and a coastline that could be profitably fished. Sir William was at this time the richest commoner in England, but he was still ambitious, or you could say – just plain greedy.

If he'd had the unlikely urge to climb 839 metres to the top of Mangerton Mountain he could have viewed the 50,000 acres of land all of which belonged to him. Nestled away in the south-west corner of this chunk of land was the little place then named Neidin, soon to become the colony of Neidin that would later be called Kenmare. Petty had his eye on it.

Before I leave the tourist information centre I ask about a bus timetable because, having already driven the twisting hilly road between Killarney and Kenmare that weaves its way between Mangerton Mountain and other peaks to the west, I have no appetite for a similarly torturous long bike ride before I'm about to start a 16-mile walk.

'They've just changed to the summer timetable,' he says; then he rustles papers about in several locations for a good five minutes looking for one, before giving up.

'If you go to the bottom of the road...' he waves a hand in the direction, '...it will be on the bus stop,' he says. I go and look, but the times are only given from Kenmare; I need to know times from Killarney, but this is a problem for tomorrow.

Today I head back to the library.

The land Petty had acquired was rocky, boggy and wooded, but Petty knew that iron ore lay underground in bedded masses and veins. He also knew there were five great woods in the area that would yield timber to be used for the charcoal required to smelt the ore. The rivers could be utilised to drive the hammers and bellows, and to cool the molten ore. Everything was to hand for iron-making.

Petty founded several ironworks in the area, the first in 1667 at Glanerought, one mile north of the centre of Kenmare. A new forge had been built there but never used and Petty set about its refurbishment (not personally of course).

The region was at that time inhabited by the native Irish, all of whom were Catholics, but Petty's colony would primarily use specialist labour; Protestants imported or sometimes poached from other English-owned ironworks that had been springing up all over the country since the beginning of the 17th century. Native labour was thought to be unsuitable for this sort of work – but was alright for labouring. Petty believed though that his projects would somehow anglicize the Irish – he was to be proven wrong.

Petty's ironworks encountered many problems: poor management and accounting, high labour turnover, the quality of the iron produced, process faults, bad workmanship, pilferages, fraudulent transactions and mine collapse and flooding. All were endured.

Petty despaired, but persevered with the enterprise, appointing and dismissing a succession of agents; the last was a gentleman named Richard Orpen.

Orpen's father was a local Protestant planter who came to Kerry aged seven after Richard's grandfather had been killed at the battle of Naseby. Richard was a protégé of Petty, taken by him from school, to eventually become his chief agent. He lived near Kenmare in a house known as the White House.

Just before I came over to Ireland my local library managed to obtain a copy of *The Orpen Family*, a book that indicated the location of the White House when it was visited by its author G.H. Orpen in 1927. My hope is that the house (or its remains) is still there and if so that I'm able to find it.

'I'm looking for a particular road,' I say to Breeda the librarian. 'It used to be called White House Lane – there was a siege there in 1689.'

'All the old maps are held at Tralee,' she says with an air of regret.

'How far away is that?' I ask, showing my complete ignorance of Irish geography.

'It's a long drive, maybe 40 kilometres,' she says, looking bemused.

'Oh!' I say. I can't hide my disappointment; the last thing I need is a long drive in the camper, especially if the roads are anything like those between Dursey Island and Kenmare.

'Wait a minute,' she ponders. 'They may be able to help upstairs in the Roads Department.'

Upstairs, the council office looks a bit like a bank. At the counter the young girl appears dumfounded when I repeat the question to her, but she disappears, asks around, and I'm led past the counter to a back room. Here I meet two gentlemen who introduce themselves as Ryan and John. It seems they perhaps like a knotty little problem. I tell them that I think the White House is off Killowen Road, which is apparently also the R569 that we can in fact view by looking out the window.

I read somewhere that it's part of the Irish psyche to avoid saying 'no', which probably also extends to never admitting to not knowing something that should perhaps be known. At any rate, Ryan brings up Google Earth on the computer and hand-sketches me a map.

'There's an old tower,' he says. 'Turn right out of here, then left and left again into Lodge Wood, then right – and it's at the end.' But now John submits an alternative.

'There are some old cottages,' he suggests. 'I think they're called Killowen Cottages, the place you're looking for could be near there.' This seems a better bet because the R569 runs parallel to the River Roughty, and it fits with something I'd read in *The Orpen Family*: 'The tide flowed around the house called Killowen'.

I first look for and find the tower that Ryan suggested might be the White House – but it doesn't feel right. So I walk back onto the R569 and turn left to walk east. The cottages appear after a plod of almost a mile, but there's no sign of a ruin that might be the White House. I pull my anorak from the rucksack as the drizzle begins and start to walk back in defeated and miserable disappointment towards Kenmare.

After a few minutes a car pulls up alongside me. John lowers the window.

'We've since looked on the map and we know where it is,' he says. 'Hop in, I'm going that way.' I quickly do so out of the drizzle and he turns the car around and drives about a mile further east.

'It's down the lane, across the fields,' he says, adding as I climb out the car, 'It's private land, but you should be alright.'

I thank him, but notice he turns the car around and drives back towards Kenmare. One knotty little problem solved by the Roads Department.

Richard Orpen's respected position at the ironworks soon enabled him to assume the mantle of local squire. Unfortunately this also entailed the duty of collecting rents and of debt collection – a role which did not exactly make him top of the pops with his Catholic tenants.

Orpen protected the Protestant community vigorously by bringing in for punishment several Catholics (referred to then as Papists) for various offences. In particular there was a Daniel MacTeig Duff, who in 1680 was adjudged to have been one of those who'd murdered and robbed Edward Gilks, a smelter, of 40 shillings (a tidy sum then). Orpen was quite brave (or stupid) in coming into the wild countryside to carry out his duties to arrest such men. One night, however, Owen Sulwan (described as 'a loose gentleman') attempting to get some revenge, ran Orpen through from behind with a sword, for which he swung.

Other offenders Orpen prosecuted severely; they received various sentences ranging from hanging to being burnt in the hand or being jailed. These events did nothing for Orpen's ratings in the popularity stakes amongst the Catholics.

Then suddenly, everything was about to change.

'Where ignorance is bliss, 'tis folly to be wise', wrote Thomas Grey on the prospect of entering Eton College and leaving his childhood behind. But folly can sometimes be the lack of wisdom

Charles II, an enthusiastic amateur chemist, possibly paid the price for his years of experimenting with mercury in his laboratory. His official cause of death, on Friday 6th February 1685, was that he'd had a stroke, but it's now felt he died of a kidney disease known then as Bright's disease. One of the rumours circulating at the time was that his brother James had conspired to poison him.

James came to the English throne as James II. He was an out and out Catholic. In Ireland he appointed Richard Talbot, soon to be made Earl of Tyrconnell, who headed up the army and promptly filled it with Catholics. They were also appointed to the Irish administration, judiciary and as sheriffs in all of Ireland except County Donegal. Their new-found status incited the Catholic-led army to become party poopers on Guy Fawkes Night 1686 in Dublin, when they put out the Protestant bonfires (celebrating the foiling of the 1605 plot) and broke the windows in the Lord Mayor's house. There's no record of how the bonfires were extinguished, but it's rumoured the Protestants were somewhat peed off by the events.

In June 1688 the impact of the Catholic monarch meant that things got a whole lot tougher for Richard Orpen in the little colony of Neidin. He reports the events in his 'succinctly' titled *An Exact Relation of the Persecutions, Robberies, and Losses, sustained by the Protestants of Killmore in Ireland: With an Account of their Erecting a Fortress to Defend themselves against the Bloody Insolencies of the Papists*. In this account Orpen relates how the officers of Tyrconnell's army had no money or resources and were 'forced to filch and steal black cattle and sheep', so that by the end of 1688 the colony had no cattle left and their barns and granaries had all been robbed.

Meanwhile in England, James II's pro-Catholic actions had so incensed some protestant noblemen that they'd invited William of Orange over to help out. William landed in England at Torbay on 5th November 1688. Cutting a long story short – William and Mary were offered the throne and James fled to France.

Orpen found this stuff out from Sir Richard Aldworth who was in Newmarket, County Cork. An army from England was expected anytime to sort things out, but meanwhile frightened Protestants were sheltering in Bandon as Tyrconnell's pro-Catholic policies in Ireland still prevailed. Aldworth advised Orpen to join them. But there was 40 miles of rugged country to cross and all the horses had been nicked by the Papists (leaving perhaps only a pony belonging to a – later to be born – Scotsman called Alexander Shanks). So the decision was made to stay put; and, bringing with them what provisions and arms they had, all the families of the colony crowded into the house that Petty had built for his chief agent. There were 42 families; 180 people in all, of whom 75 were fighting men. The house was located by the River Roughty, at a place known as Killowen, called the White House.

The gate is open. I enter a field of wet, knee-high grass. There's no evidence of any sort of building, or of Whitehouse Lane, as described when the ruin was visited in 1927 by G.H. Orpen. Very soon my jeans are soaked as I forge a line through, leaving a tell-tale trampled trough of grass like a vapour trail in a clear blue sky. I could almost do with a machete. I steer left towards a field edge where I startle and cause some trepidation to some cows sheltering behind trees – this startles me too. Then, as the field fence corner runs left the land ahead opens up and I catch my first sight of the ruin – about 300 yards away. It's tucked in front of a small group of trees that border land that falls away, down to the river. A grey-sky mist hangs gloomily over the river valley. Stalking closer to the ruin, half expecting a shout from an irate farmer, I see that the centre of the house has somehow collapsed and doesn't exist leaving only the two ends of the ruin. There is a growth of foliage and ivy climbing the walls, the surface of the upper reaches of which appear to have disintegrated or been eroded by the weather. But the lower part of the ruin is still definitely white. So I now know I've found the White House – and I feel privileged. I'm sure very few people have made the lengthy tramp across private land to see it. Even in the unlikely event that a few people may have stumbled across it by accident, would they have known its history? When I finally reach the ruin I just stand for a moment and quietly reflect that here in January 1689, over 324 years ago, a siege had taken place.

Orpen and the others crowded into the White House fearing that a bit of serious agro was about to kick-off. So the families brought to the house with them just a few items for protection. These Orpen described as: 'blunderbusses, musquets, carbides, and fowling-pieces, 40; cases of pistols, 20; swords, 36; pikes, 12 and scythes, 6'. Next they took the precaution, with the help of some of their former Irish labourers, of turning the place into a kind-of fort by building a clod-wall to circle the house. It was formed over a large area roughly in the shape of a pentangle with 14-foot-high walls, 12 inches thick. Within the fort they built some wooden huts for the families. It took them nine days to complete the work.

Tyrconnell had designated 25th February 1689 as the day by which all Protestants should be disarmed – and at one o'clock in the morning one of Orpen's lookouts thought he spotted something moving around in the dark across the field and let off a shot to wake the others. He wasn't wrong; 3,000 Irish soldiers were creeping towards them. They backed off on hearing the shot and waited until dawn – when an Irish captain came forward and was let into the garrison.

'You are requested to surrender your arms, ammunition and horses,' he ordered – or something like that, naively innocent of the fact that the Irish natives had already nicked them (although Orpen *did* probably still have a couple tucked away). The captain had brought a letter from Orpen's 'helpful Catholic friend', Sir Valentine Browne, which promised that if they surrendered they would be treated OK, but if they refused they'd be subjected to 'fire and sword'. Given Browne's past track record, they didn't trust him an inch and told the captain where to get off. He got off quickly, back to his troops and the garrison braced themselves for an attack.

Orpen, still expecting the promised army from England 'anytime-soon', managed to smuggle a spy out of the garrison to travel into County Cork and find out what was happening. The spy returned four days later, reporting that the Protestants of Cork were disarmed, that Castlemartyr to the east of Cork had also surrendered as had Bandon to the west (almost).

Orpen briefly considered going north himself to Londonderry, but of course had only one pony (called Shanks maybe). Anyway, it was a good job they didn't try because all the passes had been secured by the Catholics and they wouldn't have made it.

They appeared to be somewhat snookered; 75 against 3,000 were not good odds and there was also the possibility that ships would soon sail up the River Roughty and blast off their cannons at them. What to do? Not many options were left really. Orpen surrendered, first having established that their goods would not be plundered, that they could retain their swords (an optimistic request anyway perhaps) and that they could leave Ireland at their leisure. Lady Petty's brother had seen the writing on the wall for the colony some time before and had thoughtfully left two small 30-ton barques moored nearby.

All of Orpen's requests were granted (except for the retention of their swords of course), and horses, arms and ammunition were duly surrendered. But no formal agreement had been signed. So immediately the Irish officers allowed their men to plunder the garrison, and the colonists were turned-out miserable and starving.

One of the soldiers, a man named McHugh somehow heard that there was money hidden under the floor of the parlour in the White House and started to rip up the floor. There was indeed money there, but when he had almost got to the spot, Mrs Orpen, who was pregnant at the time and was sitting in a large easy chair in the corner of the room, laughed at him.

Ah! thought McHugh, it's under the chair is it – right! He swore at her and ordered her to move, but she refused. He threatened to cut the baby from her womb if she didn't move. She still refused. Now he was really mad and pulling out his pistol pointed it to fire at her. Just then Orpen appeared and pushed the pistol aside, so that the ball missed his wife and lodged in the wall of the room.

I touch the wall of the house, search without hope for the pistol ball hole, gaze up the chimney, then walk around the outside of the house and take some photographs. For about 10 minutes I think of the events that had taken place in this now desolate and undisturbed spot. Then I start back, walking as much as possible in the trampled-down-grass-trough I'd already created.

The colonists were packed into the two barques – except for eight families who it was planned to retain there to operate the ironworks – because the natives didn't know how. Orpen's ordeal wasn't yet over however, the sailing party were not in fact allowed to sail because somebody had nicked the sails! Consequently the colonists were kept in harbour for eight days, packed like pilchards, with the ship's hatches closed.

Eventually, Orpen was obliged to pay a bond of £5,000 on condition that he sailed to Cork and there surrendered. The Protestants sailed, but didn't head for Cork; their goal was instead Bristol. There were no experienced sailors or navigators aboard and the voyage took them 15 days. Three souls died from exposure during the voyage and the rest were in a pretty poor state, both mentally and physically, when they arrived. The Mayor of Bristol organised collections for their relief.

I leave Kenmare in the afternoon and drive to Killarney on the less scenic route that avoids the National Park and the narrow bendy mountain roads. Before picking up the major N22 road, I take the very road from which I approached the White House earlier that day. As I drive past I glance over to the field. The farmer, probably having discovered my trail of trampled-down-grass, has closed the gate.

Four
The Kerry Way to Australia

'Let us drink a good health to our schemers above,
Who at length have contriv'd from the land to remove
Thieves, robbers and villains, they'll send 'em away,
To become a new people at Botany Bay
From: *Botany Bay: A New Song*, attributed to George Villiers

Friday 21st June – Afternoon and evening – Killarney

I drive to Flesk campsite at Muckross, south of Killarney and book in. The helpful guy on reception (who undoubtedly is a 20km walk Olympic gold medal winner) gives me a lot of information. He tells me about the pitch, toilet block, laundry, on-site restaurant, nearby Chinese takeaway and the best places for Irish music in Killarney. Then he says it's a 10-minute walk into the centre of town. It took me twice as long – and I don't dawdle.

I get a good pitch because I'll be here for seven nights – the rate is reduced for a week-long stay. By using Killarney as a base, I've discovered that the walk from Kenmare to near Nad (south of Banteer) can be done by using public transport, avoiding those torturous bike rides. The plan is to get the bus back to Kenmare tomorrow.

So I walk into town to check out the bus times. It starts to rain.

There isn't a bus on Saturdays the lady tells me, but I'm in luck; the new summer timetable is just about to come into operation and there's a bus on Sunday leaving at 11am. Not so lucky really because it means it will then be almost afternoon before I can start the walk. It also means I have to re-plan Saturday. The good luck, I suppose, is that at least there *is* a bus.

I microwave a ready-meal and decide to take the gold-medallist's advice and hit O'Connor's bar on the High Street in Killarney. I get there just before 10.

It's billed as a traditional pub that offers traditional music on a

Saturday night – and so it does. But I almost have to fight my way inside and then hustle for a place at the bar before attempting the even more difficult task of attracting the barman's attention for a drink. This I achieve only after I pester.

'Can I get a drink, mate?' I ask.

When I do get a pint, some of it's jerked out of the glass by a neighbouring body before I even take a swig. The place is just too damned crowded.

The walls, pillars, ceiling and bar itself of O'Connor's are papered with bank notes from all parts of the world, the majority from the USA; presumably they'd been donated by satisfied customers, or those wishing to leave an impression – and with more money than sense – all here trying to find their roots. Some notes have scrawled on them, usually in felt-tip pen, little anecdotes or states where the donator lives. O'Connor's seems to be populated by the nationalities of the bank note donators in roughly the same proportions, confirmed it seems by the accents I hear. They're mainly American (although some may well be Canadian), with a smattering of Germans and the odd French thrown in. But I'm almost sure I'm the only Brit here. The Irish also appear to be in a minority; apart from the bar staff and the folk group, I don't hear many other Irish voices.

The group play the traditional Irish instruments of uilleann pipes and tin whistle, supplemented by the usual guitars. The fiddle player arrives a little later. They are good. I people-watch contentedly whilst I listen; at the doorway a grey-haired lady, who I assume (perhaps incorrectly) is American and staying at a plush hotel in town, is clearly flattered by being chatted-up by a young guy. But when he goes outside, she raises her eyebrows to her friend. Good try, buddy.

One of the group plays a poignant solo version of 'The Auld Triangle' that was used to wake up prisoners in Mountjoy Gaol. The song, from the opening of *The Quare Fellow*, a play by Brendan Behan, has been recorded by umpteen people over the years. I wonder how many of the audience are listening to the words. It appears that they're too busy jumping up and down click-flashing photo-souvenirs of the group. I'd read Behan's *Borstal Boy* when I was a teenager but had only just found out the song was written for him by his younger brother Dominic whilst Brendon was in

Mountjoy serving time for an IRA organised attempted murder of two policemen.

I struggle to the bar to buy a second pint, then at 11.30 leave to race-walk back to camp. I'm joking; I walk slow now after a couple of pints. Two American or Canadian ladies, mistaking me for a local (some chance around here) pull up in a 4x4 and, lowering the window, the driver asks me a question.

'Can I ask you a question?'

They don't look like they want my business, more like they're lost.

'You can,' I say. 'But I probably won't know the answer – I'm not Irish.' Without a word the driver winds up the window and they speed off.

Just before I get to the campsite I catch up a family of four. I'm sure that they're not going to be Irish but as they are almost at their hotel I get a nice surprise. The father says to me in a broad Irish brogue:

'Grand evening!' I liked his sense of humour – it had just started to drizzle and I hadn't brought my anorak.

'Yes, what's the forecast for tomorrow?' I ask.

'Not great, showers,' he says. 'Have a good night.'

'Thanks... and you,' I say.

Saturday 22nd June – Morning – Killarney

With plans forcibly changed, I bike instead into town and get to Killarney library just after 10am. I'm looking for anything I can find out about a place called Gortdromakiery, the birthplace of Edward Eagar. Why him? When I was planning the walk I keyed in 'Killarney famous people' on the Internet and his name came up as both a lawyer and convict – an intriguing conundrum. So I dug some more and found one of his descendants had written Edward's biography, which gave Gortdromakiery as his birthplace.

Éamon the librarian is very helpful and a flood of books and maps appear on the desk. We discover that, though there are lots of variant spellings, Gortdromakiery, in Gaelic is *Gort droma Ciaraid*, which translated means 'field of the ridge of Kerry'. Éamon produces yet another book which shows Gortdromakiery as an area of land known in Gaelic as a *baile*; defined as a small geographical division of land. It's located just to the south of Guitane Lough on his map, which also tallies with my Discovery map. The *baile* lies six miles, as the sober crow flies, approximately south-east of Killarney. It's on the slopes of Mount Stoompa, which peaks at 705 metres, and is circled on my map with brown contour lines. It's obviously hilly, so instead of biking I decide that this afternoon I'll walk there.

Eagar was born in 1787, so Éamon and I check the *Griffiths Valuation* book for 1853, the closest record that exists to that period. We find that amongst the 24 inhabitants of Gortdromakiery at the time, 14 of them were called Donohoe, three were called Loony (probably named after the duck rather than the crazy bin), but there were no members of the Eagar family then recorded as living there.

Edward Eagar, whilst growing up in Kerry, would have begun to slowly become aware of how privileged he was. It may have taken him some time to realise this as his childhood would likely have been spent somewhat isolated on his father's Gortdromakiery estate. His only contact with the outside world would have been with the locals hired in to farm the land. Edward was very lucky to have been born into the landed gentry. Shortly he would become a gentleman. Nobody thought he would also be a convict.

Edward was part of a large family, as was usual in those days, but his childhood at Gortdromakiery would have been brief, according to the scant records available. How much he would have been allowed to venture from the estate is debatable. He'd have doubtless visited Muckross Abbey, then called Mucrus, and maybe would have heard of the hermit who'd lived there amongst the tombs and coffins – who it's said regularly got pissed. It's also possible Edward might have visited Killarney itself, then still a village, but which within 20 years would grow into a town inhabited by 5,000 souls. It was there that Lord Kenmare, who owned much of the land in the area, resided in his walled mansion.

To travel to somewhere as far away as Cork was a real undertaking. The journey was described in a guide of 1834 as being: 'but forty-five miles and one furlong from Killarney'. You would have had to board the coach at the crack of dawn though in order to get to your destination before nightfall.

At the age of 13 Edward was sent to Trinity College, Dublin – where all aspiring gentlemen of Ireland were despatched. Here he remained for about four years.

His family had always had connections with the law. Francis Eagar, Edward's great-grandfather, had married Eleanor O'Keef, whose brother was a barrister-at-law (who somehow managed to arrange for his remains to be buried at Westminster Abbey). His uncle, Harmon Blennerhasset, was also a solicitor so, when Edward left Trinity at the age of 17, it was quite natural for him to become one too. He started in this line of work as Harmon's apprentice.

What influence Harmon had on Edward is an interesting question given the subsequent history of the pair. Harmon was 23 years his senior, had also been educated at Trinity and, having recently inherited the family estate, was loaded. Then he blew it all; within a period of three years he sold his Castle Conway Estate at Killorglin (of Puck Fair fame) 'for a song' and buggered off to New York where he managed to blow the rest of his fortune. Why did he leave Ireland? There were two reasons. He'd joined the secret Society of United Irishmen, but then had got cold feet when the British began attacking members of the Society. Oh, and there was the slight matter that he'd married his niece, which kind of upset both Catholics and Protestants in the area. All this had happened after Eagar had served his short apprenticeship with him.

Edward Eagar himself soon became registered as a solicitor and attorney to His Majesty's courts and set up his practice. Then about four years later he decided to make a career change. He became a forger.

Saturday 22nd June – Afternoon – Killarney

At the campsite, I change into walking gear and trek a mile south passing the horse-drawn tourist carts known locally as jaunting cars that are parked up in a lay-by awaiting customers. At a road junction I turn off to walk east. This road I must take again in a few day's time to link up with the Blackwater Way. Two miles of road walking later I find the turning that the map indicates leads towards Gortdromakiery – not that it's signposted. I frantically check the Discovery map, thinking I've somehow missed the crucial turning, knowing that if I see the water of Guitane Lough I've gone too far.

There are signposts for a hostel, but none for Gortdromakiery, so I keep walking. The lane passes a scattering of houses then starts to climb uphill. The upper slopes of Mount Stoompa rise up dark and remote, in stark contrast to the lush green trees lower down in the foreground. As I climb, I eventually get a glimpse of Guitane Lough. The Discovery map shows the lane turning acutely right, climbing to where it terminates at a red triangle, indicating a campsite (but in this case is a hostel).

Where the hell is the village of Gortdromakiery? Were those few houses I passed it? I pause a short way before the hostel to look back down at the houses and the lane I've just walked. Should I ask at the hostel? But what do I ask? I can't think of a logical question; I can hardly ask if they happen to know where a certain forger lived in about the year 1800. Anyway, I'm a naturally introverted sort of guy and not too comfortable with knocking on doors without giving notice.

So I take a few photographs, then turn and walk back down the lane. It starts to drizzle, which adds to my depression. It's a bit like the feeling you get as an away football supporter, whose team's been beaten 6-0 and who's facing a long, wet drive home on a dark winter's night. Not only haven't I found Eagar's house, but I've not even found the village of Gortdromakiery – and there's not a soul about to ask.

I dawdle back down the lane deep in these kind of depressive thoughts – what else could I do? Semi-subconsciously I register that, by a gate, a 4x4 is parked. I can't recall it being there on the way to the hostel. Then, a little further on, as I pass a tall hedge, I hear:

'MOOOOO'

I nearly jump out of my skin. I don't know how you could do that – but I almost did it. It's the loudest moo I'd ever heard and it came from behind the hedge. A chorus of moos quickly follow. I'm intrigued and so walk back to the gate. Here I find a farmer and a small herd of black-and-white cows. I catch him in the act of rounding them up, waving a stick wildly in the air.

'There's some very loud mooing going on,' I say. 'Frightened the life out of me.' He chuckles. 'I've been looking for Gortdromakiery,' I continue hopefully.

He's wearing a raincoat (of course), a baseball cap, and a

distinctive 'RAF type' moustache – though I doubt he intends flying anywhere.

'It's all around here,' he says with a smile, waving his stick in a circle. Of course – I remember now from the library, 'field of the ridge of Kerry'; there *is* no actual village – it's just an area. I prattle on, more in desperate hope than anything.

'Actually, I've been looking for anything to do with somebody who was brought up here a few hundred years ago – a guy called Edward Eagar.'

He bursts out in laughter at this, and points his stick in the air. Then he tells me that his daughter, who's a solicitor (coincidentally), has been doing some research on Eagar. I tell him then what I know about him.

'Yes, he was a bit of a rogue – he used to collect da rents and keep 'em,' he says. 'His house was over dere amongst da trees,' he tells me, pointing his stick vaguely back towards the main road. 'I tink ders a plaque on the wall about Eagar,' he says, his accent sounding more Welsh to me than Irish. I try to get more detailed directions to the house and he tells me there's a track that runs off left, opposite some houses on the right.

I ask his name. It's Patrick O'Donoghoe. Now there's a thing – there were, I remember from the library, 14 Donohoes residing in Gortdromakiery in 1853. So Patrick was likely a descendant from these families (or possible from just one family) because the 'O' prefix signifies a grandson of Donohoe. I thank Patrick, shake his hand, ask if I can take his photo and then let him re-bond with his cows.

Now of course I *have* to find Eagar's house. Following Patrick's scrappy directions is not easy. I turn left where I think he might have meant and come across a car in a small stream (either abandoned – or someone was very bad at parking). Nearby a sign declares: NO UNAUTHORISED PERSONS ALLOWED BEYOND THIS POINT. I feel uncomfortable; there's no evidence of a living soul about, but everything somehow seems creepy. There are three possible houses, but they all look too modern. There's no way I'm prepared to walk up private driveways, knock on strange doors and ask if there's a plaque in the house expounding the virtues of a convict called Edward Eagar. So – I just behave like a timid spy and take long-distance photographs of the houses, two of which are partly screened by trees. Then I sulk off back to the main road – very angry with myself.

I try to cheer up, but it doesn't help that dark clouds are starting to gather over Mount Stoompa. Then sure enough, as I head back towards Muckross, a few large drops of the wet stuff descend upon me. Just before I get to the campsite I stop at a Spar shop for provisions.

'Do you know what the weather's going to do tomorrow?' I ask the young lad who serves me.

'Yes, I do,' he says, almost triumphantly. 'Rain! But the forecast for next week is good.'

As I get back to the van, the wind and rain starts in earnest. It's perhaps as well I didn't knock on strange doors, or strange things might have happened. At the very least I'd have got soaked. Anyway, I'm not at all sure that Patrick wasn't just giving me a bit of the old blarney? If he'd been a sheep instead of a cattle farmer I'd be thinking maybe he'd been trying to pull the wool over my eyes. Doubt I'll ever know.

Sunday 23rd June – Kenmare to Muckross
Killarney bus station is almost deserted; a few buses are parked up, some young people are hanging about with cases and rucksacks, but it doesn't look like much is about to happen just yet. Perhaps everyone is still at Mass. The ticket office is closed. I read a timetable that tells me there's a Monday to Friday service only. Had the lady yesterday been correct? Is the summer service starting today? I start to worry.

A man drinking coffee from a paper cup looks like he might be a driver.

'Is there a bus going to Kenmare today?' I ask.

'Yes, there is, at 11 – you're bang-on,' he adds. Within the next minute he's in the cab.

The bus is a 58-seater. It's 10.55 and I'm the only passenger. But then an Irish couple – old-age pensioners – show their bus passes and join me. My 10 euros 90 cents is the driver's entire takings for the trip (it would have been zilch if my UK bus pass had been valid here).

The old couple (same age as me probably, I'm afraid) are on a fleeting visit to Kenmare. The bus will turnaround and head back to Killarney within an hour, which will just give them enough time to find somewhere open for a cup of tea. The bus takes the less-scenic route that I'd driven (in the other direction) two days ago.

In Kenmare on Friday I'd seen, outside a tourist shop, an amusing postcard that I'd later regretted not buying. It depicted a skeleton, wearing a flat cap sitting on a wall by a bus stop. Underneath, the caption read: 'Waiting for an Irish bus'. The shop is unfortunately closed today, so my regret is now permanent.

I walk along Main Street and Shelbourne Street to the tourist information centre in the square, where I remember seeing a signpost for the Kerry Way. No need to check the Discovery map. I have ahead a 14-mile walk to Flesk campsite and its midday, so I know I'll be late getting in, but I feel happy – you could even say carefree. I saunter down a backstreet, cross a river, walk along a main road and then take a smaller road. When I'd looked at the map on the bus I saw that the Kerry Way went for a while on roads before reaching open country, so everything seems OK. I come across a fingerpost and take a track that climbs through some trees. And there I am, as expected, in boggy open countryside that continues to climb through a field populated by sheep, and then climbs a series of rocky outcrops.

After about a quarter of an hour, two young walkers, lightly kitted and obviously on a day's jaunt, catch and overtake me, going at pace. I'm now beginning to think that something's not quite right and, if they hadn't zoomed past so quickly, would have asked them if I was on the right track. I walk on though, still climbing; then unexpectedly, the path turns left and starts to drop. Shit! That's definitely not right. Reluctantly I pull out the map and compass. It appears I'm heading south-west and, looking onward, I can see this without doubt because there's water: the Kenmare River inlet no less. I should be walking north-east to Killarney, but instead I've been walking for an hour in the wrong stupid direction. It's now 1pm.

I run back down the series of rocky outcrops, slip on my arse a few times, frighten the life out of the sheep as I thunder through their field, drop a few times into the bog, then speed-walk on the road, to make it back to the (now over-familiar) signpost in Kenmare square, all in 45 minutes flat. Almost two hours and a lot of energy have been wasted.

But now – where is that missing signpost for the Kerry Way to Killarney? There isn't one is the answer; it's expected that everyone will be walking south-east. I spend another 15 minutes with compass and map trying to figure out which road to take... and by now it's 2pm. The correct road, it turns out, is the one I'd walked a good few times before – between the centre of Kenmare and the shopping complex where I'd parked the camper.

When I finally reach unfamiliar territory, the road begins to climb and narrows to a grass-centred lane that runs on for about two miles to a crossroads. Here I stop and stuff down some sandwiches. The map tells me I'm near a place called Gowlane. There's a good view from here back to the Beara Peninsula – but I don't have much time to appreciate it because I'm straight off.

I follow an obvious stony track ahead that climbs again steeply up between Peakeen and Knockahaguish Mountains. Unlike whilst on the Beara Way, I see quite a few walkers, perhaps because it's a Sunday and it's a very popular walk through Killarney National Park. I pass two young girls who struggle to navigate stepping stones across a stream – they take an age, trying to keep dry feet. There are a few such crossings along the Way. At Galway's Bridge the Kerry Way splits; the track to the left eventually reaches the west coast at Glenbeigh, but I turn right towards Killarney.

For the first time now I can use *The Irish Coast to Coast Walk* book I purchased – even though the damned thing is written entirely for those walking in the other direction (from east to west). Between here and Dublin it seems I'll have to try and read it backwards. The route-maps are OK though.

As the track rises between Cromaglan and Stumpacommenn Mountains a diminutive grey haired old lady (well, again probably my age) passes me going in the other direction. Twenty minutes later she appears by my side. She's been going 'like a train' having been down to Galway's Bridge, turned and caught me back up.

'I've hurt my arm,' she says, 'otherwise I'd be off hill walking.' That's what this is, I think to myself – but say nothing. She tells me that her husband is waiting for her in Killarney and rushes on ahead, soon disappearing from view. She's fitter than me, my right knee and left ankle are both painful now and I'm starting to flag.

I see nobody else all afternoon until I reach a car park and then descend to the impressive tourist-thronged Torc waterfall.

But the worst for me is still to come. When I think I've nearly made it, the Kerry Way signs disappear. The path just seems to go on and on, seemingly bearing no scale-relationship to either the Discovery map or the *Irish Coast to Coast* book. I arrive eventually in the car park of Muckross House and need to find the N71 road, but I'm disorientated; perhaps I should just say I'm knackered! One of the few cars left in the car park at this hour starts to pull away. I stagger towards it and desperately rap on the window. The young couple inside are naturally wary of attack by such an old, odd character that I probably appear to be now. The window *is*, however, cautiously lowered and, feeling suitably embarrassed, I'm nonetheless guided in the right direction – even though it's apparent from their accents that they're either Dutch or German. Thanks, folks – whoever you are.

Eventually I make it to familiar territory, passing the road junction where I turned east yesterday afternoon and where I must continue the E8 walk on Tuesday. There's not a single jaunting car left in the lay-by. I arrive wearily at the campsite at 7.30pm.

Monday 24th June – Cork

Today I'm driving the camper to Cork to try and find out more about Edward Eagar's conviction for forgery. I already know that Eagar had been charged with 'uttering a forged bill of exchange' and was brought to trial in Cork during the summer assizes on Monday 31st July 1809 at the age of just 22.

From the park-and-ride, the bus drops me close to the River Lee. I make a mental note of where I have to wait for the return journey. With the aid of a free tourist map, I make my way to the Central Library on Grand Parade and here spend some tedious hours searching through the microfiche records of 1809 newspapers. But nowhere can I find any mention of the trial of Eagar. I speak to a librarian who tells me that the official court archives and convict records between 1791 and 1835 were destroyed when the Four Courts in Dublin was attacked at the start of the Irish Civil War.

Now it's apparent that I'm not going to find a record of Eagar's trial. I'll never know the details of the crime, the amount involved, of who brought the prosecution, or what motivated him to commit the crime. I *do* know some other stuff though.

Eagar was tried before Justice Robert Day, who knew him personally; Day's diary reveals that Eagar was the grand-nephew of an acquaintance of his.

Day was a circuit judge who'd travelled around Cork as long before as 1794. In 1797 he became the Provost of Tralee and in 1801 he did 'the Orange north', as he described the tour in his diary. After some time spent in England, Day undertook the Leinster circuit in 1808, followed by the summer circuit of Munster in 1809.

On Saturday 29th July he was in Killarney, and apart from a bad road trip between Killarney and Millstreet, which he described in his diary as 'the cursed road', he seems to have been on a bit of a jolly. He's entertained by the High Sherriff in Millstreet, he breakfasts at the castle in Macroom the following day, and stays overnight in Cork that Sunday night. But on Monday morning 31st July it was back to business.

His first job was to swear-in the Grand Jury. They were charged with hearing the prosecution evidence and deciding if this was sufficient to put the defendant on trial. If they found so, they declared a 'true bill' and the case became a serious one. Trials were quick in those days. Defendants were expected to explain away the evidence presented against them. It was not to be that way for poor Eagar. He was found guilty. Forgery was a serious crime.

Property crime in England had escalated from the middle of the 18th century; its rise mirroring the growth in population. But English common law (which was also applied in Ireland) was seen on the Continent as being too liberal. So to improve the English image abroad, and to protect the wealthy from property crime, draconian laws were introduced. Between 1660 and 1819 a total of 187 new capital statutes became law. By the year 1800 there were 220 'crimes' for which you might expect to be sentenced to death. If you got caught picking a pocket and happened to have lifted more than 12 pence you could be hanged. If you liked the warmth of a gypsy fire and stayed by it for more than a month you also risked the rope; gypsies and vagabonds were hanged. It's a good job they didn't celebrate Halloween in those days or everyone who'd worn a mask or blackened their face would have been parading up the scaffold steps. If you did such things you were thought to be poaching or about to commit a burglary. Stealing property was viewed as being far more a serious crime than attempting to murder somebody, which in 1803 was classed as a mere misdemeanour. In the 18th century the increase in paper transactions such as cheques, notes and bonds made forgery more prevalent and forgers too were hanged.

Justice Robert Day therefore had little choice. His obituary in the *Kerry Evening Post* on 10th February 1841 described him as 'The good old Judge', and commented that: 'His decisions were those of justice tempered by mercy; and many a trembling wretch was rescued from ignominious death and reserved for repentance and forgiveness'. But in a case of forgery, and even though he personally knew Edward Eagar he had no alternative but to don the black cap. Day's diary entry simply reads: 'Edwd (sic) Eagar, grand-nephew of Rowley Hassett, capitally convicted of forgery'.

Eagar was taken to reside temporarily in Cork Gaol pending his execution.

There were two gaols in Cork in 1809: the County Gaol and the old City Gaol, both of which no longer exist. I'm not sure in which one Eagar had been held, or where either had been located.

The (new) City Gaol is today a tourist attraction, though it didn't open until 1824, 15 years after Eagar was sentenced. It's the closest I can get to see what sort of conditions he'd have had to endure. I find it using a tourist map after a long walk that culminates high above the city (compensated by good views), in a climb up Sunday's Well Road.

As I'm about to climb the steps into the gaol, a man at the top is standing as if he's on guard; his eyes drill into me, he has a wild look about him.

'Hello?' he says, more as a question.

'Hello,' I reply. From the one word I speak he apparently detects my English accent, because now he rants at me.

'You don't want to go in there – it'll make you sick,' I try not to catch his wild eyes. 'It's terrible what they did to the women in there,' he shouts as I'm about to pass him. 'Torture and rape – it will make you sick.' I'm at the entrance now. 'Your king and queen did it,' he shouts after me.

'Sorry about that,' I say, and walk in, making a mental note to complete the comments panel on the gaol's website and advise them they'd best sack their concierge.

The tour is excellent; I get an audio-earphone set, and as nobody tells me I can't take photos, I do so. The cells are cold and austere; raised boards on the floor for beds, and no other furniture or adornments. Depicted in one cell by wax manikins is the scene of a young person with long bright copper hair, tied by the wrists to the side of the cell being whipped by a wild-eyed warder who reminds me a bit of the 'concierge' outside. He got it wrong, by the way, if this was the scene that inspired his comment about the women in this gaol, because I found out later that the young person being whipped who perhaps looks like a young woman was in fact a boy.

Before entering the theatre to see the video, I ask one of the staff if she knows where the old gaols were. I'm not optimistic as she's young, but I'm surprised by her comprehensive answers. She tells me that the old City Gaol was on North Main Street where the Gate Cinema is now, and where she thinks Eagar was most likely to have been held.

The Gate Cinema is a multiplex just like many in Ireland, the UK and all over the world, but I bet there aren't many with a history like the site on North Main Street, Cork. I take a look at it, but don't take a photograph and I certainly don't have the time or money to go inside. Before it became the gaol that housed Mr Eagar it was known as North Gate Castle, fortified in order to protect entry into the city over the River Lee via North Gate Bridge. I wonder how many of those people going in to watch the latest release realise its gruesome history. I think of Eagar being led into his cell for the first time – a dire situation for such a well-bred gent.

The situation was indeed terrible for Edward Eagar: the prison was overcrowded and unhygienic. John Carr, an English barrister and travel writer toured Ireland four years before Eagar's conviction. He gave a graphic description of Cork and its people in his book *A Stranger in Ireland*. He commented that: 'The poor of this city are very numerous and bear a dreadful proportion to the population'. He visited the city's two workhouses described as 'The County and City Houses of Industry', as well as the old City Gaol where I think Eagar was held. The workhouse inhabitants Carr numbered as being 82 prostitutes: 'each of whom had a chain and log fastened upon one leg, and without shoes and stockings'. There were also, he continued: '230 male and female decayed house-keepers and an assortment of 108 idiots and the insane'. Carr was surprised that the prisoners in the old gaol had not been moved to the new one, which he said looked like a mansion, as at the time it was already under construction and some of the cells had been completed. But the local builders must have worked quite slowly in those days because the new gaol wasn't in fact opened until 1824, 19 years after Carr's visit. Carr described the old gaol as: 'a shocking place, having no yard, and the prisoners looked very unhealthy; they were not ironed'. This meant of course that they were not shackled in irons or fettered – it had nothing to do with putting creases in trousers or with West Ham football club.

Being put in irons is something I expect Eagar would have had to endure. They were generally worn around the ankles (which would make it a bit difficult to play football and probably still does, especially if you play for West Ham!). In the mid-18th century it had been at the gaoler's discretion as to how many fetters were attached; if a gaoler knew a prisoner was rich (like Eagar) he'd fit him up with quite a few and extract payment for the removal of each one. This practice, known as 'the choice of irons', had only been stopped a decade before Eagar's incarceration.

Eagar would have had to share accommodation with other prisoners. The place would likely have been damp, rat infested and the air would have been none too good, being perhaps a bit noxious and feculent as the gaol probably had no sewer.

The prison routine would begin with a bell being rung before six in the morning and end with lights out at 8.30pm. Silence was the rule; no whistling, singing or humming (not that that was likely) but the occasional bout of flatulence might have just been tolerated. Infringement of prison rules brought out the whip. There was nothing like a good whip around in those days! The joys of the treadmill had not yet been invented, but another amusement was called the 'shot drill' in which a heavy ball had to be lifted to chest height, two steps be taken and the ball replaced to the ground, a process that could be imposed for about four hours a day. If there had been health and safety regulations, the hazards would have been identified as pulled muscles, trapped fingers, crushed feet and a good whipping if you dropped the ball on the warden's foot. Generally though most of the time would be spent doing boring work; a favourite being picking fibres from a length of rope – oakum thus collected was used for stuffing mattresses or was mixed with tar and used for sealing the seams on ships. Oakum picking was not a subject, however, that Eagar would have covered at Trinity College, Dublin. He would also have had to get used to the prison diet, which probably consisted of some meat, milk and potatoes, and stirabout – porridge of oatmeal and cornmeal boiled in water and stirred. But as he would still have retained some powerful contacts and had a bit of brass, he'd maybe have been able to supplement this diet with a few delicacies.

His worst tribulation was, however, not the prison conditions or the food, but the constant mindfulness of his fate – to be hanged by the neck. He was a well-educated man and had no doubt heard of the infamous William Dodd, an English Anglican clergyman, who'd got into debt and had forged a bond for £4,200 – a tidy sum in 1777. Despite a petition signed by 23,000 people (perhaps a waste of time – petitions) he was publically hanged at Tyburn where around 100,000 Londoners looked on.

The place of execution in Cork was appropriately called Gallows Green, and Eagar, having studied law, would have known of the place and of its history. The road to the gallows, taken by the carts from the prison was named Gallows Green Lane (it's now known as Greenmount Crescent, where a mass grave was found in 1990). The majority who met their fate there had committed theft of some kind, but many United Irishmen involved in the 1798 rebellion were also hanged at the Green. Murderers received the additional punishment of being quartered or beheaded, whilst murderesses were burnt, out of modesty – so their naked bodies were not on view to the spectators. Catherine Murphy was the last Irish woman to suffer this fate; she was executed in 1789 for counterfeiting.

Eagar would have known the execution procedure too. At Cork

Gaol and Gallows Green the events weren't too dissimilar from those for prisoners held at Newgate in London. There, after prayers, the condemned person would sit in a cart facing the rising sun and be transported to Tyburn, the place of execution. Here, he would recite 'the hanging psalm', don a white shroud and climb the ladder. Few escaped death because English law said that the condemned shall hang until dead – and if you didn't die at the first attempt you were liable to be strung up again. Eagar no doubt dwelling heavily on those mental scenes of his pending demise, and being a solicitor, lodged an appeal for clemency (he wisely decided not to bother with a petition).

Eagar was a Deist, so he believed in God but followed no particular religion. He didn't read the Bible; in fact, before his trial, he spoke words to the effect that he thought it all a load of rubbish. According to the prison chaplain, the Reverend Boyle Davies, who assessed him soon after his conviction, he'd led a life of very great depravity. But God is the only one who will now know exactly what that depravity entailed and the details of his crime – which only the destroyed records could have revealed. Davies visited him several times, bringing with him on one occasion a Methodist preacher. They said prayers, but Eagar was still at first sceptical and unrepentant. They implored him to repent. Then, in a moment of inspiration, they read him a verse from the Bible; Hebrew 4:16. 'Let us therefore come boldly unto the throne of grace that we may obtain mercy, and find grace to help in time of need'. These words suddenly struck a chord with Eagar (maybe the one he could feel around his neck). He broke down crying, fell to his knees and put his hands together in prayer. The preacher possibly then gave him a copy of the 'sinner's prayer' to read, which begins: 'Dear God in heaven, I come to you in the name of Jesus. I acknowledge to you that I am a sinner, and I am sorry for my sins and the life that I have lived; I need your forgiveness. I believe that your only begotten son Jesus Christ shed his precious blood on the cross at Calvary and died for my sins, and I am now willing to turn from my sin'.

Suddenly then Eagar was filled with joy, peace – and the love of Christ. He was in the words of the Reverend Boyle Davies 'a new creature'. Davies later wrote: 'I think there was as remarkable an instance of divine mercy displayed in him as ever man experienced.

Such indeed was the Love of God shed abroad in his heart. Before his trial, he was no way awakened, but when Death stared him in the face, he was seized with very strong conviction'.

The chaplain and preacher reported the spectacularly successful conversion to the Bishops of Cork, and this may well have done the trick for Eagar because they had influence with the judiciary. Sceptics have expressed doubt that Eagar's conversion alone was what got the result for him; it's been said that his well respected family together with the bishops' influence and the fact that he knew Judge Day personally may well have had something to do with it. But for whatever the reason, Eagar's appeal was successful and his death sentence was commuted to transportation for life to the colony of New South Wales.

Edward Eagar spent 16 months in Cork City Gaol before being chained to another prisoner, dressed in convict clothes and taken on a cart, guarded by a military escort, to the nearby Cove of Cork (Cobh). Here he boarded the convict ship *Providence*, bound for Port Jackson, Australia. There is a possibility he may have spent some of his prison term aboard *Providence* before she sailed. He was, however, certainly aboard when she moved out of the harbour on 10th December 1810. She took nine days to clear Cobh. So finally Edward Eagar left Ireland and, as it turned out, left for good on about 19th December 1810.

I've left the camper at Black Ash Park & Ride, and, this morning, made a definite mental note of where to pick up the return bus – by the River Lee. It would be dead easy, I thought. But now I can't find the bus stop. I find *a* bus stop, wait there a while and then decide it's the wrong stop. I find the tourist information centre and ask them, but they don't seem to quite understand which stop I'm looking for. I waylay various likely looking persons in the street and ask them – four to be exact; they all give me different directions, none of which locates for me the desired bus stop. It's that old Irish trait again of not being able to say no, or of not admitting that they don't know. Finally, a foreigner (like myself) in a bookshop directs me successfully, but it's taken a search of over an hour. Now, on the bus back to Black Ash, I look at the map of the city and realise that the difficulty's been caused by there being north and south branches of the River Lee, with Cork City being 'confusedly' situated in the middle on an island. It's obvious! Pity I hadn't looked more closely at the map an hour ago. I seem to have a propensity towards getting lost (you may have noticed). 'Directionally challenged' is a polite name for such a person – but 'silly old fart' seems to fit the bill in my case!

Tuesday 25th June – Muckross to Guitane Lough

My knee that I twisted on the second day of the walk – a week ago – has been giving me some pain over the last two days. I rubbed some gel into it last night and this morning it seems a little better.

I pass the lay-by reserved for the jaunting cars for a third time. It's early, and only one horse and cart is there ready for the tourist onslaught. I reach the road junction and turn east. A jaunting car trots past at a brisk pace on the way to work. The driver, wearing a flat cap, nods good morning.

I'm repeating Saturday's three-mile walk out to Guitane Lough, where, just before I reach it, is the turning off to the right which leads to Gortdromakiery country where Edward Eagar had played as a child.

Eagar was one of about 40,000 Irishmen and Irishwomen shipped off to New South Wales, Van Diemen's Land (Tasmania) and Western Australia.

Hangings were just beginning to go out of fashion in 1809 for a number of reasons. Firstly the judges, being a bit squeamish, were reluctant to enforce the death sentence for minor crimes, well... crowd attendances had dwindled anyway once the novelty had worn off (they'd have rather have gone to a football match if it had been thought of by then). There was also the problem of all those corpses to be deposited at village crossroads; the cross placed there, of course, prevented the subsequent rise of those unholy un-dead into heaven. But this practice upset the locals who avoided these places by making detours across the fields. Oh! And King George III also jumped on the bandwagon by exercising his Royal 'prerogative of mercy' – it was good for his public image of course. So all in all hanging became a 'no-no'.

'No problem,' George proclaimed (or words to that effect), 'we'll put 'em all in gaol, or on the hulks.' But there *was* a problem – the gaols and prison ships were all chock-a-block.

Prime Minister William Pitt and his government chewed their nails; then some progressive fellow suggested a brainstorming session might do the trick. It did. They came up trumps with a solution to all their problems. It got rid of the offenders, improved mobility by freeing-up the crossroads, improved air quality by getting rid of all those rotting corpses – *and* you didn't have to build more of those bloody expensive prisons. Transportation was definitely *the* answer. And so it was that the First Fleet of convicts sailed from Portsmouth, England less than 22 years before Eagar had boarded the *Providence*.

Providence received around 185 prisoners on board at Cork, including prisoners from Belfast, Dublin and elsewhere. The crew numbered 56, mostly Spanish, and about 39 soldiers made the passage, employed as guards. The ship's log recorded that only five prisoners and four soldiers had died – a mortality rate of around 3%. This was such a brilliant achievement that it drew mention from the *Sydney Gazette* who praised Captain Barclay for his 'humane treatment'. It was an understandable comment given the record of previous sailings. The Second Fleet for instance, sailing in 1790, had lost a quarter of its prisoners at sea. Of those that *did* make it ashore at Sydney Cove, half were in a pretty shocking state, many later dying from sickness and other after-effects of maltreatment on-board.

The First Fleet had taken 252 days to get to Australia from England – *Providence* took 162 from Ireland. She sailed first to Falmouth in Cornwall for a rendezvous with the frigate *Narcissus* who accompanied her, for protection, to Tenerife. To make use of the prevailing winds and currents she detoured 'slightly' to Rio de Janeiro, Brazil, where she lay at anchor for three weeks and took on provisions. From there she called in at the Cape of Good Hope. The captain knew where they were eventually heading, but for the convicts on board as far as they were concerned they were sailing to an unknown future in a strange land.

The present was a trifle dire too. Life on board for Eagar and the other convicts was definitely not a bed of roses; they were kept for the most part on the lower decks, lit only by dim lanterns. The air was foul, smelling of a combination of animal and human excrement.

When the ship reached the tropics things got even 'better'; they then entertained a few visitors who crept up from the bilges and out of the woodwork: cockroaches (lovely creatures), rats, lice, fleas and bedbugs galore. When there was no land in sight the convicts were given a little break and allowed on deck for a spot of fresh air and deck games. Well, the *only* game actually was to swing a hook (but fatty canvass probably wasn't much of a tasty bait) to see if they could catch something fishy to supplement their staple diet of 'salt horse', or as it was officially named, brined beef.

How did Eagar, born a gentleman, cope with the passage? How did his recent conversion to Methodism sustain him? Did he attempt to convert fellow convicts? The answers to these questions are unknown, but in all probability he would have mixed with all classes – petty thieves, rustlers, highway robbers, arsonists, burglars, pickpockets and vagrants. The Cork prison chaplain, Reverend Boyle Davies, mentioned two other 'gentlemen' on board who Eagar would likely have met. He wrote a letter to the Reverend Samuel Marsden, Senior Chaplain to the Colony of New South Wales in which he described them as a Mr Coates who had been convicted of robbery in Dublin and from whom Marsden had been unable to extract any form of repentance. Not much hope there then, Edward! The other was a Michael Casey who'd been with Eagar at the time of his conversion and who'd seemed affected by the profound change that had occurred in Eagar. Casey had been convicted of bigamy, so maybe Eagar *did* make a convert during the voyage. 'You must swear not to marry anyone else,' Eagar had perhaps said (or something very similar). This would have been a bit rich given that Eagar was to do the very same thing a decade later. One person Eagar definitely *did* speak to on the voyage was a Mr Nowlan, who was identified as 'an extra prisoner' during the muster carried out just before the prisoners disembarked at Sydney Cove. There's some confusion, however, with regards to his name; it could have been James Nowlan or perhaps John Nowland – maybe the copying clerk had bad hearing, was pissed or just didn't give a toss. Nowlan (let's say), had been tried in the County of Kildare. What his crime was and how long his sentence was is both a mystery, but Eagar certainly made an impact on him because 17 years later Nowlan appointed Eagar as his lawyer.

After a voyage of almost seven months the *Providence* was hauled into her final anchorage on 6th July 1811. The convicts clinked ashore at Sydney Cove in their chains feeling unsteady with that solid clay feeling strange beneath their feet. Here, muster was called. The majority, from the 'criminal class' and with no skills were to endure a life of near slavery. These men were assigned to chain gangs and a life of hard labour building roads or ploughing the land. The majority of the women were sent to the female factory at Parramatta where they carded and spun wool into yarn. Convicts would frequently be flogged and persistent or gross misconduct would see them sent to an even worse fate in Van Diemen's Land where solitary confinement for up to a fortnight was 'tempered' with floggings – with a 'conservative' limit of 100 lashes. Worse still was banishment to remote Norfolk Island (advertised today as: 'peaceful quietude blended with sub-tropical air').

But Eagar, still retaining his gentlemanly privileges, would miss all this 'fun'. The Reverend Boyle Davies, undoubtedly affected by Eagar's conversion in Cork Gaol, had written to Samuel Marsden and in his letter (the receipt of which preceded Eagar's arrival in Sydney) he'd recommended Eagar for connection with the church. Just two days after the muster at Sydney Cove a Mr William Cox took Eagar, along with 16 other selected convicts on a short trip of about 40 miles north-west to Windsor. Three days later a lottery was held to see which of the lucky candidates whose names had been put into the hat (provided they'd been industrious, sober and deserving) would be selected to the relatively cushy positions of servant. Eagar, due to the Reverend Boyle Davies' recommendation and Marsden's acceptance of it, appears to have missed this ordeal. He was assigned to the even cushier position of tutor to the five children of an Anglican minister, the Reverend Robert Cartwright, chaplain to Hawkesbury District. At the same time he received the coveted 'ticket of leave', normally only given after at least four years' good conduct. It seems that Eagar had really fallen on his feet (even if he was in effect standing upside down).

My feet pass the right-hand turning that leads up to Gortdromakiery, and continue eastward towards the Blackwater Way. There's no official way-marked route yet joining the Kerry Way with the

Blackwater Way and I open the rucksack to check the *Irish Coast to Coast Walk* book. It confirms what I already know; it's all minor-road-walking, almost 12 miles to Shrone and the start of the Blackwater Way, then I have to walk another three miles north to Rathmore where there's a train going back to Killarney. The one I'm aiming for leaves at just before 6pm. If I miss it, the next is at just before 8pm, which, with a tidy walk from Killarney station back to the campsite at Muckross, would probably mean I'd miss the meal I'm promising myself in the pub restaurant on the site. As I slide the book back into a side pocket of the rucksack my fingers touch the small tuft of wool picked up and stuffed in there on Dursey Island. I've only carried it on the route for about 70 miles so far; only another 3,600 or so to go then to Istanbul and the waters of the Bosporus!

My first view today of the waters of Guitane Lough appears off to my right, and beyond are the dark slopes of the Mountains Stoompa and Crohane. My thoughts then are, for one last time, with Edward Eagar, who never ever returned to this land of his birth.

If you key in Eagar's name on the Internet a number of sites come up featuring the Edward Eagar Lodge, a Wesley Mission in Sydney that gives temporary shelter and offers a support programme to homeless people of all ages. The lodge is named as a tribute to the one-time criminal, whose conundrum of a life made twists and turns that saw his dichotomous fortunes regularly change from triumph to scrape, and back again to triumph.

Eagar soon settled down in Windsor. He organised Bible classes and, after a year, formed with others the inaugural membership of the Sydney Methodist Church (which is now the Wesley Mission). He also organised the first mission to convert the aborigines to Christianity (don't know if this worked) as well as buying the largest individual holding in the formation of what would be the Bank of New South Wales.

In 1813 he wrote to England requesting that a minister be sent for the church, and two years later one duly arrived. Macquarie, the governor of the colony, was impressed and gave him a conditional pardon – though this still meant he couldn't return to Ireland without the probability of being hanged. So Eagar made the best of things, setting himself up as an attorney and marrying Jemima McDuel, with whom he was to have three sons and a daughter.

His legal practice did well for the first two years until the judge of the newly created Supreme Court of Civil Judicature, Jeffrey Bent, and a very dubious character to hold such a position, refused to hear cases conducted by ex-convict lawyers. This prompted Eagar to make yet another career move and become a merchant trader and agent (a bit of a 'Del Boy' you could say). In 1818, on the recommendation of several reverends, he was rewarded for his endeavours when the governor granted him an absolute pardon.

But Eagar's diverse business interests were soon to land him in his next series of scrapes. Between 1814 and 1828 he instigated 13 court cases, whilst another 10 were brought against him. His record was: won 13, lost nine and drawn one – that being an unrecorded judgement. In 1819 he was charged with driving carts through the streets of Sydney without the cart having a name or number, and was fined 10 shillings. That same year he and his servants and partners were charged with stealing timber – but the charge was eventually dismissed. He was also into all sorts: paper making, ale brewing and the supply of Irish and Tahitian pork to the government. He was unable to secure a monopoly of this trade with King Pomare II of Tahiti, due to a court decision and he lost a lot of money in the process, but by 1828 his firm were still reported in the *Sydney Gazette* as being 'the principle merchants in New South Wales'.

Eagar's legacy was, however, that he championed the emancipist and civil libertarian cause of the convicts; he fought for their rights to be tried by jury (which he himself was denied) and for their self-government. For his pains he was charged with making seditious speeches and being a revolutionist. Eagar countered by suing the Supreme Court Judge who'd made the allegations for character deformation. In 1821 he took the fight for convict emancipation to England, presenting a petition to the Secretary of State in London in June 1822. This time a petition *did* work: trial by jury for convicts was granted in 1823, but it took a further 20 years of persistence before all of Eagar's emancipist goals had been achieved.

Eagar took only his daughter with him to England where he then spent the rest of his life. He didn't seem to have had too bad a time there (although he *did* spend two weeks in Fleet Debtor's Prison).

Obviously forgetting what might have transpired between Michael Casey the bigamist and himself aboard the *Providence*, Eagar lived with a 16-year-old girl, whom he later married. His excuse was that the case in London had taken a long time to be resolved! The first Mrs Eagar meanwhile remained in Sydney and eventually moved in with somebody else. Eagar's new wife, Ellen Gorman, probably lived quite happily with Eagar because she bore him 10 children. He died aged 79 in London. I couldn't find the cause of death recorded anywhere, but maybe he'd died from exhaustion!

Five

The Blackwater Way

'There's a far-famed Blackwater that runs to Loch Neagh
There's a fairer Blackwater that runs to the sea –
The glory of Ulster,
The beauty of Munster,
These twin rivers be.'
From *The Rivers* – by Thomas Davis

Tuesday 25th June – Guitane Lough to Shrone (and then Rathmore)
At Guitane Lough a tourist coach has pulled into the roadside for a prearranged meeting with a sheep farmer. I eavesdrop as a huddle of questioning tourists gather hard up against a fence listening intently whilst the farmer demonstrates how his well-trained sheepdogs round up the flock to perfection.

A quarter of a mile up the road it seems that a faction of the flock have decided not to go along with the farmer's well-rehearsed script and have made a break for freedom. They head up the road towards me pursued by two frenetic dogs and one frantic farmer yelling orders. One of the dogs cuts into the flock and herds about half of them first into and then out of fields and gardens from one side of the road to the other. The farmer meanwhile drives past them in his 4x4 and parks it to form a road-blockade. But, upstream of him around 20 of the woolly absconders still trundle on past me nonchalantly and find a tasty shrub or two in the hospitable garden of a bungalow. A car travelling in the opposite direction is forced to stop and wait for the episode to be resolved and the road to be cleared. The driver lowers his window for a chat. We find the situation far more amusing than the farmer.

The driver asks me about my walk and where I'm from. I tell him I have a house in Spain that I'm renovating and that my partner has a house in the UK.

'Life's good,' he says with a smile. I agree. I do indeed feel lucky.

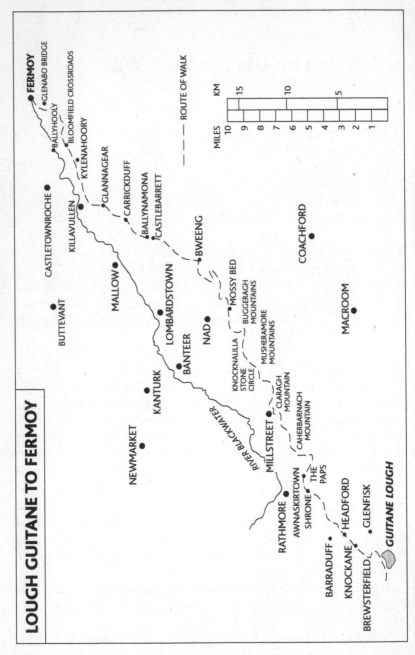

LOUGH GUITANE TO FERMOY

FERMOY
GLENABO BRIDGE
BALLYHOOLY
BLOOMFIELD CROSSROADS
CASTLETOWNROCHE
KILLAVULLEN
KYLENAHOORY
GLANNAGEAR
CARRICKDUFF
BALLYNAMONA
CASTLEBARRETT
MALLOW
BWEENG
BUTTEVANT
LOMBARDSTOWN
MOSSY BED
COACHFORD
BUGGERAGH MOUNTAINS
NAD
KNOCKNALILLA STONE CIRCLE
MUSHERAMORE MOUNTAINS
MACROOM
KANTURK
BANTER
CLARAGH MOUNTAIN
CAHERBARNACH MOUNTAIN
RIVER BLACKWATER
NEWMARKET
MILLSTREET
THE PAPS
RATHMORE
AWNASKIRTOWN
SHRONE
HEADFORD
GLENFISK
BARRADUFF
KNOCKANE
BREWSTERFIELD
GUITANE LOUGH

- - - ROUTE OF WALK

KM
15
10
5

MILES
10
9
8
7
6
5
4
3
2
1

74

Statistically some of my school classmates will no longer be alive. Some, I know died as teenagers in motorbike accidents; one, chased by a police motorcyclist, lost an argument with a double-decker bus. Two of my oldest friends died recently of brain tumours – so yes, life *is* good; I've been lucky.

I bid the car driver and the situation farewell and am on my way. The road I'm walking has little traffic, no designation, and would be classed as a lane in England. But talking of luck – a lady driver pulls up alongside and offers me a lift; it never happens when you're really desperate for one. I decline gracefully, trying to explain that I *want* to walk.

The road bends sharply several times left and right. For a short while it joins the N22, but I soon turn off it to walk through the hamlets of Brewsterfield, Knockane and on towards Headford Roadside shrines of the Virgin Mary remind me I'm in a fervently Catholic land.

Just before Headford I inadvertently add about a mile to the walk, which I only discover when finishing up in somebody's backyard. I've misread the map by turning right too soon (the book having of course to be read backwards and being of little help). I can now see, on closer inspection of the map, that a railway line passes over both the lane I've taken and the road I want, which is a little further on. As I walk back to the T-junction I notice the lane sign that clearly reads: CUL-DE-SAC. Yep!

I sit by a railway arch on a wall to take a sandwich lunch. It was around here at Headford Junction Station just over 92 years ago that the Irish Republican Army (IRA) ambushed a train carrying British soldiers.

The ambush took place on 21st March 1921; it was the largest engagement to take place in Kerry during the Anglo-Irish War – otherwise known (especially in Ireland) as the War of Independence. The war is recognised to have begun in January 1919, so the situation in Ireland was well established by the date of the ambush. Kerry was occupied at that time by the British army, including the infamous Black and Tans. The situation had been intensifying since towards the end of the previous year.

The train was carrying 28 Royal London Fusiliers who'd embarked at Kenmare on route to Tralee, and would need to change trains at Headford Junction to pick up a train travelling from Mallow. The ambush could have been much more successful for the IRA, if not for three occurrences: the IRA were organised into brigades that were sub-divided into battalions, each of which comprised a number of columns situated in towns and villages. The Kerry battalion in the area had three columns local to Headford: north at Barraduff, east at Gortderrig (at the foot of the Pap Mountains) and south at Glenfisk. The Officer Commanding (O/C) the battalion stayed the night before the ambush locally at Knockane, to the west of Headford, and he'd appointed a scout to find out from the station staff whether the train leaving Kenmare would be carrying troops that morning. The scout was having a bad day – perhaps he'd had a few too many whiskys the night before; anyway, first he made it late to the station, then he dithered around a bit before finding out that the train *would* have the fusiliers aboard. For reasons known only to him, instead of then reporting to the battalion O/C at Knockane as arranged at 10.30am (perhaps fearing a bollocking for being late), he instead reported to the O/C at Gortderrig called Dan Allman, whose 30-man column alone then carried out the ambush. *The Times* erroneously reported two days later: 'The number of ambushers is estimated at about 100, of whom 15 had taken up positions in the station-master's house' (three actually, according to the IRA). The second occurrence also influenced the outcome in favour of the British: it was the custom that, once detrained, the British soldiers would form two ranks with two flanking rows of five men each side. They were required to stand in this formation until the arrival of the train from Mallow, due in about 45 minutes – sitting ducks for an attack by the IRA. What occurred, though, was that before the attack could take place, one of the soldiers was dying for a slash and dashed for the public lavatory where (presumably before he'd got unbuttoned) he discovered, much to his surprise, Dan Allman and three other IRA men. In the ensuing scuffle, Allman shot the soldier, which kind of ruined the surprise attack planned for the remaining 27 fusiliers. The third occurrence really saw the luck of the Irish desert them: fierce close-quarter fighting ensued and at one point when the IRA appeared to have the upper hand they shouted:

'Tommy, surrender.'

'No surrender, Paddy,' was the defiant reply. But then the 'cavalry' rode over the hill in the form of the awaited train from Mallow with 200 soldiers aboard. Game over. The IRA sensibly withdrew.

The ambush resulted in the deaths of seven British soldiers, two IRA men (including Allman) and one civilian.

Estimates of the numbers killed during the entire War of Independence vary but are thought to be over 2,000. Could all that bloodshed have been avoided? It was unlikely, given the complex political, religious and historical path leading up to the conflict.

It's difficult to know how far to go back to get to the root of things. The Irish were never, it has to be said, happy about being under the thumb of the British, whilst Britain for her part was certainly spooked by the Irish Rebellion of 1798, in which the French played a hand. A French invasion, by any route, was always a threat and these events pushed the British towards uniting Britain and Ireland via the Act of Union, which became law in 1801.

The British government's insensitive disregard for Ireland during the famine years of 1845–49 stoked the fires for the overthrow of British rule and contributed to a continuing mood of armed insurrection. William Smith O'Brien and James Stephens were involved in an abortive rising in 1848 and 10 years later Stephens, together with John O'Mahony, set up an oath-bound secret society founded for the overthrow of British rule. It was later to be known in Ireland as the Irish Republican Brotherhood (IRB) and in America as the Fenian Brotherhood. The Fenians made two failed attempts at rebellion in 1865 and 1867.

William Gladstone, a Liberal, took over from Benjamin Disraeli as British prime minister in 1868 and, on hearing of his summons to meet Queen Victoria, declared that his mission was to pacify Ireland. It has to be said that he gave it a good try. Gladstone saw four periods of office as prime minister, during which time he tried twice, both times unsuccessfully, to introduce a home rule bill for Ireland. On his first attempt in 1886 he split his party, which resulted in the Conservatives being returned to power. He was still trying at the age of 83 with the Second Home Rule Bill, which was submitted in 1893 but was rejected by the House of Lords (largely comprising of Conservatives).

Ireland itself was also pushing for home rule during this time. In

1873 Isaac Butt was instrumental in the creation of the Home Rule League, but his approach was perhaps too gentlemanly. Fenians Michael Davitt and John Devoy took a more aggressive stance and in 1879 formed the Land League. At their inaugural meeting Charles Stewart Parnell was (at Davitt's invitation) elected president. The Land League ostracised estates with bad records, notably that of Captain Charles Boycott, a land agent who attempted to get rents reduced then, when he was 'boycotted', wrote a letter of complaint to *The Times* – thus introducing a new word into the English dictionary. Butt's and Davitt's parties later amalgamated.

Parnell and Gladstone worked closely together for eight years, Gladstone promising to present a home rule bill in exchange for support from Parnell's party. This relationship was to change, however, upon the death of Captain William O'Shea's estranged wife's aunt.

Auntie's death was to change the course of history. The butterfly's flapping wings *did* affect the path of the tornado. She was wealthy and, perhaps because she didn't much like the captain, left her estate not to him as he expected, but to her niece, his estranged wife Katharine. O'Shea was a trifle upset about this and either to try and change the situation, or purely out of spite, he filed for divorce, citing Katie's affair with Parnell, which he'd in fact known about for some time as Parnell had fathered three of her children and had been living with her for some time in various locations along the south coast of England. Parnell didn't contest the divorce case and the verdict was delivered against him.

Because of attitudes at the time, Parnell came under pressure to stand down as leader of his party, not only from the Roman Catholic bishops, but also by a moralising Gladstone who (and although he'd known about the affair himself for some time) in the face of public opinion, threatened to abandon the Irish/Liberal pact and scrap the Home Rule Bill. Parnell, however, refused to resign as leader, which caused his party to split on the issue and form two separate factions, pro- and anti-Parnell. The majority were far and away anti-Parnell. He subsequently married Mrs Katie O'Shea, but the strain of trying to regain his political status eventually told on his health and he died a broken man a year later, with Katie beside him, at their rented home in Hove, Sussex, on the south coast of England.

What would have happened to Ireland had Parnell lived beyond the age of 45 will always be a matter of conjecture. The nationalist cause didn't come to fruition until the signing of the Anglo-Irish Treaty in December 1921 – and then certainly not to everyone's satisfaction. As Parnell was a Protestant, he surely wouldn't have accepted the partition of Ireland and maybe things would have been resolved differently and a lot sooner. If Parnell hadn't died when he did, perhaps the IRA would not have been formed. Certainly things would have turned out differently had it not been for auntie's will.

Lunch is a short interlude. I walk on under the old railway arch of the Kenmare branch line that had brought the fusiliers to Headford Junction. The line was closed in 1963. The stationmaster's house is now a private residence.

A little way along the road I come to Con Spillane's bar which at first also seems closed, but I decide to see if lunch can be washed down with a glass of beer. The place *is* open but deserted, to the point that nobody is behind the bar. I call out loudly several times and eventually 'Mr Spillane' arrives from a back room. He's not the chattiest of landlords; surprisingly he asks me no questions and serves me without a hint of cheer. Perhaps I woke him up from his afternoon nap. I make some enquiry about the weather, to which he informs me, again without humour that it is of course going to rain. Then he disappears into the back room again.

The road walk to Shrone passes scatterings of detached houses and bungalows where, at some, dogs stand guard – not always behind shut gates. Some lay stretched out, too lazy to raise more than a watchful eye, whilst others set-to with wild barking, probably more from trepidation than aggression. On two occasions things get a little hairy. On the first I'm surrounded by a pack of three that follow me for a while; the Jack Russell is particularly persistent, barking furiously and not giving up for about 300 metres, still continuing the occasional growl and bark upon his retreat. On the second occasion a large dog (I'm too worried to note the breed) sniffs me from behind then sidles up alongside menacingly. My strategy in these situations is to keep walking slowly and never to make eye contact. It works; he gets fed up once I leave his familiar territory and wanders back home.

It's another six miles to Shrone according to the map. My right knee and right shoulder both hurt again so it seems a lot further. By now I must be somewhere near the village but it's difficult to tell as there's no signs (Shrone it seems to me is another 'area' like Gortdromakiery). I reach a distinctive crossroads and a school, after passing a long scattering of properties. I check the map – it tallies. This must be the centre of Shrone.

My plan is to join the start of the Blackwater Way from the lane I'm walking. I pass a farm with yet more aggressive barking dogs and notice from the map that the lane does a loop and returns to the crossroads. The Blackwater Way is shown branching off it at the head of the loop. I reach the ladder-stile, which in my book marks the start of the trail (well, actually the end as I'm reading the book backwards). My book says that the trail ends abruptly. It surely does; there is just a fingerpost pointing east across soggy, uneven bog-land. I peer into the distance; I can see no discernible path and no further fingerposts. Everything is desolate and bleak, including, now, my mood. Nobody knows I'm here. I've seen nobody for hours. I climb the stile and descend into the wet.

After five minutes of tediously picking my way and balancing precariously upon clumps of uneven grass to avoid the deep boggy pits, slipping and slithering on them and the rocks, I cover very little distance.

To catch the 6pm train I must navigate this terrain for some time it seems and then ascend part-way up a mountain. It's three miles to a place called Awnaskirtawn where a lane leads to the Rathmore Road. From there it's another five miles of road walking to reach the station at Rathmore. Eight miles in two and a half hours could be possible but I calculate that, even if I don't manage to get myself lost, over this sort of terrain I won't make it on time to catch the train. Reluctantly and dejectedly I turn around, walk back and clamber over the ladder-stile to rejoin the lane and complete the loop back to the crossroads. By the road route it's still a seven-mile walk to Rathmore, but at least I know where I'm going and it's easy walking. It still takes me two hours – but then I have an hour to kill until the train is due.

I sit in the Sun bar in Rathmore with a pint and contemplate the next day's walk which will include getting to and from the

Blackwater Way. It will be over 25 miles, three miles of which will be backtracking (breaking one of my rules). If I could get a taxi back to that isolated ladder-stile I'd save six miles, leaving a manageable, but still challenging 19 miles to walk. I call at the post office (always a good shot when in trouble) and the lady gives me the telephone number of a local taxi firm.

Back at the campsite I calculate I've clocked up around 22 miles walking today. The train tomorrow leaves Killarney at 7.34am, so I need a taxi for eight o'clock.

'I'm sorry,' he says, when I phone, 'I can't do that.' He's obviously on a school run – but I'm a bit taken aback.

'I can maybe do nine,' he adds. 'Where is it you're wantin' to get to?' I tell him my story.

'Oh, it's the Paps you'll be walking then is it?' he enquires.

'Yes,' I say – not wishing to confuse things.

It'd been a long day.

Wednesday 26th June – Rathmore to Millstreet

I'm up at 5.30am – it's a lovely morning. On the walk into Killarney groups of Japanese tourists are already up and taking photographs of each other.

I sit opposite a German couple on the train. The man stands up to look closely at the rail map.

'A lot of stops,' I say.

'No, this is a no-stopping train,' he replies.

'I hope not,' I say. 'I'm only going one stop.' He looks worried.

'We are going to Dublin,' he says. 'The man told me this would not stop – he sold me no-stopping tickets.' Now it's me who looks worried.

'I hope it *does* stop, I don't particularly want to go to Dublin and back.'

'You can pull the cord,' he jokes. I force a polite chuckle. A few minutes later he concedes, and I'm relieved.

'I think you *are* right – it stops – we will get there next year. It is being pulled by a jaunting car.'

The couple are apparently from Cologne. I thought Germans were supposed not to have a sense of humour!

The train stops at Rathmore at precisely the scheduled time of

7.57, but now I have over an hour to wait for the taxi – and there's nothing to do. I consider sitting under the little waiting-canopy and reading, but this seems a waste of time on such a nice morning, so I meander along Station Road to the main road. Everything is closed.

I decide, although feeling slightly guilty, to *walk* back to the Blackwater Way – back the three miles of almost dead straight and boring road I'd slogged along yesterday. I switch off the mobile just in case the taxi driver calls – at least I'll save the fare. The only downside is that I would have asked him to take me back to the ladder-stile and the official start (or end) of the Blackwater Way, but to *walk* back to that point is another three miles, and I'd then still face the same uncharted, boggy challenge as yesterday, adding at least five miles to the otherwise scheduled 24-mile walk for the day. So at the end of the straight road, when I reach yesterday's turning point, instead of turning west back towards Shrone, I turn east along a lane heading for the track up to Awnaskirtawn. It feels like I'm breaking my rule number three by deliberately shortcutting the defined trail. But the distance walked will be the same and I'll be satisfying my other two rules of not backtracking east to west and of starting from exactly the same point as reached the previous day. It seems I must be a pragmatist after all.

Ancient vibrations are, however, something I shall miss. My book tells me I would have walked close to 'The City', an ancient fort where Irish pagans performed druidic rituals before the arrival of Christianity. I reckon, judging from my distant view yesterday of the land ahead, that it would have taken some time for the Christians to stumble on this desolate, barren site anyway. An annual Christian pilgrimage apparently takes place at the fort, dipping into Irish folklore and mythology, celebrating the conversion to Christianity of one of the pagan war goddesses who gave her name to the site. I hope the pilgrims wear good waterproof boots and bring a compass.

It's still not yet 9am as I ascend the lane, and at the point where it joins the stony track to Awnaskirtawn and the Blackwater Way a man stands and watches my approach warily, as if I've just landed from Mars. He asks me where I'm from. I interpret this to mean where I originate from, but think later that perhaps he meant where I'd come from that morning.

'Portsmouth,' I say. He's English, originally from London and he lives in a cottage that we are approaching. Perhaps he heard my footsteps or was just out for an early morning stroll. He seems as surprised as I am with our meeting at this hour in such a remote spot. I have the feeling that I'm the first Englishman he'd spoken to for some time.

'How do the midges affect you?' he asks.

'They tend to be in the shade, and if I keep moving there's no problem,' I say.

I shortly reach the Way and pause to look back at the route I would (and perhaps should) have taken had I waited for the taxi. It runs alongside a forest. I join the Way and head east. It's similar to that of the previous day: rutted, boggy and not at all an easy walk. However, the narrow path, sprinkled with prickly gorse, myrtle, and shielded on both sides by foliage, is well defined. It emerges onto open land and I get my first sight of serried rows of rectangular peat strips, which I have to delicately tread across. Fingerposts *are* in place here, but are sometimes widely spaced and difficult to spot. The Way leads over marshland and crosses a stream, then heads towards a col where it snakes up to reach the lower slopes of Caherbarnach Mountain. It's a challenging but satisfying climb. Now I stay at this elevation for almost three miles following the fence (which the book tells me is electrified – and I don't test), with views to my left of flat countryside stretching for miles away into the distance. Somewhere out there in the valley is the River Blackwater and the railway line that I'll travel later today.

Higher up on the mountain are two horses. I pass them lower down and, when I turn back to look, one rolls his head high in the air and neighs loudly. In the valley far below I hear the faint reply of another horse. The two above gallop wildly down the mountain as far as the fence.

A rocky track leads down to a road – more of a lane really – which I stay on for another three miles until I reach Croonig's Crossroads.

Along the road section I meet an Irishman of about my age, wearing a straw hat (for the sun – it's a hot day) and a fluorescent jacket (in case of the odd tractor) over a tee shirt of black-and-white hoops. He's just trimmed his hedge and is sweeping up the clippings. We chat for a while. He tells me he worked in England for years, offers to fill my water container and asks if I'd like a bun. Very kind of him, but I decline as it's almost time for my packed lunch.

Sheep, it's of no doubt, are stupid creatures. A high bank rises from the lane to a field and one has somehow got itself entangled in the perimeter fence on the lane side. When it sees me, it tries to get back to the field but then gets itself even more trapped, with its head stuck inside a large wire square of the fence. I drop my backpack and make several unsuccessful attempts to scramble up the bank – each time the sheep goes crazy, forcing itself even more tightly into the wire square. On my third attempt I make it up onto the bank and set the stupid thing free to dart away. It's my good deed for the day, perhaps making up for upsetting the taxi driver.

I turn right at the crossroads and, after another mile of uphill lane-walking, stop for lunch, before setting off across open countryside to skirt Claragh Mountain.

The train from Millstreet is scheduled to leave at 5.47pm. There's plenty of time. The afternoon is pleasant and warm, time enough for me to stop, read a little and take the sun. The path remains elevated, with the flat-lands and distant mountains beyond to my left and behind, there's a clear view back to Caherbarnach Mountain.

The remainder of the afternoon is uneventful – except that I finish up in somebody's back garden after missing a fingerpost. I eventually find the path, which leads up through a wood and then begins its drop towards Millstreet. Before I start the descent I pause to read an information board.

This is truly bog country as the names of places hereabouts bear witness to: Musheramore means big rough bog; Musherabeg means the small rough bog; Carragh is named after a marsh or swamp, and has a famous bog from which turf has traditionally always been saved, whilst Gneeves also has many turf cutting allotments. A day in the bog, cutting peat sods, still holds many memories for Irish folk. The lines of peat I'd seen today verify that it's an activity that is still obviously pursued. The turf was, and perhaps sometimes still is, cut using a specially designed two-sided spade called a *slane* (nowadays though cutting is highly mechanised). The little cut sods are then turned to be dried in the sun (or more likely the wind), then later they're stacked upright in what is known as 'footies', supported by each other, for further drying. But peat burning is now considered to be environmentally unfriendly – a dirty fuel releasing large quantities of carbon dioxide. Conservationists also say that the natural habitat of plants and insects are destroyed by the cutting. There's been a Brussels Directive issued and an EU ban in some areas – which has sometimes been openly defied by groups of economically-squeezed working people. 'For peat's sake' – the debate is liable to continue for some time.

After dropping steeply, the Way cuts across meadows, passing the fenced-off, ivy and foliage smothered ruin of the once grand Georgian Mountleader House. Not occupied since the late 1970s it was built by, and was the seat for years of, the wealthy colliery owning Leader family. From here it's a short walk down to the main road. There's another information board at a crossroads here that tells me about Mountleader House and also that I'm still on the route taken by O'Sullivan Bere. He passed through Millstreet, the board tells me, and received hospitality from the O'Keeffs at Boinng Castle. The crossroads is the point where I will rejoin the Blackwater Way another day, but now I have a road-slog into the small town of Millstreet and then have to endure a further road-walk out to the railway station. Overall, it's a good three miles.

My right knee has been extremely painful for miles and, when I hobble into the centre of Millstreet, I finally decide to do something about it and buy a knee-support bandage in a chemist. The young girl assistant is very attentive and I roll up my jeans whilst she painstakingly measures my knee – a not too pleasant task for her. I check my watch before I set out for the station; there's time for a quick pint at the Bridge bar.

The bar is busy, which I find surprising for late afternoon on a Wednesday. I'm inspected momentarily but then ignored; my walking boots and rucksack obviously give-away my identity – a feckin foreign walker. The conversation, having momentarily stopped when I came in, continues again as I'm being served. All the locals, as they undoubtedly are, are men except for one apparently unaccompanied woman. The men, perhaps unemployed (or maybe night workers) clog up the bar as horse-racing is being shown on two TVs. There's a deal of raucous and suggestive conversation between the woman and several of the locals, but the others sit quietly reading newspapers or watching the racing. I perch on a bar stool next to a man reading *The Mirror*. Nobody speaks to me. I feel uneasy; about as welcome as a pork chop in a synagogue. They know I'm English as soon as I open my mouth to order the pint. Perhaps I'm paranoid, but feel somehow that Ireland and England's history still in some way reverberates here; these are the sons and grandsons of the Volunteers, the nationalist military organisation formed in 1913, that later joined together with other organisations to become the IRA.

The emergence of the IRA was the result of a long and twisted chronicle of events that followed the death of Parnell. His and Gladstone's home rule dream now began to turn into a political nightmare and, as Ronan Fanning well illustrates in his book *Fatal Path*, the British government were about to take further steps along such a path.

Gladstone's successor, Archibald Primrose achieved the last of his three life's ambitions when he became prime minister; the other two were to marry a rich heiress and to own a Derby winning racehorse. He took a complete U-turn from Gladstone's Irish policy, showing a total disregard for Irish nationalist views. He was a big fan of Oliver Cromwell and campaigned for government funds to be made available for the erection of a statue of Cromwell outside Westminster Hall in London. No surprise that this little venture didn't get the Irish vote in the House of Commons then (the statue *was* eventually erected following a donation from an anonymous donor – discovered later to have been none other than Primrose himself). After just over a year as prime minister, Primrose lost a vote in the Commons, took the hump, and tendered his resignation to Queen Victoria, who invited Conservative and Unionist leader Lord Salisbury to be prime minister (pretty clear what her politics were then). In the election that followed, the Conservatives won a thumping victory and stayed in government for the next 10 years, which pretty much stifled any constitutional home rule ideas the Irish had.

When the Liberals regained power in 1905 they were led by Henry Campbell-Bannerman, who promised John Redmond (leader since 1900 of Parnell's previously fractured party, now reunited as the Irish Parliamentary Party) that he would progress the home rule question. Campbell-Bannerman resigned in 1908 due to ill health and was succeeded by Herbert Henry Asquith, a barrister by profession and a declared anti-Catholic.

In 1910 there were general elections in both Britain and Ireland in which the Irish Parliamentary Party (IPP) held the balance of power, giving Redmond an opportunity: he threatened that unless Asquith pushed for home rule he'd ensure that the Liberals would lose many seats in Westminster. To prevent a reoccurrence of the House of Lords (still packed with Conservatives) exercising their prerogative to veto a home rule bill, the Irish put their case forward for the abolition of the Lords veto. This was a bit of a catch-22 conundrum as the Lords could always veto the bill to abolish the veto.

The crisis came to a head over whisky. David Lloyd George, then Chancellor of the Exchequer, proposed an increase in the tax on whisky to which the Irish naturally objected. The consensus of opinion was that Lloyd George, in order to keep the Irish vote and a Liberal majority in the Commons, would propose *not* to raise the tax. He didn't, however, take that course. What he *actually did* was to keep the tax increase and then threaten to resign and join the Irish unless the government approached King Edward VII for a guarantee that Liberal peers would be created so that the Lords could no longer veto any future home rule bill – a clever move by Mr Lloyd George.

Asquith had never been enthusiastic about home rule; he and Redmond shared, if nothing else, a mutual distrust of each other. Lloyd George also basically opposed home rule, on religious grounds – he apparently just didn't much like Catholics, whilst the recently promoted Winston Churchill was opposed to it from an imperialist standpoint, although he also had a view that strong Catholicism destroyed countries.

Just weeks after Edward VII had agreed to create more peers the King upped and died following an attack of bronchitis caused by a series of heart attacks. George, Queen Victoria's grandson, then became King George V and, finding himself in the middle of political mire, suggested (upon being given guidance from Asquith) that the Conservatives and Liberals should chew things over in a Constitutional Conference. Redmond was unfortunately excluded, as was the leader of the (Orange) Irish Unionist party – Edward Carson.

At the conference, crafty old Lloyd George, without consulting the prime minister, proposed secretly to Arthur Balfour, the opposition Tory leader that a coalition of the two main parties would enable the Irish question to be handled without threats from either nationalists or Orangemen. Balfour couldn't accept this of course because when it became clear that home rule in some form was still on the cards, he knew it would upset his political alliance with Carson who was fiercely opposed to home rule. Carson, suspicious (with good reason) that some sort of a deal might be hatched for home rule, spearheaded the establishment of a secret committee with the object of obtaining arms. They soon began arriving in Ulster. Carson was preparing for revolution. In the event the Constitutional Conference foundered over the home rule question.

Asquith, with the Cabinet's approval, asked the King to dissolve Parliament and prised from him a secret undertaking that, if the Liberals were returned to power, up to 500 Liberal peers would be created. These peers would enable the progression of a Parliament Bill which was finally enacted in August 1911. Its result was that the Lords could only veto the Third Home Rule Bill for a maximum period of two years. However, they still managed to do their best to delay it as much as possible in January and July of 1913.

Meanwhile, in September 1911, Carson began to declare his hand when Orange lodges and Unionist clubs from all over Ulster met at a rally. Arming and drilling began and shortly after, the framework of a constitution for a provisional government of Ulster was drawn up.

Balfour, as leader of the opposition, was succeeded by Andrew Bonar Law whose Ulster Presbyterian background made him very much amenable to Carson's cause. In July 1912 the Unionists held another rally, this time at Blenheim Palace, England and in September a large number of them (variously estimated at between 200,000 and 500,000) signed the Ulster Covenant, pledging to use *all means* to resist home rule. In December that year Carson's Unionists followed up this trial of strength by raising an amendment to the Third Home Rule Bill for the exclusion of nine Ulster counties.

In January 1913 things were beginning to move too swiftly for Prime Minister Asquith, forcing the home rule question to the fore. The Third Home Rule Bill was defeated by the House of Lords, whilst in Ireland the Ulster Volunteers – a Unionist militia – was formed. The Bill was reintroduced in July, but the Lords again kicked it out. In August the King, who seemed more attuned to the situation than Asquith, met him on *The Royal Yacht*, and urged him to exclude Ulster from the Bill. Asquith twiddled his thumbs and stalled for time again.

The Ulster Unionists had been agitating against home rule since November 1910, but it took until February 1914 before Asquith finally broached to Redmond the government's scheme for the temporary exclusion of Ulster for a period of five to six years, with the provision for automatic exclusion after that. By this time Irish nationalists, frustrated by British politics and the delay of the Third Home Rule Bill (and knowing what the Ulster Unionists were up to), decided it was time to make a move themselves. The initiative came from within the Irish Republican Brotherhood (IRB), who was committed to the use of force. In November 1913 they encouraged in Dublin the formation of the Irish Volunteers, under the chairmanship of Eoin MacNeill, a university professor. It was set up explicitly to safeguard the granting of home rule and within months the movement had spread throughout the country.

The atmosphere in the Bridge bar still feels hostile – but perhaps it's my imagination. The guy next to me closes his *Daily Mirror* and offers it to me. I feel a wee bit more relaxed; perhaps everyone around here is just naturally reserved and allows a stranger privacy by their silence. I catch up on the sports news, down the pint, pick up my rucksack and set out suitably refreshed to tackle the one-and-a-half-mile walk to the station.

History is all around me here: I pass, somewhere along this road, the site of what was once a football field where a certain Patrick Pearse, a teacher by profession and later a leader in the Easter Rising of 1916, addressed a crowd at the *Feis* in August 1915.

The records of The Bureau of Military History 1913–1921 held by Military Archives (BHM) of witnesses involved with Millstreet for these times tell something of the formation and development of the Irish Volunteers. Before its formation many of its future members were also part of the Gaelic League, an organisation dedicated to the restoration of the Irish language. Mathew Murphy, future captain of the Millstreet battalion of the IRA in fact met Patrick Pearse whilst he was engaged in Gaelic League language competitions during *Feis*. Pearse had joined the League at the age of 16 in 1879. The Gaelic League in Millstreet was formed in summer 1912.

The Millstreet battalion of the Irish Volunteers originally comprised 17 men. All were also supporters of the All-For-Ireland Party – a Munster based nationalist movement that campaigned to get agreement amongst all those parties aiming for home rule.

Humphrey O'Donoghue, later a lieutenant in the IRA, joined the Volunteers in 1914 after hearing the speeches of Pearse and others at an *Aeriocht* (open air concert). The Volunteers held weekly parades in fields at night and on Sunday evenings he said 'they practised close-order foot drill, involving marching, manoeuvring and the handling of arms'. The problem was, they didn't seem to have too many arms, just dummy wooden guns, some three pronged spikes and a few pikes.

In April 1914, the Ulster Volunteer Force set up by the Ulster Unionists had *plenty* of arms: 25,000 rifles and three million rounds of ammunition had been shipped from Germany, landed at Larne and Bangor and had been distributed throughout north-east Ulster.

Two months before the Ulster gun-run there'd been discussions between Asquith and Redmond with regards to the exclusion of Ulster from home rule. Pressure was soon brought to bear on the negotiations when 60 of the 70 officers at the Curragh Camp near Dublin stated that they would resign their commissions rather than fight in Ulster. The events were labelled as a mutiny – it was more of a conspiracy. Fearing that Ulster might only be *temporally* excluded from home rule the War Office's Director of Military Operations, a diehard Irish Unionist, Major-General Henry Wilson and a mate of Bonar Law, had been told by him that any officer who resigned over Ulster would be reinstated by the next Conservative government who were trying to force a general election. This information Henry Wilson passed to General Hubert Gough, the officer commanding at Curragh.

These events did not go unnoticed by the Irish Volunteer movement which had seen a growth in numbers from under 2,000 at the end of 1913 to 160,000 by the summer of 1914, and in June

Redmond issued a statement that urged that *he* must have control of the Volunteers.

In late July the Irish Volunteers landed 1,500 rifles and ammunition, purchased in Hamburg, at a small fishing port north of Dublin. The subsequent events were in stark contrast to the unopposed Ulster Unionist landings of arms at Larne and Bangor. The King's Own Scottish Borderers, who were pretty pissed off because they'd not managed to disarm some Irish Volunteers, opened fire on a taunting crowd of civilians, killing four and wounding 30. This did nothing to help Redmond's cause for co-operation with Britain; neither did the fact that his party had reluctantly been forced to agree to (what they understood would be) a trial exclusion of Ulster for six years.

On 4th August 1914 Britain declared war on Germany, an event that shelved the enforcement of the Home Rule Act for its duration. In order to try and hasten enactment of the Act Redmond called the country to support Britain's war effort. But differences of opinion were beginning to appear within the Irish Volunteers. The All-For-Ireland Party were not too impressed with the passing of the Act, which had finally struggled over the finishing line and gained royal assent in September; they abstained from voting and denounced it as a 'partition deal'.

These differences soon became evident in Millstreet. It seems there were two companies: the O'Brienites (the official unit affiliated to the executive composed of All-For-Ireland Party members), and another company of similar strength made up of Redmondite supporters (otherwise known as the Ancient Order of Hibernians). Clashes between the two factions had almost occurred in June 1914 when the municipal election result went in favour of the O'Brienites, to the surprise of the Redmondites. A large force of the Royal Irish Constabulary (RIC) expected trouble and stood by with batons drawn.

Throughout Ireland the majority of the Irish Volunteers adhered to Redmond's appeals to enlist but a minority (around 6.5%) split away and remained as the original Volunteers under the leadership of Eoin MacNeill. But, unbeknown to many of its members, it had been infiltrated by the secret Irish Republican Brotherhood (IRB).

In December 1913 Patrick Pearse was sworn into the IRB; in 1914 he became the Volunteers' Director of Military Organisation and by

1915 he was on the IRB's Supreme Council and its secret Military Council. On 22nd August 1915 Pearse visited Millstreet to meet IRB members and the Volunteers. It was the town's *feis* and sports day; there was tug-o'-war, pony racing and championship dancing. Oh, and an address by Patrick on the resurrection of Erin. The Royal Irish Constabulary were keeping an eye on Pearse but he somehow managed to slip through their net and made it to the football field to give a talk to the several thousand people gathered there. The crowd consisted of all ages, ranging from old Fenian campaigners to young boys. The RIC were a trifle demoralised when they realised that Pearse had eluded them, even more so when they were obliged to stand guard outside The Railway Hotel, whilst inside Pearse partook of a good evening meal.

The Easter Rising of April 1916 came as much of a surprise to Redmond as it did to the British government. It was carried out by Pearse and members of the IRB who'd combined forces and plans with James Connolly, leader of the Citizen Army – a group of trained trade unionists in Dublin.

Even players whose support was crucial to the success of the Rising were kept in the dark. Eoin MacNeill, now the commander-in-chief of the Irish Volunteers, only discovered three days before the Rising that preparation for a general mobilisation of the Volunteers was to be part of the plan. The Rising was planned for Easter Sunday 23rd April. But the IRB kept MacNeill in the dark for as long as possible because they thought he wasn't in favour of an all-out rebellion.

MacNeill was, however, convinced that a rising was necessary when he was presented with a document (known as the Castle Document) that detailed British plans for the introduction of Martial Law and the arrest of Irish activists. He was also assured that Sir Roger Casement, a retired British Consul, was in the process of acquiring from Germany an estimated 20,000 rifles, 10 machine guns and some five million rounds of ammunition. But MacNeill soon began to realise that the Castle Document was a forgery, and on top of this learnt that Casement's mission had failed and there would be no guns. He responded by putting an advertisement in the *Irish Independent* giving orders to all Volunteers: 'No parades, marches or other movements of the Volunteers will take place'.

MacNeill's orders made the IRB decide to put the Rising back a day to Easter Monday, the 24th. What MacNeill's actions would have been had he'd found the arms to have been landed successfully is an interesting question.

In the event, MacNeill's counter-orders published in the *Irish Independent* caused chaos and confusion, especially amongst the local commandants who, without the aid an efficient communications network, had no real idea of what was going on. The result was that there was not a Rising in Cork or Limerick; instead of a planned 10,000 participants there were only 2,000 – in Dublin, Enniscorthy and Dunshaughlin only.

Captain Cornelius Meany, who lived in Mushera, east of Millstreet, reported that he'd attended a meeting on Easter Sunday 23rd April in Cork and had received orders to undertake a route march with all arms, ammunition and equipment. He was instructed to bring rations and trench digging implements but hadn't been told where the parade would be held. The companies from Millstreet, Rathduane and Keale all met at Millstreet and marched three miles south where they carried out open-order drill. There was no order to cancel the parade that day; as far as they were concerned it was just a run-of-the-mill parade, so clearly MacNeill's orders hadn't got through. That night Meany met Jerry Twomey who told him that something was coming off the next day. Twomey was thought possibly to be an IRB man – and was so in the know. On the strength of this information Meany mobilised the company late that night, but nothing was forthcoming and the men were sent home. There were rumours of a Rising on the Monday night (it had in fact occurred that day), so Meany mobilised the company again on the Tuesday morning. They hung around all day in some woods, but were then sent home as no orders had been received from the Brigade.

I catch the train at Millstreet station and, back at the campsite in Killarney, remember to switch on my mobile. There's a message from the taxi driver from early this morning saying he can meet me in a quarter of an hour. I feel guilty. Sorry, mate, I just couldn't wait.

Six
More Bog Country

In the bogs of Claraghatlea North just west of Millstreet Town
The hare sits in the rushes in her coat of chestnut brown
Of man with gun and man's dog and fox she lives her life in fear
And her's is never a deep sleep as she rests with one pricked ear.
From: *In the bogs of Claraghatlea North* by Francis Duggan

Thursday 27th June – Campsite at Killarney
Today is my last day on the site. It's a day to catch up on some chores. Around 8.30am I call at the local store for groceries. In my basket is a bottle of wine to accompany this evening's meal.

'That,' says the lady serving, as she puts my bottle to one side, 'I can't serve you until half-past-ten in the morning.' I was surprised, and somewhat disappointed. In the UK booze can be purchased in supermarkets 24 hours a day, except on Sundays, and this prompted me to think about the Republic's view on alcohol consumption.

The 'Olympic walking gold medallist' on reception had told me that outside the bar on the site it's possible to get Internet reception, so I pick up my laptop and, after sifting through two weeks' accumulation of emails, check out a few drinking facts whist I wait for the bar to open.

The first website I find claims that the British are to blame for Ireland's drink problem; a survey of 3,500 students by the University of Dublin claims that the problem may date back to when the country was under British rule. A map of the Republic shows that the heavy drinkers resided in the counties of Dublin, Cork and Waterford. This claim drew some comical comments on the site: 'The British taught the Irish how to drink – don't think so!'

A perhaps more serious report for the Health Service by an economics lecturer attests that between 1970 and 2003 alcohol consumption doubled in Ireland – one of the largest increases in the world during that period.

But it seems to me that the periods of time when alcohol can be bought can't be as relevant to consumption as is its price. Surely if you can't buy booze before 10.30am, and you're *that* desperate for an early morning tipple, you'd make sure you bought enough the night before. Several of the websites I view confirm my thoughts and agree that the fundamental law of economics links price with demand. So next I check out the relative cost of alcohol in various countries. Out of a list of 145, Ireland are the fourth most expensive whilst the UK are fifth. If you fancy a pint in Singapore you'd better go to the bank first – they came out top. I'm surprised to find that Iran is one of the cheapest places to get blathered – but only if you're a Christian Armenian (who distil their own sometimes dodgy stuff called *araf* from raisins). If you're a Muslim and get caught in Iran they give you 160 lashes the first time – and if you're stupid enough to get done for a third time they do for you properly and string you up. Curiously enough Lithuania and Estonia rank 74th and 85th respectively as the cheapest of countries in which to purchase alcohol (some way below the world average), yet according to another Internet site they are the world's most dominant drinking population (measured by the overall litres of alcohol consumed per person), so you might expect them to be around the 140th most expensive. Perhaps there's naff-all else to do there. So I key-in: 'What do Estonians and Lithuanians do for fun?' Estonians it appears enjoy whipping each other with towels on the ice lakes, whilst Lithuanians like to go on picnics and shoot things.

On a more serious note: from surveys conducted by Alcohol Action Ireland, the Irish are of the opinion (85% of those surveyed) that the current level of consumption in Ireland is too high. I shall add, in a very small way, to these statistics when the pub opens at half-past-ten.

The remainder of the day I spend shopping, sorting out some problems on the camper, followed by a long-delayed clothes wash in the campsite's launderette. Being completely undomesticated, I need mobile phone assistance from my partner Polly in the UK. She gives me detailed real-time instructions, but I still manage to screw things up and think I've somehow broken the machine when the view window turns opaque with foam – but it's just because I've added too much detergent.

Friday 28th June – Millstreet to Boggeragh

I leave the campsite at Muckross at 7.30am and drive to the village of Nad (meaning nest of the eagle) six miles south of Banteer; it's about a one hour drive. Nad is three and a half miles north of the Blackwater Way but parking to offload the bike may be a problem there, so I stop in the Nad pub car park and lock the bike to a steel post. Then I drive back to Banteer to catch a train back to Millstreet.

On the station wall is a warning sign about trespassing. At the ticket office I ask if it'll be OK to park for the night in the station car park.

'I wouldn't advise it,' he says, giving me an ominous look, 'a car got damaged a few weeks ago – there's no CCTV.' My plan is to wild-camp tonight either here or in the car park at the Nad pub, the advantage of the latter being that I might get an evening meal there.

The 11 minute train journey gets me to Millstreet by 9.45. I slog back to the centre of the town and then on along the main road towards Macroom and the information board at the crossroads I'd reached the day before yesterday. By 10.30 I'm back on the Way. It heads slightly west uphill on a lane that narrows and then grows grass along its centre. There are good views of Claragh Mountain as the lane continues to climb. But the weather today is not so good and the mountain-top is hidden by a skullcap of hanging cloud. The map tells me I should stay on the lane for about three miles. I see nobody, except two young girls taking turns to swing on a rope in a garden.

It seems like a very long time I'm on this road heading south. I keep checking the map trying to work out where I am and looking for a lane that peels off east – but I don't find it. I reach a road junction that confirms I've gone wrong and then I get scared to hell by an aggressive dog. Things are starting to go awry already. I pull out my compass for the first time and sorrowfully confirm that I'm still walking south when I should be going east. I'll end up in Macroom soon if I don't turn off. But there's no way I'm going back past that bloody dog to find the turning. Basically I'm lost yet again. The overall scheduled distance to walk today is 26 miles and it now looks like this will increase.

Then, a piece of luck; the first car I've seen on the lane approaches and I step into the crest of the road to make sure the lady driver has to stop. We check the map together and she tells me that if I continue a short way further on the lane I shall come to another that goes east. Thank God I don't have to have a growling contest with the dog.

'You'll be passing Knocknakilla Stone Circle,' she says. 'Turn off down just down there left,' she says, indicating back the way she's come, 'and then turn right.'

The unplanned diversion adds only about a mile to the day's walk. I reach the stone circle along an undulating road, forested on both sides – and frankly both boring and tiring. My right knee is still hurting even though it's strapped up tight with a bandage. I'm already feeling weary, and it's not yet lunchtime. The circle is a short climb off the road and through a kissing gate, but I'm so tired I consider passing it by – but I don't.

A fenced enclosure surrounds the monument. A grey-haired man is standing in the centre of the enclosure staring into space, obviously absorbing the ambience of the place. He doesn't seem to notice me; neither of us acknowledges each other or speak. The noticeboard is written firstly in Gaelic, followed by English. The complex, it tells me, consists of a stone circle, two standing stones and a stone mound. They were erected in the Bronze Age and used for unknown rituals or ceremonies – which make me curious about what actually must have gone on here. I stay only a few minutes in the circle; I'm too conscious of the long walk yet ahead. The grey-haired man is still standing in exactly the same spot and staring into space when I leave; he's obviously gaining something very profound from the experience.

At a T-junction I turn left on the road and sit down on a rectangular block of quarried stone at the entrance to Millstreet Country Park to take my sandwiches. No vehicles have passed since the lady car driver. There's a faint sound of voices from within the Park, but I see nobody and there are no parked cars in the entrance. All soon becomes a spooky silence again. Opposite me, the Way leads into open countryside and onto the slopes of Musheramore Mountain. But I can't see it because everything is obscured by a thick shroud of cloud that seems to be spreading towards me as I watch. Somewhere there, is the path I must take to Mushera. A feeling of complete isolation permeates through me. I'm committed to the walk and to the path. There's no way I can go back and admit defeat and there's no way I'm prepared to deliberately break my rule number two by taking a shortcut. I *have* to enter the turbid mist and grope my way from fingerpost to distant fingerpost with constant reference to the compass. Then I'm bound sure to get hopelessly lost, and the already challenging walk will turn into a nightmare. With these doubts in mind I save, as a contingency, a sandwich for later, linger as long as possible over the last mouthful of the one I'm eating and drain the very last drop of orange juice from the carton, squashing the carton flat with my boot – all delaying tactics.

But I've found in life that things always turn out really bad when they happen unexpectedly; when you expect the worse, it never reaches the nadir of your imagination – and so it was. I saunter across the road peering warily into the mist ahead and start up a shallow fenced gully towards what looks like a continuation of the footpath ascending into the cloud and mist. But at the end of the gully the Way points left, not up – as I'd expected, in fact staying out of the cloud. I continue north along a soggy grass track that runs for a while parallel with the road I can still just make out. Then, edging ever east, I start to climb and suddenly enter the mist. But the fingerposts have been well laid and the furrowed path is obvious. According to Paddy Dillon's book there are some extensive views here over the 'rolling moors of north Cork' – but not today. Today, I can see only a few steps ahead.

Eventually I descend from the mountain and just as suddenly as I entered the mist, so I leave it and emerge through some trees to an empty car park and onto a stoned track. It's single vehicle width, an old bog road according to my book. Vehicles have pushed the stones into piles at the edges and centre of the track leaving two clearways in between; I walk along one of these – it's easier on my feet. The track continues across moorland and then through a forest for about three miles before turning onto a narrower track that climbs through yet another forest for what seems like ages. It's described in the book as 'a forest ride'. I wish I *was* riding through it instead of walking, as it's both boring, and painful for my feet.

At last I emerge onto a wide green lane fenced on both sides, where I encounter a lone, lost, stupid, frightened, woolly friend. What does it do? Instead of passing me, or letting me pass it, it scuttles on in the same direction in which I'm walking, stops, looks back, determines

I'm still approaching, and so scuttles on again. It repeats this process numerous times despite my attempts to surreptitiously creep past it. Finally it's snookered, trapped by a gate that bars the way to a road. So now, as I continue slowly, it runs around frantically in circles in total panic. I don't know what to do either – but it solves the problem. Somehow (although dimensions seem to preclude the likelihood) it manages to squeeze through the bars of the gate and bolts away up the road.

Soon I'm walking on the narrow cut of a badly rutted road. By now it's around 4.30pm. The first car I've seen since this morning creeps past at about four miles an hour, driven by a lone man. I squeeze into the side for him to pass, and he raises a finger from the steering wheel in acknowledgement. As the cut opens out I realise where he's going. A huge field full of sliced black peat strips stretch far into the distance. This is highly mechanised peat farming. At the back of the field is a vast extent of wigwam strips stacked up in their second drying phase, whilst in the foreground the remainder are horizontal, except for a scattering of wigwams bordered by triangular orange markers. After turning at a junction of tracks, I glimpse, through the half-lit murk, the final stages of the process; cut and dried turves are being loaded onto tractor-drawn carts and are then being taken towards the road where several of the workers' cars are parked.

I turn east away from the peat farm and sit by a stream to eat my remaining sandwich. A group of peat workers walk towards me and I'm anxious about my wallet containing money and cards which are in the rucksack. My book 'reassuringly' points out that this is 'a particularly remote part' of the walk. But before the group get to me they move off into a field to inspect their stacked sods. Phew!

More little piles of turf appear as I walk on with little name tags attached, awaiting the collection of their owners. Further on again a crude hand-painted noticeboard instructs that behind it lies NO. 59, a: PRIVATE BOG PLOT – a 'stern warning', lest anyone should try their luck at the peat poaching game.

There is but yet more forest track walking before my tiredness tells at a (by now) confusing track junction with no marker sign for the Way. I make the wrong decision and take the high track heading east and skirting the Boggeragh Mountains. The official route detours south first into, what looks like, an inhospitable wasteland. Later (too late now – no retreating) I realise from the map that it too would soon have swung east. Anyway, both options meet the R579, Banteer to Cork road. This juncture I assume to be Boggeragh; it's the end of today's 'on route' walk and is a good point to bike back to tomorrow. I earmark a suitable locking point for it. Three miles of dodgy walking on this busy road then gets me back to the car park of the Nad pub and the camper.

I buy a pint in the pub and, at a welcome wood-burning fire (it *is* June after all!), change out of my walking boots and socks into cycling attire and sip the pint as I go. Two young men sit opposite me eyeing the process, but saying nothing. The barmaid, chatting to another girl, suddenly interrupts her flow.

'You're busy over there,' she says. I'm just *too* weary to make conversation.

'Yes,' I mumble and continue to haul out my fluorescent vest and helmet for the dangerous seven-mile ride to the station at Banteer. I get bad (perhaps unjust) vibrations from the pub and decide I'll spend the night in the station car park instead. When I'm outside I hear the girls laughing. Paranoia again – but it confirms my decision.

Banteer is busy. Some function is about to commence near the crossroads and people have parked in the station car park to attend it. But when they go home, and after the last train pulls out at 9.35pm, I spend a peaceful night there. I eat-in frugally and successfully (given my poor cooking abilities). It's my first attempt at using the stove fired by a bottle of Calor gas (purchased from my old company and pension provider).

Saturday 29th June – Boggeragh to Ballynamona

The plan today is to drive to Ballynamona, cycle back to Boggeragh and walk back to the camper at Ballynamona. It's a simple plan. I calculate it's a walk of about 19 miles on the Blackwater Way itself.

Ballynamona is a small village approximately four and a half miles south of Mallow, just off the N20 road to Cork. The Way crosses the N20 here, which is why it makes an ideal break point. I at first miss the turning off the dual carriageway and have to drive back – a good start.

I park on the road, opposite Murphy's bar, already changed into cycling gear and with rucksack packed. But I'm not entirely sure where I am in relation to the Way. I ask two draymen making an early morning delivery of Guinness to the pub, showing them the map. They don't seem to know where they are either (or they can't read).

As it turns out (and I later record in my log) I'm about to make several serious mistakes. First mistake: noticing the back bike tyre is a bit soft, I unpack the pump, add some air and squeeze it with my thumb – it's about right. Second mistake: I decide I don't fancy cycling back along the busy bypass to Mallow and then west along the N72 to Lombardstown before heading south; this anyway seems a roundabout route. Third mistake: I don't take a compass reading before I set out.

So off I go pedalling and pedalling over crap roads, swerving to avoid potholes and rumbling over uneven surfaces, up hills and down hills, stopping only to wipe the sweat from my brow and check the map. The map doesn't help me decide where the hell I am though because there are few features of note and no villages. Even if I *were* to pass through a village I'm pretty sure there'd be no sign to tell me so. With no disrespect to the National Mapping Agency, and their blurb of: 'Ensure you always know your place in Ireland', I certainly didn't know my place – and their map didn't seem to help much either. I continue up and down more hills, able to use only six of the 18 gears this bike is supposed to have. I'd tried to use the other 12 gears but the chain had come off every time. At a crossroads I signal to a car driver (the first I've seen this morning). He puts on his specs and peers at the map. He has a thick local accent that I have great difficulty in deciphering, especially as he speaks at a hundred-miles-an-hour. You can only say 'pardon' so many times before it becomes impolite. One of the few phrases I do understand is:

'Sure, even the locals get lost around here.' He's very friendly though and extends his hand for me to shake; a nice old boy, who's perhaps gratified to meet a crazy, lost Englishman in his lost Irish lanes – a good topic of conversation for the pub later.

I keep going over the crossroads. Fourth mistake – I should have turned right. There are yet more hills and the day is beginning to warm up considerably. Now I'm sure, after checking the compass, that I'm heading south-west, when I need to be going north-west, but I resist taking several lanes that lead off in that direction for fear they might lead me around in some foolish circle. (That decision was *not* a mistake I later learn.)

A young lady is parking in her driveway. I get to her just before she disappears indoors and show her the Discovery map. It appears that I'm much further south than I ever could imagine; somewhere near a place called Knockanare, and only about seven miles north of the village of Coachford.

'So many hills!' she exclaims, when I tell her where I've biked from. Don't I know it! She tells me I should ride on; then turn right and right again.

'Stay on the main roads,' she shouts, as I pedal away. I know now I should have done that in the first place. I've acquired a sudden hatred of cycling.

Finally I reach the R619 and go north for eight miles, and yes, there are still more hills. On a particularly stiff climb I'm embarrassingly overtaken by a serious lady cyclist (or maybe she's just got a better bike than me), but finally I reach Bweeng, soaked in sweat, after 24 miles of cycling. By the shortest route it should have taken me 7½ miles to get here.

I check the map and discover my fifth mistake of the day: staying on the main road sure enough avoided bad road surfaces and navigational problems, but if I'd headed north-west back at the Tailor's Cross Roads (with a few turn-offs) there was a reasonably direct route to my walk start point at Boggeragh. Now I see that the Glennaharee River and lack of bridges forces a lengthy diversion. I estimate that nine miles of pedal pushing still remain. It's past midday by now. I check the map carefully before leaving Bweeng and then hit a stiff hill climb that never seems to end.

Something's wrong – everything seems heavy – shit! Now I have a puncture in the back tyre.

I push the bike on for a while trying to think what to do. To mend the puncture will eat up yet more time which is fast running out. I'll then not make it back to the start of the walk until mid-afternoon – then there's a 19-mile walk to tackle. The map indicates the road I'm on is actually part of the Way, so I decide to ditch the bike and *walk* in a westerly direction to the start of the day's walk at Boggeragh; at least it's a more direct route than by the road.

I come across a fingerpost for the Way by a barrier; it's a suitable pull-in point for the camper when I drive back here tomorrow to fix the puncture. I hide the bike behind some trees – adding it to somebody's fly-tip rubbish.

But I'm confused – which doesn't seem to be so unusual for today. I can't figure out in which direction along the Way I should be walking. After half an hour I realise, when some masts appear on the top of a hill, that I've made the wrong choice. In an hour's time I'm right back by the concealed bike again. Now I go in the opposite direction, but can't find the Way's fingerpost, so overshoot – more lost time! Finally I backtrack again, find the fingerpost and am on a long stony climb up a forest track which is hard on the feet, especially as I'm now into a forced brisk march.

A huge expanse of the forest has been felled and I pass a vehicle on the track engaged in this process. Unfortunately I know I shall pass it again in an hour or so on my way back. The walk is already a labour not to my liking. I turn left along a rough road and at a little house I ask a young lady, whose watering flowers in her garden, if she'll top up my water bottle. I need all the fluid I can get; it's sweltering. I explain my woes. She's slightly bemused and maybe slightly worried when I tell her she might see me passing again in a while.

There's an interesting section of tricky, boggy walking through a wood near a place called Mossy Bed. I stop here to gobble my sandwiches at a stream that then has to be leapt across – an exercise to be shortly repeated in reverse. When I finally reach Boggeragh the time is 2.30pm. Now at last today's walk can start for real.

A third of the total distance I must now walk is ground I've already covered in the other direction. I don't hang around. The walk is a painful grind both physically and mentally. My knee still hurts and now my feet are sore from the stony track. I tackle the distance by an incentive scheme I invent for myself consisting of brief stoppages at a quarter past each hour, at which time I alternately take a portion of chocolate and a swig of water. There's a road accident on the R619 out of Bweeng; a tail-end shunt. The Gardai shepherd me around it. Somebody has had a worse day than me. I feel sorry for them, but it's the only incident that breaks up my labouring slog.

At Castlebarrett the ruin of the 13th century castle comes into view. In the 15th century it was owned by the Earl of Desmond and in the 17th century by the Jacobite Barrett family before Cromwell's army wrecked it. For me it signifies the near end of the walk. Around the next bend I catch sight, at the bottom of a hill, of the welcome old camper. I check my watch: it's 7.30; it took me four and a half hours to get back from Boggeragh. From there it's been a 19-mile trek at just over four-minute-mile pace. Not bad going for an old boy who will be 68 in two day's time.

Murphy's bar and the thought of a pint of lager have kept me going. I march into the bar (well, in truth it's more of a stagger) like Captain Anson in the 1958 film *Ice Cold in Alex*.

Seven

Starlings and Rooks

'I write it out in a verse –
MacDonagh and MacBride
And Connolly and Pearse
Now and in time to be,
Wherever green is worn,
Are changed, changed utterly:
A terrible beauty is born.'
From *Easter 1916* by William Butler Yeats

Saturday evening 29th June – Mallow

Mallow is a town whose population has doubled over the last half century to around 12,000. In the past it's been renowned for its spa, as an agricultural centre and for its dairy produce, as well as for the significant events that took place here during the War of Independence and the Civil War. It's now a thriving business centre.

I drive in across Mallow Bridge, spanning the River Blackwater and turn left. I'm on Park Road, named after the park and sports fields it runs beside, and *not* because it's conducive to parking a six-metre-long camper van. I pull into the car park of a ubiquitous supermarket (Lidl – no secret really) in order to get my bearings and find somewhere to wild-camp for the night. There are a number of long-term all-day car parks, but I suspect they're just that, 'day' car parks. The local Gardai, I imagine, would not view too favourably a retired English walker sleeping there the night – and being told to move-on in the middle of the night, when you've settled down, is no joke. I undertake an extensive, painful and tiring foot slog in order to find a secluded nook. I back the camper slowly and with some difficulty into the spot, hard against some locked gates at the rear and tight against a fence at the side, with some trees partially shielding the camper from the road.

The camper is located on the access road to some sort of

industrial premises. Two notices are fixed to the fence; one warns against dumping, but the other is rather disquieting; it states that all trespassers are monitored by 24-hour CCTV, and that the Gardai will be contacted. Well, I'm not actually trespassing am I, if they mean inside the gates? I just hope the cameras are somewhere *inside* and not on me here now – guess I'll soon find out! Putting this worry behind me, I cook up a quick meal by gas and set out to explore the town.

Mallow's republican persuasions are evidenced by the street names I walk along. The main street is named after Thomas Davis, a poet and 'Young Ireland' revolutionary who was born in the town in 1814; then I turn into William O'Brien Street, founder of the All-for-Ireland party. Here I find Maureen's bar.

The bar is patronised by local characters, mostly congregated around a TV that's showing Gaelic football. I buy a pint, sit in a corner and try to read a book. But the conversation of the locals and the TV are both distractions and I find I'm reading the same lines over and over. Finally the TV wins out and I try to discover the mysteries of Gaelic football.

There's not much, if any, TV coverage of the sport (or of hurling, another Gaelic sport) on Britain's television. It's a fast and furious game, kind of a hybrid of associated football, basketball and rugby that uses a round ball. After a while I think I'm picking up the scoring system but need some reassurance, so I uncover my English ignorance by asking the barman.

'There seems to be two ways of scoring – is that right?' I ask.

'Yes,' he confirms, putting up three fingers. 'Three points for below the bar, and one point for above.'

'Are you impressed?' asks a man standing next to me.

'Yes,' I say, 'it's very fast.'

'They're all very fit,' he says, adding, 'and all amateurs.'

The origins of Irish games and sports date back to an ancient Celtic festival which began in 1829 BC, whilst the earliest record of the modern game of Gaelic football took place in 1670. Towards the end of the 19th century it was felt that Irish games could become extinct as they were being overtaken by English games made popular by the police and British military. There was at that time no central body to organise and regulate the traditional Irish games. Michael

Cusack, a teacher, and Maurice Davin, a farmer and former athlete with an international reputation, convened a meeting in 1884 to change that situation. They formed The Gaelic Association for the Preservation and Cultivation of Gaelic Games. This later became the Gaelic Athletic Association (GAA), with Davin as President and Cusack as Secretary. The Association gained much support from the Catholic Church in the form of the Archbishop of Cashel, Dr Thomas Croke who was an ardent supporter of sport.

Membership of the GAA grew, attracting young men throughout Ireland and it was soon seen as an opportunity for infiltration by the Fenians. There were a number of organisational crossovers and links; many Fenians were also members of the Irish Republican Brotherhood (IRB), and members of the GAA were also members of the Irish Volunteers. The GAA was fiercely nationalistic and excluded members of the police and armed forces. It succoured a generation of fit young men who were proud of their Irish identity whilst developing their organisational skills. These were all useful attributes for those nationalist movements prevalent at the time of the Easter Rising of 1916. The GAA was, as an organisation, not involved directly in the Rising but many GAA members were.

The immediate outcome of the Rising was that after six days of fighting, Patrick Pearse surrendered unconditionally. The casualty figures quoted seem to vary, but around 450 people are thought to have lost their lives and almost 3,000 had been wounded; civilians, soldiers, police and rebels. The rebels' cause was lost and, whilst being led away, some were harangued and pelted with stuff by women whose husbands were fighting on the Western Front in the First World War. For many members of the general public though the rebels had gained some credibility and admiration; although poorly armed, they'd stood up to the might of the British who seemingly had unlimited resources.

During the Rising a proclamation was made declaring an Irish Republic, stating it had been supported 'by gallant allies in Europe'. This statement sealed the fate of the rebels. In the eyes of the British government this was an admission of collaboration with the King's enemies (Germany) in wartime, and as such the rebels (as British citizens) were deemed to have committed treason under the recently passed Defence of the Realm Act.

Herbert Asquith and the British government had decided during the course of the Rising that martial law should be proclaimed over all Ireland, and in doing so they had washed their hands of the events that followed. This was to be their biggest mistake. Total power was delegated to General Sir John Maxwell, the newly appointed commander-in-chief of the British troops.

Maxwell took the view that all those associated with militant nationalism should be dealt with severely. The trials of those involved directly in the Rising were conducted without a professional judge or a jury and were done so in camera. The 'judges' consisted of a panel of three senior British officers. Each of the accused were charged that they: '...did take part in an armed rebellion and in the waging of war against His Majesty the King, such act being of such a nature as to be calculated to be prejudicial to the Defence of the Realm and being done with the intention and for the purpose of assisting the enemy.'

So, the trials of the rebels were conducted by military court martial, at which death sentences were passed. Maxwell had the final say and confirmed the death sentence on 15 of the rebels, including all seven signatories to the Proclamation and those Volunteers deemed to have been major participants in the hostilities. All of them except William Pearse, the younger brother of Patrick, pleaded not guilty, but he too was amongst those executed. The prisoners were shot in the former stone-breaker yard at Kilmainham Gaol, Dublin. Twelve young Sherwood Foresters were assigned to carry out the execution, one row kneeling and one row standing. The prisoners were blindfolded and white paper targets were pinned over their hearts – their hands were tied behind their backs. The Foresters had been given very little training and to ease their consciences they were told that the rifle fired by of one of them would be loaded with a dummy bullet.

On 3rd May Asquith had heard that the first of the rebels had been shot, and some arses had started to twitch. By about 11th May the pressure was starting to tell on Asquith; he was by now getting quite a lot of flack over the severity of the sentences and was worried about how this would affect his government's chances in the forthcoming elections. He sent a telegram to Maxwell saying that there were to be no further executions except under special and exceptional circumstances, and on 12th May (the day of the last executions) he visited Dublin. A large number (around 97) of death sentences were subsequently commuted to life imprisonment and some of the accused were in fact acquitted. Amongst those who evaded death in the stone-breaker yard at Kilmainham Gaol was Éamon de Valera (future President of the Republic) the only Irish Volunteer Commandant to escape that fate.

Whilst the court martials were being conducted in Dublin, General Maxwell had been busy organising activities elsewhere. Using intelligence built up over the years, the military and police swooped speedily to arrest around 3,400 people. About 1,800 of those captured were sent first to England. Most ended up in North Wales at the wondrous 'holiday camp' (sorry – internment camp), of Frongoch, located two miles west of Bala near the beautiful lake of the same name, close to the Cambrian Mountains.

The Frongoch camp, previously occupied by 'lucky' captured Germans, was a place where, even if the Irish had wanted to escape, they wouldn't have been able to understand a word spoken – until that is the Welsh started to give them language lessons. There wasn't much enthusiasm for escape though; the internees knew they were much better off there than in an English gaol. There was a feeling of camaraderie amongst them. Irish language courses, open air concerts, fancy dress parades and cross-country walks were all organised, as were classes in bookkeeping, maths and shorthand. It wasn't all fun though. The nights were cold and there weren't enough blankets. The sleeping arrangements consisted of a wooden trestle, boards and a bag of straw. The commandant was also a bit tactless and somewhat of a tartar, whilst the food wasn't too palatable. The occasional rat is also said to have made an appearance around the camp.

Internment in Frongoch was for Asquith and his government the worst possible decision they could have made because the camp became the bedrock upon which was built the guerrilla war that was to eventually take shape in 1919. Here future actions were planned, guerrilla tactics were taught and lines of communication were set-up. Michael Collins, who was to play a crucial role in the War of Independence, was one of the internees. The camps (there were actually two, north and south) became known as 'The University of Revolution'.

Immediately after the Rising, raids were made at the homes of

Volunteers in Mallow. Daniel Hegarty, a resident of Fair Street, Mallow, and Christopher O'Connell were both arrested on 4th May. Hegarty gave an account of what followed in his witness statement to the Bureau of Military History. After his arrest, he was taken to Cork Gaol where he was held for five days. Then early one morning he was handcuffed to another prisoner and, guarded on each side by soldiers with fixed bayonets, they were marched to Glanmire railway station and put on a special train. At Mallow station the canteen ladies offered tea to the soldiers but not to the prisoners. At Buttevant the train was stopped and sent back to Mallow to pick up some prisoners from Kerry – obviously a bit of an organisational cock-up. More prisoners were taken on board when the train reached Limerick, before they travelled on to Dublin where they arrived at around 6.30pm. From the station they were marched to Richmond Barracks, crowded into bare barrack rooms and were allocated two army blankets; one to use as a mattress and the other to cover them. They used their boots as pillows. After a day or so in the barracks they were marched to and loaded onto a cattle boat at the North Wall, Dublin Port.

Hegarty's account ends at this point, but the story of what he was to endure was taken up by another account given by Charles Browne, who was arrested in Macroom on 2nd May. On board (he records) the prisoners were handcuffed together in pairs. The ship crossing was rough, and many men spewed up (a bit unpleasant if it happened to be the bloke handcuffed to you). Next morning they were entrained to various English prisons. Browne arrived that evening at Wakefield Gaol in Yorkshire where Irishmen from all over the country had ended up. Here he and the others were initially kept in solitary confinement and although exercise was allowed each morning and evening, it was taken in strict silence. After four weeks, these restrictions were, however, relaxed and prisoners were allowed to mix and talk. Visits and parcels were also allowed. Browne observed that 'the Irish of Yorkshire saw that we were well supplied'. Towards the end of June he, like many of those detained, was sent on to Frongoch. Here he and the other internees forcibly bided their time.

Their time was soon to come. A wave of resentment began to sweep over the general population of Ireland because of the severity of the British reprisals and executions following the Rising. Memorial Masses were held for the executed rebels, photographs of them were popularly purchased, aid funds were set up for their families and songs and ballads began to appear celebrating the Rising. Republican flags and badges suddenly began to appear everywhere, rebel slogans were shouted – and young men marched, military style, at Gaelic football matches.

Events had turned around; the inroads made by the Fenians and IRB into the Gaelic Athletic Association from the 1880s were now finally coming to fruition.

Maureen doesn't put in an appearance at her bar in William O'Brien Street in Mallow and I leave after a couple of pints and navigate my way back to the hideaway. The CCTV cameras don't seem to have alerted anyone, but I still feel uneasy. I can't relax or settle for the night. The local Gardai pass, but don't see me. I sit in the cab facing the road expecting trouble and count 185 vehicles passing my adopted works entrance in a nervous two-hour observation vigil. One young girl walks past oblivious to my presence with a mobile phone clamped to her ear; 15 minutes later she's back again, walking in the opposite direction and apparently still on the same call – again she doesn't see me. Just before one o'clock in the morning a taxi driver startles me from semi-slumber; he's nipped out his cab to take his customary pee at his usual tree trunk when, glancing up, he sees a strange aberration watching him from the cab of a phantom vehicle. He's more frightened of me than I am of him.

Sunday 30th June – Mallow, and near Bweeng

'I can't serve you with these 'til after 12.30,' he says, and sets aside my bottles of brandy and wine.

'But they told me it was 10.30 the other day,' I say in protest.

'Ah, but it's a Sunday today,' he counters.

'It's 12.15 now,' I argue, 'you're only talking about 15 minutes.'

'Sorry, it's more than my job's worth – I'll put them aside for you,' he says – and does so. But I don't wait.

I take the rest of the shopping back to the camper and drive off towards Bweeng. I need to see if my bike's still hidden behind the trees or if somebody has stolen it or fly-tipped more rubbish on top of it.

My dad was not a very practical man; he could just about manage to connect up an electrical plug. I never saw him attempt any other do-it-yourself task, but as he wasn't a home owner, I suppose he had no real need to. He did, however, teach me how to mend a puncture – and I still remember.

I fill a plastic jug with water, get the inner tube out, blow it up and discover a small split at the juncture of the valve stem with the main tube. It's going to be a difficult repair because the split is right in the corner. I cut and shape a patch as best I can so that it follows the line of stem and tube, then dry the area, rough it up, apply the glue, let it set as recommended, peel the patch with some difficulty, press it hard into the area and hold the pressure. I reinflate the tube and immerse it in the water, everything seems fine – no bubbles. I dry the tube, grate and apply chalk, fit tube back into tyre and pump it up – testing the pressure as I go by squeezing it with my thumb. After about five minutes I gently squeeze it again – it's gone down slightly. I repeat the whole process a second time – same result.

It's a sunny day. I strip off my jumper and start to sweat. Midway through the third repair attempt a man drives up and parks in the lay-by to take his dog for a walk along the Way. He looks none too pleased that I'm hogging most of the space. The third repair attempt fails just as he returns, so he catches my curses. We don't speak. He drives off.

The walk ahead relies on the bike. If I can't get it sorted, the walk is over. There's no chance of using trains; the railway line veers away from the Way after Mallow and of course a bus service on the route is non-existent. I need a new inner tube.

I clamp the bike onto the back of the camper, phone Polly and explain what's happened.

'I'm in the shit! Can you do me a favour and see if there's a cycle shop in Mallow?' She checks on the Internet and gets back to me. Luckily there *is* a shop; it's on Bridge Street. This gives me a good clue as to its location, but of course it's a Sunday and it'll be closed.

I drive back to Mallow and find the bike shop. It opens at 10 o'clock tomorrow morning. I park at the supermarket and decide to spend the rest of the day here, wild-camping again at the same spot as last night. I wander around the town.

Taxis are parked up along Thomas Davis Street and I get an

idea. If I drop the bike into the shop for a new inner tube to be fitted tomorrow morning, I could drive to Ballynamona, walk on to Killavullen, get a taxi back to Mallow pick up the bike and cycle back to Ballynamona. It would be an easy 11-mile walk and I wouldn't lose another day of the walk. A lady taxi driver hands me her card with her phone number, together with other listed cab numbers. Her name is perhaps Pat as this is printed on the card; she's maybe the proprietor of the company. I decide to think on the idea.

The rest of the afternoon I while away wandering around Mallow; I sit on a bench just off Park Road and read for a time. Two scruffy looking guys take an adjacent seat; they converse in an uncertain tongue (possibly Polish, but certainly not Irish) and scoff takeaway meals. A fat young man staggers past clutching a can of Guinness he'd obviously purchased, no doubt along with a few more, at precisely 12.30 that day – or maybe the day before? I walk up to the bridge to take a close look at the River Blackwater.

Here in August 1922, during the Civil War, the people of Mallow defied threats from the withdrawing republican forces and occupied the area day and night to prevent the bridge being blown up. They were led by both the Catholic parish priest and the Anglican vicar, who both knew that their congregations would be depleted if the bridge was blown because north and south of the town would be physically separated.

The afternoon passes well enough – and in the evening I take myself for a spicy treat at D'Mughal's Indian restaurant.

Monday 1st July – Ballynamona to Killavullen

Sixty-eight years seems like a long time, but not when you realise that on this day you've been around that long; suddenly it seems like the blink of an eye. I'm not unique in concluding that the passage of time appears to have a strange exponential relationship with age; the theory is that every moment you live is a smaller and smaller representation of your whole life, which somehow makes the days, weeks and years flow past quicker. These ponderings go through my brain as I wake at 7.15am this morning.

I've not slept well because I'd still felt vulnerable in this dubious hideaway. Last night I was woken by what sounded like a low-flying light-aircraft at 3.30 – then I couldn't get back to sleep. Some early-bird pigeons suffering from insomnia made sure I stayed awake after that, before I drifted off again.

I remember to open the couple of birthday cards I've brought across with me – a pleasant few moments I've saved up to savour. I can't remember where I was one year ago on this day, but next year I shall definitely remember Mallow. By eight o'clock I'm still only partially dressed and am having a spot of breakfast – when a man turns up to unlock the padlock and remove the chain securing the double gates that the camper is parked hard against. I open the van door expecting the worst.

'Do you want me to move?' I ask nervously.

'No, you're alright – you're alright,' he says. I'm relieved.

The gates are double, and open inwards; the camper is in front of one gate, so he's still able to drive his van in via the other. I watch him through the back window as he carries out a security check before he locks up again and drives off. My daughter phones to wish me happy birthday and one of my granddaughters sings the happy birthday song to me – it's lovely.

The bike shop isn't open at 10 o'clock, and it's still not open 10 minutes later. So I sit by the bridge and worry. Maybe it's a public holiday today? Maybe the proprietor is sick? Maybe I've got it wrong and they're closed on Mondays? At 10.20 I return to the shop and this time it's open – God is in his heaven after all.

'Here's a man who looks like he's got a problem!' the lady says as I wheel the bike into the shop. I explain I'd like to pick it up this afternoon and she tells me how much it will likely cost. Everything is fine.

I drive the camper to Ballynamona and park in the same spot as two days ago, outside Murphy's bar. I've had a long think about the idea I had yesterday and phone the taxi firm. A man answers – maybe he's the Pat on the card? We agree on a rendezvous in Killavullen at five o'clock, which should give plenty of time for the walk and get me back to Mallow before the bike shop closes.

As I begin the walk, the Way climbs up and ducks under a railway bridge (the line from Mallow to Cork) and crosses the main road. Within minutes I'm strolling along a quiet lane. Today there is time to really enjoy the walk, to drink in every step, every change of scene. The beauty of walking for me is that you're never sure what terrain or feature you're going to find around the next bend or over the next rise – or whom you might meet.

At Carrigduff, a couple of kilometres into the walk, I turn onto a track and a cyclist passes me. I don't know it then, but he will be the only person I'll see (other than in a car) until I reach Killavullen. An information board stands at the juncture of lane and track and whilst I'm reading it the mobile phone gives a beep. It's a message from my son wishing me all the best for the day. I text back, thank him, and tell him of this fine sunny day and of where I am in Ireland (not that that'll mean much, unless he checks a map). Today I've forgotten the camera, but write some notes instead. The information board explains that furze can be found in abundance around here. Better known to me as gorse; it was used, the board explains, by country folk for chimney cleaning, soil tilling and for fuel. Well, you learn some new little snippet of stuff every day – even at my age.

The morning is spent on minor roads (but with few cars), on tracks, on footpaths, over open countryside and through forests; it's a pleasant mixture and there's no stress. Butterflies flutter and flit in pairs. A murder of crows and a few wayward gulls strut ungainly across a flat field; then suddenly all take to graceful flight. A notice declares the field to be 'land preserved' and warns against trespassing – an unlikely offence in this desolate spot I would think.

During a sandwich lunch I sit on a grass bank and listen to a peewit calling from one side of the track, answered by another on the other side. The peewit (or lapwing) is sadly one of the few birds I'm able to identify from its call but as I walk on towards a car park at Glannagear a chorus of different bird songs ring around me.

After lunch, while I stroll on, cows stare at me with some amazement and, as I stare back at them, I'm reminded of a poem I learned in my youth. I'd found it in one of a set of children's encyclopaedias Dad bought for me. The poem reflects the essence of my walk today; it's called 'Leisure' and was written by William Henry Davies, a Welshman who spent much of his life as a hobo – and so had plenty of time to experience the subject of his poem. I can remember the first few verses and say them over silently to myself as I walk:

'What is this life if, full of care,
We have no time to stand and stare.
No time to stand beneath the boughs
And stare as long as sheep or cows.'

A footpath leads down towards Killavullen; it seems to go on interminably and, even though I have plenty of time before the taxi is due, I keep pulling out the map to see if I've somehow overshot the road that leads off for about half a mile into the village. Eventually the path drops down to meet a likely looking road. But, as I'm not entirely sure, I cross over it, follow the fingerpost and climb up through trees on another footpath. I walk on for another 15 minutes before deciding that the road I'd crossed must be to one leading to the village. Doubling back then and descending steeply I spot a dog-walker in the parking area who's preparing to leave. I scramble and slide down a bank and rap on his window just as he's pulling away. He lowers the window warily and his dog growls at me (I don't blame it). The man confirms that Killavullen is indeed only about half a mile away along the road.

The village has a population of just over 200. At a Y-junction I join Main Street. The taxi might pick me up here – our telephone discussions weren't that explicit. But then I think it might come along the main road from Mallow and into the village over Killavullen Bridge, so I walk on towards the River Blackwater. The village was the birthplace of Nano Nagle, so an information board at the bridge tells me; she was born here in 1718 and spent her life educating the poor in hedge schools – a risky occupation in the days of the Penal laws. I'm very early for the taxi pickup, so sit on a stone wall near the bridge and wait.

Miss Annie Barrett was also born in Killavullen on 24th September 1888; her father was a Fenian. She recorded, in her witness statement to the BMH, that she usually cycled from Killavullen to her job as a telephonist at Mallow post office. Her brother was a wireless operator and it was through him that she'd become associated with the Irish Volunteers and had become a member of their female counterparts, *Cumann na mBan* (Irishwoman's Council). This was a nationalist group whose membership was comprised entirely of women and girls. In 1919 the British outlawed it along with other nationalist organisations. The inaugural public meeting of the organisation took place in Wynn's Hotel, Dublin in April 1914; *The Irish Times* reported that there were about a hundred ladies present. Agnes O'Farrelly presided over the meeting. At that time very few women were politically active. They were not yet allowed the vote either, despite the militant stone throwing, arson, hunger strikes and other such unladylike activities of suffragettes such as the Pankhursts in England. In November 1918 certain women over the age of 30 had finally been granted the vote.

Annie Barrett had turned 30 that year but because she was unmarried and, probably living at her parents' home, wouldn't have been allowed to vote. Back in 1914, however, Agnes O'Farrelly's view was that politics should be left to the men of the Volunteers and that the women's role should be to 'put Ireland first' by helping to arm their men. *The Irish Times* of 3rd April 1914 recorded that, in answer to a question from the floor as to whether the women should learn to fight, Miss O'Farrelly had stated that they could do splendid work as spies.

Annie Barrett effectively became a spy for the Volunteers at Mallow post office. In early 1919 she was appointed to the post of Supervising Telephonist. The Irish Volunteers saw much change in the period between the Rising and the outbreak of the War of Independence at the beginning of 1919 when Annie took up her new post.

The Unionists continued to put pressure on Asquith's coalition government over their Irish policy and the Third Home Rule Bill. Lloyd George led negotiations on behalf of the government. In June John Redmond persuaded the Ulster Nationalist Conference in Belfast to vote for the *temporary* exclusion of the six north-eastern Ulster counties. With Bonar Law and the Unionists forcing the issue this concession gave the green light in July for the introduction of two amendments to the Bill that advocated the *permanent* exclusion of the Ulster Unionists. Lloyd George had, it transpired, backed Carson and the Ulster Unionists' position all along. Sinn Féin, the Irish Republican party formed in 1905 by Arthur Griffith, never allowed the Irish people to forget that Redmond had agreed to the partition of Ireland. This fact and the casualties sustained by Redmond's Volunteers who'd gone to the Western Front to fight for the rights of small nations, contributed to the demise of his Irish Parliamentary Party and assisted the rise of Sinn Féin. Lloyd George replaced Asquith as prime minister on 7th December 1916, assisted by the Conservatives, which further worsened the position of the IPP.

Bonar Law, having gained more power, was able to exert pressure on the British commander-in-chief in Ireland, Sir Bryan Mahon to prohibit the Volunteers from undertaking military drilling. Instead, they did physical exercises – but managed to slip in a bit of 'disguised' drilling as well.

From April 1917 public opinion in Australia and in America forced Lloyd George to try and sort out the Irish situation. One of the outcomes of this pressure in was the release in June of the prisoners from Frongoch and British gaols. Amongst them was Éamon de Valera who suddenly found himself heralded as a hero.

A by-election was forthcoming in East Clare and de Valera was invited to run. He stood under the banner of the Sinn Féin party, and won by a majority of more than two to one. De Valera now worked with others to unify the various nationalist factions into a common cause. In hindsight this was more difficult than can now be conceived because Griffith and his supporters wanted to restore an Irish king together with houses of Lords and Commons. Eventually agreement was reached that the aim was to secure the international recognition of Ireland as an independent Irish republic.

Meanwhile the British were getting somewhat spooked by the growing prominence of Sinn Féin. In July General Sir Bryan Mahon issued a proclamation prohibiting the wearing of uniforms of a military nature and of the carrying of hurleys (the stick used in the game of hurling) in processions, presumably because they could be considered weapons. Legislation was introduced under the Defence of the Realm Act (DORA) for various offences. It was under a provision of this Act that Thomas Ashe, a teacher in Lusk near Dublin was sentenced to be imprisoned in Mountjoy Gaol, Dublin. Ashe went on hunger strike in September in an attempt to gain political prisoner status and not be treated as a common criminal. Like others (including suffragettes in England until 1913) he was force fed by the prison staff and as a result he subsequently died. His death gave rise to a national demonstration of mourning which incidentally created thousands of new supporters for Sinn Féin.

Just before the Sinn Féin convention of October 1917 de Valera did a deal with Griffiths in which he proposed that once independence had been achieved the Irish people would be given a referendum to decide the issue of a monarchy. He also talked Griffiths into withdrawing from the presidency of the party, and a few days after the convention de Valera had become both president of Sinn Féin and leader of the Irish Volunteer Force.

Unwittingly the Germans gave the biggest boost to Sinn Féin's cause in the spring of 1918 by launching a massive attack on the Western Front with half a million extra troops redeployed from the Russian front. By the end of the first day of this offensive 21,000 British soldiers had been taken prisoner and the Germans so believed that they were about to wind up the war in their favour that a national holiday was declared on 24th March. How did this help Sinn Féin? The British reacted by deciding to draft a bill to extend the age limits for military service and Ireland was included within the legislation. Lloyd George further decided that conscription in Ireland should be linked with the implementation of home rule, and on 9th April the Military Service Bill was introduced in the Commons. On 16th April the Bill received its third reading; John Dillon, who had succeeded Redmond upon his death, withdrew the IPP from Westminster and went back to Ireland to organise opposition, and Mahon, with his ear to the ground, reported that its introduction would induce an armed insurrection and that the Catholic Church was also very much opposed to it.

The Right Rev. Monsignor M. Curran, secretary to the Archbishop of Dublin, in his witness statement to the BMH, set down the mood of the country: 'Conscription set Ireland ablaze. The entire country galvanised into life. Every man, woman and child, every province, diocese and parish were determined that, whatever the cost, Ireland's manhood would in no circumstances be enslaved to fight England's battles, not to mention fighting a people who had never done us any harm'. He continued: 'Drilling is going on nightly. The number of Volunteers and Sinn Féin bodies is increasing'.

The Catholic Church issued a manifesto supporting resistance to conscription 'by every means that are consonant with the law of God'. Meanwhile, in Dublin's Mansion House members of the IPP, Sinn Féin and the Irish Labour Party convened to co-ordinate opposition to the 'conscription crisis' as it became known.

John Dillon came to the conclusion that Lloyd George's stance on conscription was a devious device dreamed up, under pressure exerted from the Unionists, to wriggle out of granting home rule.

His suspicions were perhaps vindicated by the appointment of the hawkish Field Marshal Lord French as Lord Lieutenant (but giving him the flashier title of Lord Lieutenant General and General Governor of Ireland). During the summer of 1918 the pressure was again intensified by the introduction of further restrictions under the banner of DORA. Bans were now imposed on Gaelic language classes, football matches, dancing competitions and athletic meetings. But although Lloyd George was upping the ante, he was anxious that it didn't appear so, particularly to President Woodrow Wilson and America (there were more Irish in the USA at that time than in Ireland) who was now Britain's ally in the Great War. His opportunity to make it appear that any actions taken by his government were defensive ones came, luckily for the British, due to the escapades of a certain Joseph Dowling.

Dowling had been captured in Germany in the winter of 1914–15 and had joined Roger Casement's German Irish brigade. He was landed from a German submarine at his own request, convincing the Germans that he could set up communications between themselves and Sinn Féin. Michael Collins was one of the few who knew of the approach. Dowling landed on Crab Island in Galway Bay, thumbed a lift from two lobster men in a boat to the mainland and made his way swiftly to the local pub. Here he quickly got himself legless, probably on a cocktail of Guinness and Jameson which he'd obviously missed (schnapps being not quite the same). He was promptly arrested and court martialled. Found guilty, his sentence of death was commuted to penal servitude for life. Dowling's landing was just the excuse Lloyd George needed; the incident was labelled as the 'German plot' and was quickly broadcast around the world.

The conscription crisis and the internments of around 80 prominent members of Sinn Féin (including Mr de Valera) after the 'German plot' saw a huge growth in the strength of the Volunteers throughout the country. The Mourne Abbey Company, situated about five miles south of Mallow was no exception. John Ronayne recorded in his witness statement to the BMH that: 'During the spring and summer of 1918 all members were engaged in various activities in preparation for the anticipated fight against conscription. They were watching and reporting on the movements of enemy forces, making buckshot, reloading shotgun cartridges and helping to manufacture pikes and other weapons in the local forges'. He continued: 'We also made bombs from cocoa tins filled with concrete and scrap metal and charged with gelignite. There was, of course, a detonator and fuse also inserted. I think about this time the companies were organised into a battalion. Mallow was Battalion HQ'.

Annie Barrett got involved with the Intelligence section at Mallow in 1918. She recorded that: 'I remember that I transmitted a record of a telephone call from the British Headquarters at Cork instructing all units to arrange for collection of arms in the area. As a result of this information the Volunteers staged a general raid for arms throughout the Cork brigade area before the enemy moved'. She also found out that the British code word to be used if conscription was to be enforced was *TURKEY*.

On 11th November the First World War came to an end. There was to be no conscription, but there was also no home rule.

Sinn Féin achieved a landslide victory over the Irish Parliamentary Party in the election of 1918. The Sinn Féin candidates had been selected carefully; many were in British prisons, and some didn't even know they'd been nominated until informed so by the prison staff. De Valera's name was submitted again for East Clare, where he was unopposed. All the Sinn Féin MPs of course refused to attend Westminster. The rest of Britain was left firmly in the control of the Conservatives and Unionists parties even though Lloyd George retained his Liberal seat and the premiership.

On 21st January 1919, 37 of the 73 Sinn Féin MPs (who were not in gaol) met at the Mansion House in Dublin. Here they established a constitution, and their own Irish Parliament, the *Dáil Éireann* (meaning 'assembly'), proclaiming the establishment of an independent Irish republic. Edward Carson received (tongue-in-cheek) an invitation to attend, along with the other Unionists; we don't know exactly what Carson said when he got the invite, but I bet the second word was 'off'. The remnants of the Irish Parliamentary Party didn't attend either. This same day is also the day traditionally recognised to be the start of the Anglo-Irish War (as described by the British), or the War of Independence as it's known elsewhere. However labelled, things kicked-off in a quarry two miles from Tipperary. Nine masked Volunteers who, from around this time were increasingly known as the Irish Republican Army, carried out an ambush of two RIC constables and two council workers bringing gelignite from the military barracks in Tipperary to Soloheadbeg quarry. During the incident the two constables were shot and killed.

Annie Barrett had only recently taken up her new position as Supervising Telephonist in Mallow post office at the beginning of 1919, when she was contacted by Dan Hegarty. He conveyed a message from his boss Liam Lynch, and Commandant of Cork No.2 Brigade of the IRA, in which he requested her to disassociate herself from *Cumann na mBan*. The request was made to deter the British from putting her under scrutiny. Annie did as she was asked and during the coming months and years of the war she passed on valuable information – whilst continuing to cycle daily to her switchboard in Mallow from the little village of Killavullen.

I sit on the stone wall by Killavullen Bridge reading my book for three quarters of an hour, waiting for the taxi to appear. But now it's five minutes past the arranged time and I start to get concerned. Whilst I'm looking in the direction of the bridge, the taxi arrives from the opposite direction and pulls up alongside. The driver is a lady, the same one who gave me her card in Mallow yesterday – perhaps her name *is* Pat after all. She'd come, not as I'd thought along the main N72 road, but along the more direct minor road. She'd had trouble finding me, expecting me to be at the Y-junction where I'd joined Main Street. I could have saved myself the walk to the bridge if I'd stayed there.

We drive back to Mallow along the minor road (Annie Barrett's cycle route). During the short journey she asks me where I've walked and I relay my trip and Saturday's puncture problem.

'It's dangerous,' she says with concern – because I'm walking alone. She shows even more concern when I tell her my age.

'I'm 68,' I say then, for some reason, perhaps because I'd spoken to nobody all day, I add: 'Actually, it's my birthday today.'

She drops me right outside the bike shop. I pay the 15-euro fare that shows up on the meter with a 20-euro note, and am about to give her a tip from the change, when she thrusts eight euros into my hand. I try to give her some coins back, but she's insistent.

'Buy yourself a drink tonight,' she says smiling – a lovely gesture which I won't forget. Thank you, Pat – if that was your name.

The bike shop has fitted a new inner tube, but make up for my taxi fare gain by charging me more than was quoted. Good and bad strike a balance. I bike along the flat dual carriageway to Ballynamona and then drive to the Blackwater Valley campsite at Fermoy.

Tuesday 2nd July – Killavullen to Fermoy

The campsite is situated by the side of the main N72 road; it's a 13-mile bike ride back west along this back to Killavullen, then a 16-mile walk to Fermoy along the Blackwater Way.

I set out on the bike at 8.45am. There are a few hills and the road surface is good. About a mile before Ballyhooly it begins to rain slightly and looks very black in the direction I'm going, so I stop and don anorak and leggings. At Ballyhooly it begins to throw it down. The village is supposed to have been the first to be settled in AD 923 by a small group of Africans from Nigeria who were looking to find somewhere wetter to live. I have much belated news for them – they were undoubtedly successful in finding it. At Castletownroche the water gushes down the gutters of the main street in a torrent. I'm wearing trainers – not the best of footwear for this sort of weather and, when the steep hill up the main street grinds me to a cycling stop, I squelch up it alongside a roaring gully. Before the turning off at Killavullen the rain eases and then stops. It was just a 'shower'. I'm a soggy deranged mess, a condition not improved by a lady driver who almost knocks me off my bike as she turns into a garage for fuel.

At the parking area where I finished the Blackwater Way walk yesterday I take off wet shoes and socks – but can't do anything about the bottom of my soaked jeans. I have no towel, so improvise by drying my feet using my jumper. The walking boots, socks and sandwiches are snug and dry in the rucksack because I'd learnt to my cost many years ago that everything has to be packed in there in a plastic bin-liner.

It's 10.15am when I start walking the Blackwater Way. I climb up through a wood on a track, repeating the carry-over walk from yesterday. A lady out for an early morning trot on her horse passes and wishes me a good morning. She's accompanied by a friendly bitch collie that jumps up at me affectionately. I catch the odd glimpse down to the Blackwater Valley through an arcade of trees but otherwise the walk continues in a forest of tall conifers for some while. The dense green carpet of ferns and ground foliage around the trees is broken only by occasional towers of pinkish-purple foxgloves; their drooping clusters, open and mature at the bottom, are closed and yet to flower at their tapered tips. In a clearing, tree felling is in progress; well it might be but, the bundle of logs that have been grabbed by the machine is frozen in mid-transit because a mobile phone is clamped to the ear of the man in the cab. I've noticed virtually everyone in Ireland (and elsewhere for that matter) has this affliction – especially whilst driving, regardless of whatever the law says about the matter.

I come out from the forest near Kylenahoory and watch a hare taking his grass lunch in a field. I'd never seen this before. He loops forward, stops to munch for a few minutes – then loops forward again. I watch him closely through a gap in the hedge. Now I join him, while sitting on a grass bank taking my lunch. The sun appears very briefly. Dogs bark somewhere in the distance – but otherwise all is silent. The morning has passed like life – too quickly.

I come across the third person I've seen today on yet another forest track. He's walking his little dog. I catch him up and we walk along together chatting. He explains he's not at work because he's got a bad back.

'There's no work around here,' he says. 'In Killavullen last Christmas they had a big party for 50 people who were all leaving for Australia – it keeps the unemployment figures down,' he adds with a touch of cynicism, 'and if you get a feckin job – what factories there are might close down next feckin week.' I've noticed that the use of that feckin expletive seems to be quite prevalent in the land, even in mixed company. But hey! What the feck.

'There are a lot of Poles over here now,' he says, letting the subject hang in the air.

'Yes, I've noticed that,' I agree.

It seems that, like Britain, Ireland has seen an influx of Eastern European immigrants, mainly Poles and Latvians, whilst emigration on the other hand is around 30,000 a year – a quarter of whom go to Britain and around 17% to Australia. Like Britain, Ireland is looking closely at her immigration policy and trying to address the issue of illegal immigrants. This reminds me of an amusing tale, which I relay to my walking companion. Apparently, a group of 40 Romanians submitted an application to take part in the Sligo International Choral Festival. They were accepted and booked to appear on the opening night. Unfortunately Sligo never discovered if they were any feckin good, because as soon as their plane touched down in Dublin they did a feckin runner; the awards they'd claimed to have won in Romania were feckin forged, as were their feckin testimonials – and the tape they sent over to impress the organisers of the festival was recorded by another feckin choir.

We walk on together towards Ballyhooly. His little dog scampers ahead flitting from one side of the path to the other on exciting scent hunts, while his master continues to paint a gloomy picture of the economy in the area.

'There's nobody in the pubs during the week… people can't afford it,' he says. 'And if you do go, in the morning, the feckin Gardai might stop you.'

'Oh shit,' I say, thinking of my frequent nightcaps in the camper whilst I write up the day's notes.

'No, you they won't stop a tourist; too much paperwork,' he says reassuringly.

'Thank God for that,' I say.

He tells me he'd recently been on a very cheap three-day excursion to Estonia and was shocked by the high cost of clothing and the low wages. A woman he'd spoken to there, he tells me, thought she had a good job, being paid three euros an hour. I think back to my Internet research in Killarney and remember that booze was pretty cheap in Estonia – it would have to be I guess.

The track terminates at a barrier and the Way leads onto a road. 'I go off that way,' he says, nodding to the right, 'you'll be going down to the crossroads and then turning right.' I offer my hand, and we shake; it's been an interesting 15-minute interlude, but sadly I forgot to ask him his name. Thanks anyway, mate – nice to have met you.

I sit on a wall at Bloomfield Crossroads to rest for a while with two cyclists who've had the same idea. Across the Blackwater River is the 16th century Ballyhooly Castle, bedecked with scaffolding and undergoing a renovation. From where I sit it looks like the castle is sprouting out of the top of the house below it – which is actually a fishing lodge, and was built much later. I've so far walked about halfway back to Fermoy.

The remainder of the afternoon is uneventful; the terrain is again a mix of minor roads and tracks – many through woodland and forests. A few information boards explain Irish myths and legends. The story that appeals most is the legend of the birds' parliament. The birds met to determine who would be their ruler. They decided that whichever bird flew the highest would rule over the bird kingdom. The eagle of course was the bookies' favourite but, unknown to him, as he soared above his rivals; he had a little passenger who'd sneaked onto his back for the ride. When the eagle tired, the little bird took off above him to win the contest – and so it was the tiny wren became the ruler of all birds. The information board tells me that the wren's song can be heard hereabouts in great volume – I just wish I knew how it sounded.

Walking downhill on a lane near Glenabo Bridge I'm overtaken by a young girl jogger, music blaring from her iPod. She's trailed by three golden retrievers and a west-highland-white terrier all struggling, between sniffing interludes, to keep up with her. The westie doesn't actually seem to give a shit – in fact he stops for one and follows it with a wee, then valiantly endeavours to catch up with the rest of the pack.

I joined the Blackwater Way walk 75 miles back, at Shrone, but the Blackwater River has always been away somewhere in the valley to the north. Now, a mile or so from Fermoy I finally get to walk beside it. The head of the river runs off from Knockane Mountain on the Cork/Kerry border. It flows south to Rathmore and then east – passing through places I'd walked through or close to: Millstreet, Banteer, Mallow and Killavullen. From Fermoy the river enters County Waterford and continues to flow east through Ballyduff, Lismore and Cappoquin before broadening and dropping south to enter the sea at Youghal. After Fermoy, the Blackwater Way itself goes north-east away from the river and so leaves my route at Clogheen – for me a two-day walk away.

It's a pleasant walk along the river that runs here broad and quiet. I pass a few salmon fishermen. Across some fields, a man passes me going in the opposite direction, but otherwise there's nobody until I get to the rowing club boathouse and onto the 'civilised' tarmac path known locally as Barnane Walk, passing St Bernard's Well. St Bernard, from which the name of the Walk was derived, was the patron saint of the Cistercian Order. The monastery of the Christian Brothers was located around here between the 12th and 16th centuries.

I'm almost at the end of the day's walk as I cross the Blackwater and look down on the impressive weir. The camper waits around the corner but I spend a moment or two gazing at the rushing water and thinking about a snippet I'd recently read from *Foster's Irish Oddities*:

In 1930, about 300 rooks apparently nested in two groups; one in Fermoy itself and the other a mile or so from the bridge where I now stand, on an island in the river. One evening in November of that year around 11,000 starlings wheeled around the town and poured into the rooks' nesting places, ousting them. This event was repeated each evening for the next week, which kind of got up the rooks' beaks. The starlings, thinking they were on to a good thing and would soon permanently rule the roost, raided the rooks again on an eighth evening. But this time they got a shock: instead of 300 rooks, suddenly 2,000 rooks appeared and rose up in a black mass to drive away the invaders. The starlings never tried the stunt again and eventually left the area.

In Killarney I'd bought *Rebel Cork's Fighting Story* and had been reading it since I'd left Shrone. Fermoy was featured prominently within it. It was an account written from an IRA viewpoint of the War of Independence, and I couldn't help but draw the similitude between that war and the war of the birds; the rooks being the Irish nationals and the starlings taking the role of the British soldiers. In 1919 the Irish rooks began their rise in earnest to drive away the starling British.

Eight
Ferment in Fermoy

'A dream! a dream! an ancient dream!
Yet, ere peace come to Inisfail,
Some weapons on some field must gleam,
Some burning glory fire the Gael.'
From: *Ways of War* by Lionel Johnson

Wednesday 3rd July – Fermoy
At the campsite I'd been given a trail map of the town and so I set out to explore the place. The name Fermoy means 'monastery of the men of the plain'. The town now has a population of around 6,000 and was developed in the late 18th century by a Scotsman, John Anderson.

I go through Wellington Wicket Gate and cut the corner into town by going through Town Park. There's a bust of Anderson in the park. He originated from a poor family and made a fortune as a commercial agent in New York during the American wars, losing it all again following the Napoleonic wars. In the period in-between he developed roads in Ireland and started a mail coach system in Munster, as well as purchasing land in the area and laying down the town design for Fermoy. In 1797 he did a deal with the British army for the construction of a barracks, so that Fermoy grew and prospered as a garrison town, becoming the largest in Ireland by the 1830s.

I head for the local studies section of the library in Connolly Street. Throughout the town the period of the struggle for independence is evoked by its street names: MacDonagh Terrace, MacCurtain Street, John Redmond Street, Clancy Street, Devlin Street, Kevin Barry Hill, Fitzgerald Place, Lynch Terrace, Ashe Quay, McDermot Place and Pearse Square.

Other names commemorate earlier conflicts: Emmet Street and Wolfe Tone Park, whilst New Barrack Street, north of the river, is one of the few reminders of the British presence before independence.

As I scour the library shelves, I'm acutely reminded again that I'm in a Catholic country:

'I'll be with you in a minute, Father,' I hear the librarian say.

I can find only two books relevant to my period of interest: a well-worn copy of *Rebel Cork's Fighting Story*, and *Kilworth and Moore Park – British Army Camps from 1896 to 1922*. On page 114 of this book I read that thousands of republicans were held without charge in camps. Kilworth camp, comprising wooden huts, was located six miles north of Fermoy just off the road to Mitchelstown. It was one of the largest camps, holding up to 250 at any one time taken from a wide area. The book brings me back well enough to the period.

The events at Soloheadbeg quarry in January 1919 signalled the start of IRA activities. Piaras Béaslaí (born in Liverpool as the less impressive sounding Percy Frederick Beazley) made clear in the Volunteers' newspaper what was expected of its readers; their clear targets should be soldiers, and in particular the RIC – it was effectively a declaration of war.

De Valera was at this time in Lincoln Gaol with other republican detainees. They were classed as political prisoners and so were allowed the privilege of receiving food parcels. It seems they'd acquired a particular penchant for cakes – especially those with a ferrite flavour. This was, fortunately for Mr de Valera, six years before two clever Germans, Geffchen and Richter, invented a metal detector to prevent theft from a large manufacturing plant. It took the receipt of four cakes before the correct key was received. It'd been made in Dublin from a wax impression of the chaplain's master key, produced by de Valera by melting down a candle 'borrowed', together with the key, whilst the priest was saying Mass. Michael Collins went to Lincoln to assist in the escape, which was carried out almost exactly to his planned timescale. It took place on 3rd February 1919, and by the 23rd de Valera was in Dublin, having travelled there via Worksop, Sheffield, Manchester and Liverpool.

De Valera spent only a short time in Ireland, milking the kudos. His mind had already been made up that he'd make an appeal to the American public for recognition of Ireland's independence, and to try and gain some financial assistance. He departed for America in June.

Another key player was absent from the nitty-gritty of Irish affairs during the early months of 1919 – Lloyd George. He was thoroughly tied-up in Paris at the Peace Conference with the American, French and Italian leaders setting the terms for those nations who'd been defeated in the Great War, a task that absorbed his entire attention until July. The British were slowly getting around to looking at the Irish problem: the Home Rule Act was due to come into force once the last of the peace treaties had been ratified. An Irish Committee had been set-up in April 1918 to draw up a home rule bill 'as soon as possible'. The committee was chaired by Walter Long, a staunch Unionist who'd helped to found the Ulster Defence League. His idea of 'as soon as possible' translated meant 'as long as it takes'. It took the committee 19 months, until November 1919, to issue their report the details of which were then kept secret, but which formed the basis of the eventual settlement that followed the War of Independence.

In May 1919 a motley quartet of Brits met aboard the Admiralty yacht *Enchantress*, moored at Kingstown (now Dun Laoghaire), eight miles south of Dublin. It comprised: Walter Long, now First Lord of the Admiralty; Field Marshal Sir John French – Lord Lieutenant of Ireland, who'd intensified activities under DORA; Mr Saunderson, private secretary to French and son of Colonel Edward Saunderson (the originator of Irish Unionism) who inherently distrusted all Catholics. The final member of the quartet was Ian Macpherson, a Liberal member of the Cabinet and Deputy Secretary of State for War, whose 'expertise' on deer forests in Scotland had convinced Lloyd George in 1913 that millions of acres of such lands were suitable for agricultural purposes, much to the disdain of the highlanders. It was on this 'jolly-boat' *Enchantress*, that a campaign was masterminded to defeat Sinn Féin and the IRA. Walter Long suggested it would be a damned good idea to redeploy some discharged soldiers into the RIC, and John French quite liked this concept; their ideas were to eventually mature and result in the formation of the infamous Black and Tans.

Michael Collins had a few ideas up his sleeve himself. In

April he organised a national loan to finance the war that he was helping to initiate. His idea was to gradually provoke a general state of disorder. This he achieved by a number of initiatives: he set-up two underground newspapers, organised an arms smuggling route, a bomb making factory and formed a hit squad to eliminate members of the Dublin Metropolitan Police Force – specifically those employed in the detective branch known as 'G' division, who were actively engaged in suppressing the activities of Sinn Féin and the IRA. Collins had been smuggled into the detective headquarters and spent a complete night gleaning information about their personnel and how they operated. He determined to put this knowledge to good use by forming what became known as 'The Squad', a group of assassins who specifically targeted British Intelligence 'G' division men, spies in the view of Collins. Warnings were issued for these men to 'lay off' specific investigations which, if not heeded, resulted in the detective's elimination. Four such men were killed by 'The Squad' before the year end, three more went the same way in 1920. The first to be targeted in July 1919 was Detective Sergeant Patrick Smith (known as 'The Dog'), who was ambushed near his home and shot there following a running battle.

This event prompted Macpherson, backed by French, to advise the British Cabinet to outlaw Sinn Féin by proclaiming it illegal throughout Ireland. Even Bonar Law saw the danger in this. It gave Collins grounds to extend his extremism; during August 11 attacks were carried out on the police, and their demise forced the British to increase the presence of the military.

There had been a strong British military presence in Fermoy since 1806. On Sunday morning of 7th September 1919 the War of Independence came to the town in a big way. A group of around 15 soldiers, led by a corporal, marched with rifles at the slope from their barracks across Fermoy Bridge to attend a divine service at the Wesleyan church in Walkers Row. When they reached the church they were attacked by around 25 IRA Volunteers whose objective was to seize their rifles. The attackers were armed with six revolvers and short clubs that they concealed up their coat sleeves. This was the first direct attack made upon the British army, and permission for it was granted to Liam Lynch by Collins on the understanding that casualties to either side should be avoided. Unfortunately a 20-year-old soldier, Private William Jones of the 2nd Battalion King's Shropshire Light Infantry was shot and killed in the raid.

The Times reported on 9th September: 'The audacity and success of the outrage at Fermoy, where a soldier was killed and others wounded on Sunday, have startled the whole country'.

Everyone, however, was agreed that the attack was well planned; the Sunday church procedure had been closely observed by the IRA over a three-month period. But witness statements made by the Volunteers, by eyewitnesses, and by the British soldiers of the events of the attack differ considerably.

Leo O'Callaghan, driver of one of the cars involved, reported in his BMH statement that he heard *one* shot being fired, whilst Private Benjamin Byles of the Shropshire Light Infantry reported that up to 20 shots had been fired – the truth probably lies somewhere in-between; Mrs Foster, wife of the Wesleyan minister, said that she heard at least a *dozen* shots. There are also varying accounts about *how* Private Jones was shot. Patrick Ahern in his BMH statement stated that: 'All had instructions to rush the enemy party when the order 'hands up' was given by Lar Condon'. John Joseph Hogan also confirmed this in his BMH statement: 'Immediately there was a shout of 'hands up' from the main attacking party, which included Mick Fitzgerald, Lar Condon, Paddy Ahern, John Fanning, George Power and Jack Fitzgerald'. At the inquest on Jones, however, the coroner asked the Corporal (Frank Hudson): 'Did any of these men make any observation prior to firing? Did they say *hands up*, or anything?' Hudson replied: 'No'. Hudson also stated that the attackers 'made a rush with three revolvers and started firing away. One man was in front of the crowd – a low-sized stout man with a sallow complexion. He shot at Private Jones and he fell'. Laurence Condon, who was in charge of the main attacking party, gave a different account in his BMH statement: 'We, the first three, had revolvers and we produced these. The first file of soldiers handed over their rifles without any trouble but some of the others showed fight and one who refused to give up his was shot dead and about eight or nine were badly wounded'.

Wherever the truth lay, the inquest on Jones, held the next day (Monday), found a verdict of death due to a bullet wound inflicted by persons unknown. Though they: 'Expressed their horror and condemnation at this terrible and appalling outrage in the midst of a peaceable military and civil community, between whom the most friendly feelings have always existed', the coroner's jury came to the conclusion that: 'These men came for the purpose of getting rifles, and had no intention of killing anyone'.

This verdict didn't go down too well with the boys at the barracks who, after probably imbibing more than a few beers that Monday night, decided to take their revenge out in the town. According to a report in *The Times* of 10th September, 'The soldiers were armed with hammers and pieces of iron, which they used to smash windows. The report continued: 'The whole body was led by a soldier, who gave signals with a whistle at intervals to rally his followers and direct their movements'. It appears that every shop or business owned by members of the coroner's jury was targeted. The boys and some civilian followers continued their rampage by looting and burning properties; there must have been a shortage of footwear at the time, because hundreds of pairs of boots and shoes were nicked. The foreman of the jury owned a jeweller's shop located on Artillery Quay, and the boys paid particular attention to him – chucking trays of rings and watches into the River Blackwater.

The Shropshire Light Infantry were moved to Cork a few months later but the Fermoy reprisal, labelled 'the sack of Fermoy', set the scene for the future. Within six months such reprisals would become a routine part of the war, further alienating the general public from the British forces; within a year they would be adopted as part of official government policy.

The IRA Volunteers in Fermoy had posted notices around the town warning against spies and informers and, following the attack and reprisal, no Irish person contacted the British. However the British had some idea as to those responsible, and searches, raids and the arrest of suspects quickly followed. Over a period of time 13 arrests were made concerning the attack and death of Private Jones. Eight men were arrested within a few days – including Michael Fitzgerald.

Fitzgerald had been released from Cork Gaol at the end of August having been sentenced to two months imprisonment because ammunition had been found at his house. He was not a well man.

His comrades told him to stay away from the Fermoy raid, but he came along anyway and joined in.

John Hogan, arrested nine days after the attack, gave an account of the events that followed the Fermoy raid arrests, the bones of which are that: after about five weeks in Cork Gaol, six of the 13 who'd been arrested were released, including Laurence Condon who'd led the main attacking party. Dan Hegarty was arrested around Christmas time. It took until April 1920 for statements to be gathered, and the eight remaining prisoners (including Hogan and Fitzgerald), were brought to trial at Cork County Assizes in July. The judge directed that the jury should not find a true bill against any of the accused who'd 'not been definitely identified' as having taken part in the attack. This resulted in the release of all but three of the accused – Dan Hegarty being one (who was subsequently found unfit to plead on the advice of the Crown). This left Hogan and Fitzgerald to stand trial. The problem for the Crown was that the IRA had issued an order prohibiting any person from serving on the jury. So no jury could be found and the cases were continually put back.

I walk to the Wesleyan church. Its windows are boarded out with yellow advertisements for a local newspaper and for motor parts. Nearby is a stone memorial to Michael Fitzgerald commemorating the spot where he took part in the attack. I read that he died in Cork Gaol on 17th October 1920: '... in defence of the Irish Republic. His last engagement against British Forces took place on this spot on 7th September 1919'. At the bottom, in Gaelic is: '*Mairfidh a chlú*'. I check around the monument to see if there are more details of the action or perhaps some mention of Private Jones – but there aren't.

Back over Fermoy Bridge I make my way towards the barracks' sites, following the town trail map given to me at the campsite. I pass the impressive WWI memorial plaque. Around 49,000 Irishmen died in the First World War, identifying with the plight of Belgium and 'small countries'. More Catholics enlisted than did Protestants; all were encouraged by John Redmond to do so: 'in defence of the highest principles of religion and morality of right'. I continue up Church Hill and reach Bridge Street. There's not much left of the 'new barracks' where once soldiers stood to attention on parade in serried rows. Rugby and football (soccer) are now played here. Across the main road, the gated entrance of the 'old barracks' leads into the Gaelic football grounds.

For light relief I think to try the pitch and putt course, but bringing your own clubs is apparently an essential requirement. Balls to that! Perhaps you have to bring them too?

The campsite is deserted when I return, unsurprisingly given the site fee which, even after I managed some negotiation was, I thought, still too much. So, I sit in the sun outside the camper and read *Rebel Cork's Fighting Story*. There's a short account about Michael Fitzgerald, written by P.J. Power, but the chapter that really captures my imagination is written by George Power and is entitled: 'The Capture of General Lucas'. The events took place on the banks of the Blackwater River one evening in the summer of 1920.

By this time the war had escalated, de Valera, who perhaps might have been a moderator, or otherwise may have changed the course of events, was conducting his own propaganda, political and financial war on behalf of the Irish cause from the luxury of the Waldorf Astoria Hotel in New York. He'd spent the previous six months travelling throughout the States making speeches with the aim of gaining America's recognition of an Irish Republic and its inclusion within a proposed League of Nations.

During this time Michael Collins was waging his own brand of guerrilla war against Britain: the attack, capture and burning of RIC barracks had become a common occurrence – but so too had reprisals by the RIC and British army. Collins' 'Squad' continued the execution of spies, informers and prominent opponents of the cause. Off-duty RIC constables feared for their lives. In March, Thomas MacCurtain, the Lord Mayor of Cork, was shot at his home in front of his wife by men with blackened faces who were seen later to enter the local police barracks. French and Lloyd George tried to claim that he was murdered by his own extremists.

At around the same time the concept dreamt up aboard Admiralty yacht *Enchantress* the previous year came to fruition – the Black and Tans arrived in the country. Lloyd George's government's attempt at constitutional reform meanwhile got out of the starting blocks when

The Government of Ireland Bill was passed in Westminster – but it wouldn't be enacted until the end of this long and bloody year.

In April there were riots in Limerick city, and a two-week mass hunger strike in Mountjoy Gaol was supported by a general strike that gained IRA prisoners political status and the release of around 90 of them. Following these events the British hardened their views. Arthur Balfour stated that 'they would not permit justice to be defeated by the threat of suicide'.

Liam Lynch, Commandant of the Cork No. 2 Brigade of the IRA and instigator of the Wesleyan church attack, had great respect for Michael Fitzgerald who was still in Cork Gaol pending trial. On several occasions he'd drawn up plans to rescue him, but on each occasion had felt that the casualties from such a venture would be too great. At the end of June, however, he had a brainwave and decided that if the British could capture IRA officers then he could do the same to British officers. His objective was to use such a capture to bargain for the release of Fitzgerald.

The opportunity Lynch had been waiting for came in the form of Brigadier-General Cuthbert Henry Tindall Lucas. Aged 41, Lucas had been in the army for 22 years, had served in the Boer War and fought at Gallipoli and at the Battle of the Somme during the Great War. On Saturday 26th June 1920 Lynch's intelligence organisation reported that Lucas had been seen frequently fishing on the River Blackwater at Kilbarry, five miles east of Fermoy. Whilst Lucas and two other British officers were fishing, Lynch and three more IRA men occupied their fishing hut and arrested Lucas's batman. They then rounded up and disarmed the Brits. The events that followed made Monday's edition of *The Irish Times*. The article's headlines read: 'DARING CRIME IN COUNTY CORK – THREE MILITARY OFFICERS KIDNAPPED – ARRESTED IN THE NAME OF THE IRISH REPUBLIC – COLONEL DANFORD, D.S.O., BADLY WOUNDED – GENERAL LUCAS CARRIED OFF BY HIS CAPTORS – NO NEWS OF HIS WHERE-ABOUTS'.

The Irish Times was edited by John Healy, a staunch Unionist, so its reporting was naturally pro-British. The Cork correspondent telegraphed his report through to the newspaper's Dublin office and had obviously been groping around for the facts. To start with he falsely reported the location of the kidnap, saying it to be near Castletownroche, which is about 15 miles distant from Kilbarry. He then went on to say that the capture occurred in the early hours of the Monday morning (to make his reporting seem current) when in fact it had happened two days before. Given these errors, little credence can be given to his other reported details. The batman had been given a letter to deliver, addressed to 'The Deputy Commandant, Army of Occupation, Fermoy' and he was released to deliver it, whilst the three officers were driven away in two cars. The report continued '...one of the officers contrived to jump out, and run in the opposite direction to that in which the cars were travelling at fairly high speed. There was an instant order to halt, and the Republicans opened fire on their escaped prisoner, with the result that after a few rounds he was brought to the ground, seriously wounded in the shoulder and head'. In a later message, the correspondent embellished the heroics of the officer, reporting that: 'When Colonel Danford was attempting to escape, he is said to have fired his revolver at his captors, with what result is not known. The raiders instantly returned the fire, bringing him to the ground'. How did Danford obtain a weapon if he'd been disarmed earlier?

The facts as recorded in *No Other Law*, written by Florence O'Donoghue, vary considerably from that of *The Irish Times*. In the book, O'Donoghue records that the first car travelled ahead carrying Colonel Tyrrell with two IRA men. In the second car travelling behind was Liam Lynch seated in the front with the driver, whilst in the back Lucas and Danford were seated either side of Lynch's companion, Patrick Clancy. Lucas and Danford had a brief conversation in Arabic, a language in which they were both fluent, and then, at a prearranged signal, sprang simultaneously on Lynch and Clancy. As the fight went on inside the car, the driver lost control, crashed the car into a ditch and was knocked unconscious. Lynch and Lucas were fighting together, as were Danford and Clancy – all now at the roadside. Having finally overpowered Lucas, Lynch saw that Danford had a grip on Clancy's throat and shouted, 'Surrender or I shoot.' Danford ignored the command, Lynch fired and the bullet hit Danford in the face. The first car realising there must be a problem, turned back to find the others. It was decided that Colonel Tyrrell would be left to attend to Danford whist General Lucas was taken away first to Lynch's HQ at Mourneabbey, then to a house in Lombardstown, on the southern slopes of the Blackwater Valley, where he spent his first night of captivity.

According to the book, the driver of the crashed car, having recovered, was sent to the nearby village of Rathcormack for a doctor, but according to the report in *The Irish Times*: 'The two officers (Tyrrell and Danford) were practically all night on the roadside, and at length they managed to get a car to drive them to Fermoy military hospital which they reached at 10 o'clock today'.

Whatever the events actually were, Fermoy suffered again with another reprisal. *The Irish Times* reported: 'MILITARY OUTBREAK IN FERMOY – SEQUEL TO KIDNAPPING OF GENERAL LUCAS – DESTRUCTION OF SHOPS – THE OFFICIAL ACCOUNT'. It continued: 'Sunday night about four hundred of the military stationed at Fermoy turned out and broke plate glass and other windows. Looting took place at some shops. About midnight a body of soldiers broke out of barracks and went through Barrack Hill to Queen Square cheering. Every plate glass window on Queen Square was smashed and the property looted. The jeweller's shop of Mr Cole was wrecked completely. The gas jets were lighted in the shop and many valuable articles were taken away, whilst what was left was badly damaged. Next door the cycle shop of Mr Noble came in for the same treatment. Bicycles and two motorcycles were thrown into the river'. It seems that the jeweller's shop on Artillery Quay was owned by the foreman of the jury in the inquest on Private Jones the previous September, so it again came in for attack. But Mr Barber had learnt from his previous experience and had installed some strong shutters which the soldiers couldn't break down.

As well as enjoying the excuse to get drunk and run riot, the military were out searching for General Lucas. Shouts of: 'We want our fucking General back' were heard. While the premises of Mr Sweeney, a member of the Urban Council, was being searched, an officer was alleged (as reported in *The Irish Times*) to have said that if the General was not back tomorrow (Monday) night, 'Up goes the town!' It didn't help the situation that local youths were singing: 'Can anyone tell me where did General Lucas go', to the air of 'The Blarney Roses'.

The New York Times reported that the search for Lucas continued without intermission by soldiers and police, whilst airplanes swooped low over woods and mountains. There was speculation that he might have been taken to Limerick and was perhaps being held in a cave in the Galway Mountains, quoted as being: 'one of the finest natural prisons in the world'. It was thought more likely, however, that he would not be held in such primitive conditions but would be comfortably housed, and accorded the privileges befitting his rank.

It appears, from the BMH witness statement of Joseph Good, that Lucas had been moved from Lombardstown to Mitchelstown. Good was one of a party of eight from the West Limerick Brigade area who went down to Mitchelstown to collect him. He recorded: 'The whole party of us, including Sean Moyllana and Liam Lynch, came back from Cork to Templeglantine, where General Lucas was lodged for the night'. On the way, according to Tom Malone (alias Sean Forde) they ran out of petrol near Abbeyfeale and Lucas had to help them push the car to the tops of the hills so that they could let it run down. They eventually struggled their way to Abbeyfeale where they obtained petrol and stayed for the night before finally making it to Templeglantine.

Templeglantine is a village near the town of Newcastle in County Limerick, close to the borders with Counties Kerry and Cork. Good seems to have struck up quite a bond with Lucas at Templeglantine as he recorded: 'Lucas and I had numerous conversations together. During our first conversation Lucas was looking down over the valley from a hill at Templeglantine. It was a beautiful view and we could see a number of counties from where we were. He remarked: *This is a country worth fighting for.* I thought this was a peculiar remark, and reminded him that another general, his predecessor, Cromwell, had passed a similar remark'.

Lucas was held only a few days in County Limerick before being transferred on to the East Clare Brigade. Good recorded that '... some of us escorted Lucas to the banks of the Shannon. Michael Brennan arrived in a punt or boat. It was night-time and there was no attempt to blindfold Lucas, who was observing the stars. Mick Brennan took Lucas across the river, and I remained in Limerick'. Lucas certainly got to see a good part of Ireland.

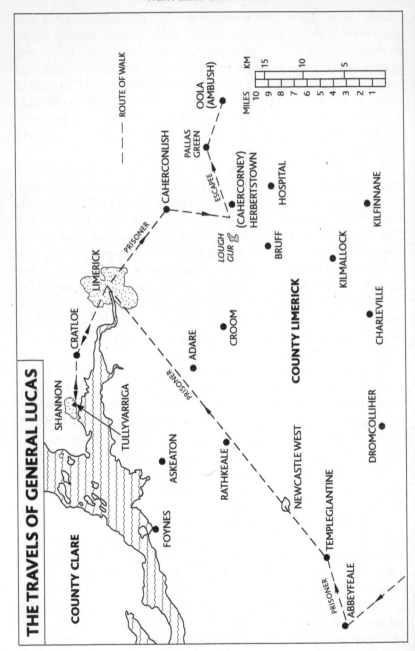

THE TRAVELS OF GENERAL LUCAS

COUNTY CLARE

COUNTY LIMERICK

- - - - - ROUTE OF WALK

OOLA (AMBUSH)
PALLAS GREEN
CAHERCONLISH
(CAHERCORNEY) HERBERTSTOWN
HOSPITAL
KILFINNANE
ESCAPEE
PRISONER
LIMERICK
LOUGH GUR
BRUFF
KILMALLOCK
CRATLOE
CROOM
ADARE
CHARLEVILLE
SHANNON
TULLYVARRIGA
PRISONER
ASKEATON
NEWCASTLE WEST
RATHKEALE
DROMCOLLIHER
FOYNES
TEMPLEGLANTINE
PRISONER
ABBEYFEALE

MILES KM
10 15
9
8
7 10
6
5
4 5
3
2
1

140

Whilst in captivity in County Clare he was allowed to write letters, which were of course censored. He wrote, however, that he had no complaints as he was being well looked after, and added that no anxiety should be felt about his circumstances. In Clare he was accommodated in the village of Cratloe, just north of the River Shannon, and in Tullyvarriga, near Shannon town. However, because there was a report of a planned British raid in the area the IRA again moved him back south across the Shannon into the custody of the Mid-Limerick Brigade. All the transfers were made at night.

Lucas's experiences while with the Mid-Limerick Brigade are detailed by Richard O'Connell: 'I put them up at Dr Corby's house in Caherconlish...' During this time, on one occasion Mick Brennan and O'Connell were taking Lucas for his daily walk when in the middle of a field they were attacked by a three-year-old bull and had to run up to a ditch. Lucas wrote a description of the event afterwards in a letter: 'Imagine! Two officers of the Irish Army and a British General! A bull frightened us!'

Whilst at the Dr Corby's house, Lucas discovered from a letter on the mantelpiece where he was being held, but when he was free later, never gave out that information. O'Connell reported: 'Lucas was a very decent man and he proved that afterwards'. Whilst he was there Lucas's wife in England had given birth to a son which was reported in the newspapers. His captors had by now become endeared to him, so to celebrate they produced some 'liquid refreshment' and a box of cigars.

General Lucas was moved again around various safe houses near Limerick, but his captivity came to an end on 29th July in the village of Cahercorney, near Lough Gur. The IRA had proven their point – that a British general could be held by them undetected for some time. Keeping him had by this time become a bit of a burden; supplying him with a bottle of whisky each day, playing bridge and tennis with him, taking him on fishing excursions, and moving him, had all become a drain upon their resources, so it's difficult to say how easy they made it for him to escape. Richard O'Connell, who was with him at Cahercorney, recorded: 'In the room he was in, the window was barred with ordinary bars that you would see in a farmhouse, but one of the bars was missing. The McCarthys in their younger days had taken one of the bars out to enable them to get in and out of the window when they were late out. It was through that window that Lucas escaped. When he was gone, there was little made about his going. No one was very sorry about his escape. He was a nice fellow and we liked him. Besides that the business of holding him a prisoner was a considerable lot of trouble'.

News of the General's escape was sent around the world. He apparently squeezed through the window, perhaps bending bars. Then, in the darkness of early morning and in torrential rain, he walked roughly south-west for three hours through fields, hedges and scrub, climbing over walls and wire fences. Just after dawn he met a peasant who cheerily directed him towards the RIC barracks at Pallasgreen situated midway between Limerick and Tipperary, where he arrived cold, wet and bleeding. But the General's Irish adventures weren't quite over. He was put aboard a military mail lorry on its way south which was then, after travelling about six miles, ambushed by the IRA near Oola. Two British soldiers were killed in the action which lasted about 30 minutes.

General Lucas finally arrived at his home in England to see his family and get first sight of his new son on 6th August. He had, previous to his capture, taken a hard-line with Sinn Féiners, proclaiming that they should be shown no mercy. The experiences during his capture mellowed his attitude; perhaps he'd gained some insight into the psyche of the Irish. When interviewed by reporters after his escape he disappointed them by saying only: 'I was treated as a gentleman by gentlemen.'

The drunk who enters the Thai Lanna Orchid restaurant in Fermoy that night certainly doesn't behave as a gentleman. He perhaps needs to use the toilet or wants a takeaway, but all he keeps saying is:

'*Ni hao*,' which I know is Chinese for 'hello'. The young waiter apologises to me when he leaves. The restaurant manager tells me they've only just opened up and so offers me a choice of free cake as a sweet – I choose the chocolate. When the waiter brings the bill he apologises again for the drunk and I point out his misguided greeting.

'Yes,' he says, 'but I'm not Chinese, I'm Thai.'

'I know,' I say, 'so what's hello in Thai?'

'*Saw wah dee*,' he tells me.

I repeat the word to myself all the way back to the campsite just in case I ever get to go to Thailand.

The gate of the site has 'thoughtfully' been locked, and I have to climb over the wall.

It's been an interesting day. My mind is still wound up with the history of the War of Independence that seriously touched Fermoy some 93 years ago, so I take a sleeping pill to stop me churning these events over. It works.

Nine

It's a Long Way to Go

'It's a long way to Tipperary,
      It's a long way to go.
It's a long way to Tipperary
To the sweetest girl I know!
      Goodbye Piccadilly,
Farewell Leicester Square!
It's a long long way to Tipperary,
      But my heart's right there.'
From: *It's a Long Way to Tipperary*, by Jack Judge and Harry Williams

Thursday 4th July – Fermoy to Araglin

I'd set the mobile for a rude awaking at 6.30am but I'm still groggy from the effects of the sleeping pill. I cobble together some breakfast; this morning with electric hook-up I have the luxury of toast – tomorrow I'll wild-camp. An early start is what's required, but now I suddenly remember the site gate is locked and begin to fret. But at 7.15 the caretaker unlocks it and I'm away.

It's a long way to Tipperary (I can't get the song out of my head this morning) – actually it's only a 17-mile walk from Fermoy to the County Tipperary border. Araglin sits just inside County Cork. According to Paddy Dillon's *Coast to Coast Walk* book it has a shop and pub.

I think I may have found Araglin, but it's not much of a place; the shop and the pub are both boarded up. I park the camper on a rough gravelled area just off the road in front of what looks like the back of a farm-building with a rusty corrugated roof.

The bike ride back to Fermoy is easy – mostly downhill and following the Araglin River valley for much of the way. On the other side of the river is the county of Waterford.

The walk begins as a reversal of the route I've just biked but then edges around the north of the town to meet the main Dublin Road and turns north along it. After a little while the Way takes a diversion to pass first Kilcrumper Old Cemetery, and a bit further on the New Cemetery. In one of these are the remains of Michael Fitzgerald and Liam Lynch lying side by side.

In August 1920 John Hogan, Michael Fitzgerald and the other prisoners in Cork Gaol went on hunger strike for the reinstatement of political status. Fitzgerald had been held in Cork Gaol since September 1919. John Hogan recorded: 'Early in August 1920, together with other political prisoners in Cork Gaol, I went on hunger strike. The sentenced prisoners amongst us were removed and deported to various prisons in England within about eight days while, three days later, I was removed with 17 other untried prisoners to Winchester prison... Maurice Crowe who was in charge ordered the hunger strike to cease after he had consulted the general body of the prisoners.'

The release of prisoners from Mountjoy Gaol in April following hunger strikes had had an adverse effect upon the morale of both the RIC and the British army. It had served to further escalate the war and had hardened British attitudes towards hunger strikes.

Michael Fitzgerald was not transferred to Winchester but was kept in Cork and continued his hunger strike. He was allowed to die there after 67 days without food on Sunday 17th October 1920. Patrick Ahern stated that he'd visited Fitzgerald that very day posing as his brother Patrick so that, if Michael regained consciousness, any message he wanted to send could be taken. Ahern was led to the hospital wing where he found Fitzgerald unconscious. Still claiming to be his brother, Ahern managed to remain in the cell until about 8.30pm. His statement then reads: "...When three nuns and Father O'Flynn (I think) came along. They began to say the Rosary and were accompanied in their responses by the relatives of the other prisoners. At the same time I could hear the crowd outside the prison who were also saying the Rosary. Just before the end of the fifth decade one of the nuns turned to me and said 'he's gone', it was then about 9pm. A few moments later the Cork Volunteers' Pipe Band which was outside the prison began to play 'Wrap the green flag round me".

Fitzgerald's death and the position of Terence MacSwiney, Lord Mayor of Cork, who was also on hunger strike in Brixton Gaol, was the subject of debate in the House of Commons two days later. The Secretary of State for the Home Department, Mr Shortt, was asked if the King could be advised to exercise his prerogative of mercy and order MacSwiney's release. Shortt refused. He also confirmed that no form of feeding had taken place, to which Mr Jack Jones, the National Socialist Party MP for West Ham chipped in sarcastically that he was being fed on 'Coalition soup'.

Lieutenant-Commander Kenworthy, an Independent Liberal and anti-coalitionist, raised the issue of Fitzgerald having not being tried. He was told by Sir Hamar Greenwood, the Chief Secretary for Ireland, that a *true bill* had been found against Fitzgerald, but that due to the absence of jurors through intimidation it was impossible to proceed with his trial. The Restoration of Order in Ireland Act, Greenwood said, which would have enabled the government to try him, had come into force on 9th August, and that two days later Fitzgerald had gone on hunger strike, thus preventing his trial. Kenworthy suggested that there was no evidence against Fitzgerald – to which Greenwood replied that: 'There was evidence of the most decisive nature against this man'. The evidence that Greenwood referred to was undoubtedly that given by Corporal Frank Hudson who'd said at the inquest into the death of Private Jones that the man who'd shot him down was 'low-sized'. Fitzgerald fitted that description.

The result of the British hard-line policy on hunger strikes led to the further estrangement of the Irish general public towards the British. On 25th October Joseph Murphy died after 76 days of hunger strike, whilst MacSwiney perished on the same day in Brixton after 74 days. MacSwiney's death received worldwide attention and had international repercussions; Americans threatened the boycott of British goods. Sinn Féin banned hunger strikes after MacSwiney's death until the 1970s.

The day after Fitzgerald's death, his comrades transferred his remains to the church of Sts Peter and Paul in Cork where Mass was said. There was a strong British military presence at the service and a question was raised by Major Howard, Liberal MP for Seaham, County Durham, in the House of Commons regarding their conduct. He asked if soldiers fully armed had entered the church after Mass, if an officer had handed a document to the priest and if outside the church he'd announced through a megaphone that he had orders to fire on people if more than 100 persons followed the remains, soldiers being drawn up ready to act on the order. Sir Hamar Greenwood defended the actions of the military on the grounds that funerals had in the past been used for parades by the IRA, which had led to breaches of the peace. He said that the officers' and soldiers' demeanours had been 'highly respectful, decorous and reverential throughout'. Soldiers, he said, had removed their helmets when entering the church. This account varies considerably from that given in *Rebel Cork's Fighting Story* in which P.J. Power says that the officer approached the priest with a drawn revolver and that soldiers walked over the seats in the church.

Thousands are said to have defied the British order as Fitzgerald's remains were taken by road to Fermoy and placed in St Patrick's church there overnight. There were huge crowds at the funeral the next day at Kilcrumper Cemetery where again the British military showed up in some strength. In the afternoon three IRA Volunteer comrades of Michael Fitzgerald each fired three volleys from revolvers over the Republican plot where his remains had been buried.

All is very peaceful here now as I walk amongst the gravestones and Celtic-cross headstones this morning searching unsuccessfully for the plot. I'm unsure even if it's in the Old Cemetery and walk wearily on to the New Cemetery. A sign outside warns motorists about leaving valuables in their cars. Here, a lady is laying flowers at a grave and a man is cutting the grass. I've seen a photograph of the republican plot on the Internet, so I know that the headstone I'm looking for has a Celtic-cross. But the search is again fruitless. I think of asking the man if he knows its location but, fearing that my English accent might lead to some sort of an issue, I don't have the courage. Instead I walk on to Ballyroskillakeen Cross Roads.

The Blackwater Way now crosses the new M8 motorway, which unlike those in the UK, is almost completely devoid of traffic. It's been all road and pavement walking so far this morning, of which

I'm none too pleased – and this continues into the village of Kilworth where I take a sandwich break. Kilworth was once on the old Dublin to Cork road, and the Way follows the old Coach Road out of the village. I cross a bridge and head on into Glensheskin Wood on a track that runs for a time along the side of the River Douglas that flows down to meet the Araglin River.

An information board gives a few useful facts to be remembered for a pub quiz. Bats, it says, are the only mammal capable of true flight, and there are apparently 977 species of them in the world. Only nine of these live in Ireland, but three species are apparently roosting in this woodland's bridges.

A red flag in the wood at a junction of tracks warns me that the Irish Defence Force's firing range is close by. The ranges were opened by the British in May 1896 when the lands here were purchased from the hard up Lord Mount Cashel. Unfortunately the sale, which was just prior to the introduction of the Land Act, meant the loss of the homes and holdings of tenant farmers.

The Way continues through the forest on a track and then a road to reach a crossroads and the deserted Mountain Barracks Inn, where I turn right and then leave the road to head uphill. I walk on tracks along ridges with rolling countryside, through forests and over stiles. The Discovery map, as always, handy, stuffed down the front of my jeans, whilst the camera is in my right-hand pocket. A small blue butterfly settles on a leaf with her wings closed; with camera poised, I zoom in and wait and wait – and then she obliges by opening her wings to be captured in a frame – it's a beautiful moment.

I've seen nobody for hours; not since I left Kilworth. The map stays stuffed down my jeans – the fingerposts alone guide the way. I go into autopilot; the only sounds are the breeze, the insects, the birds, my footsteps padding the ground, my breathing and clothes rustling with each step – there is a somnambulistic rhythm to it all. I think of nothing except the process of walking, the surrounding countryside – its smells and sounds. I have no concerns except the steps I take. I just think and live each moment as it happens. I am truly in the 'now'. I could live the rest of my life like this every day.

Then suddenly the Way turns abruptly, my precious Zen time

disappears and I'm jolted back to consciousness and sudden concerns. Am I still on the right path? Have I missed a fingerpost? Have I overshot the road that leads off the Way down into the river valley and to the camper at Araglin? I pull out the map from my jeans and try to establish where I might be. The abrupt turn may be taking me north, and if so I might be able to relate to a point on the map. But in my mindless state all sense of direction has been lost. It's overcast, and now I'm not even sure where north is. I need the compass. It's in a side pocket of the rucksack.

There's an established system of storage in the sack; Paddy Dillon's book, wallet, emergency toilet paper, wet-wipes, the detestable dental plate (only worn when in contact with humans), fruit gums, loose change, compass, plasters, wool for Istanbul and the van keys are kept in the two side pockets. Waterproofs are kept in the compartment at the bottom of the main sack, water is at the top of the main sack and everything else is stored below it.

I fumble in the first side pocket for the compass, but don't find it, so take everything out of the second pocket – there's the compass! But now I don't recall the van keys being in the first pocket, and they're not amongst this pile of stuff I've thrown on the grass either. I've lost the bloody keys – I'm absolutely stuffed – won't be able to get in the van – will have to find somewhere to eat and sleep tonight – the walk will be over! Like a loon, I throw *everything* out of the rucksack. The keys are not here! They're not here! Fumble, scrabble, fumble – throw things about – they're not here! YES – here they are right at the bottom – thank you, God. But how did I do that – put them at the bottom? It's my age, the dreaded start of Alzheimer's.

I recover my composure and put things in an orderly fashion back into the bag. Then amazingly, a deer leaps out of the undergrowth just in front of me, darts across the track and disappears.

I walk on, but am still in a daze from the deer leap and the mystery of the keys. I get maybe 50 metres along the track and remember that 10 minutes ago I was about to check where north was. So now I empty the side pockets again looking for the compass. It's not there! I go back scouring the ground. Not only can't I find it, but I can't remember the exact spot of my first panic attack. I open up the rucksack again and everything gets thrown out – perhaps I dropped it into the bottom of the bag. This time I take more care – but the compass is not there. So back I go further again – and there it is! Anyone who'd watched me over the past 15 minutes would have thought I'd escaped from a mental institution. At last I can check the compass; I am indeed now walking north. From several other turns I make that correspond with those shown on the map I establish where I am.

By Carran Hill I make a right turn and descend steeply downhill on a lane that joins a road off which the camper is parked. But I've overshot Araglin and have to walk back west around two miles. By six o'clock I'm back at the van. The 19-mile walk has taken just over eight hours.

The rough gravelled area at the back of the farm building is to be my wild-camp spot for tonight. But to make good use of the time I drive to Fermoy, collect the bike and drive on east via Mitchelstown to Clogheen (tomorrow's walk destination) where I chain it up in Brewery Lane for the night.

Back on my spot, I cook up an evening meal of noodles and beans that go down with some sandwiches. Then I make a second batch of sandwiches for tomorrow's lunch. There is no point in washing. I may smell rank, but I'm not likely to meet anyone tomorrow. I write up the day's log and count the euros I have remaining; today has been the first day that my expenditure has been absolutely zero. It's cold tonight so I wear socks and snuggle down into the sleeping bag. There has been no traffic along this road all evening, but at around midnight two cars pass and beep their horns. I worry a little – but soon drift off to sleep.

Friday 5th July – Araglin to Clogheen

This morning there's not a cloud in the sky. It's a joy to be straight into a walk; I leave at 8.30am, and am back on the Way at Carran Hill by just after nine o'clock. The Blackwater Way ends at Clogheen, a mere doddle of a 12½-mile walk according to the book. From there I will join the East Munster Way.

Some pleasant narrow lane walking proceeds up a track which continues to climb, heading towards Crow Hill according to the map. I look back to catch the back view and see a station wagon is gaining on me. There's no time to drop the pack, open the side

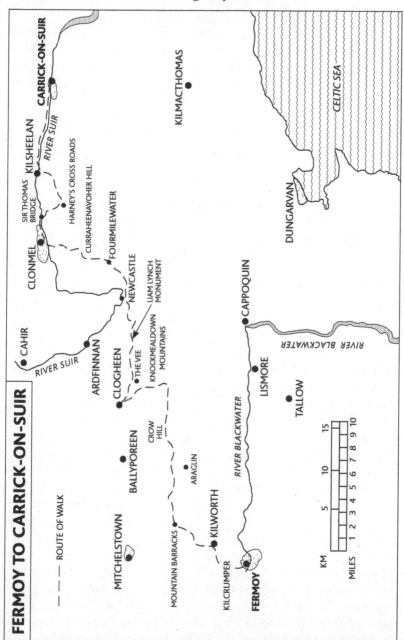

FERMOY TO CARRICK-ON-SUIR

- - - ROUTE OF WALK

CELTIC SEA

KILMACTHOMAS

DUNGARVAN

CARRICK-ON-SUIR

KILSHEELAN
RIVER SUIR
SIR THOMAS BRIDGE
HARNEY'S CROSS ROADS
CURRAHEENAVOHER HILL
FOURMILEWATER
CLONMEL
NEWCASTLE
LIAM LYNCH MONUMENT
CAHIR
RIVER SUIR
ARDFINNAN
CLOGHEEN
THE VEE
KNOCKMEALDOWN MOUNTAINS
CAPPOQUIN
RIVER BLACKWATER
LISMORE
TALLOW
BALLYPOREEN
CROW HILL
ARAGLIN
RIVER BLACKWATER
MITCHELSTOWN
KILWORTH
MOUNTAIN BARRACKS
KILCRUMPER
FERMOY

KM   5   10   15

MILES   1 2 3 4 5 6 7 8 9 10

151

pocket and slip in my dental plate before it's alongside.

'You picked a good day for it,' says the farmer, grinning from below a cowboy hat. I smile with mouth closed – what the hell!

'Yes,' I'm forced to say, revealing those gaps. 'It's a lovely day.' Two young boys sit beside him looking bemused, as you might expect at seeing the strange sight of a semi-toothless sexagenarian walker on this wild, lonely hillside.

'Between the two mountains, if you look up to your left you'll see a pile of stones,' says the farmer. I look that way and nod. 'That's Crow Hill, it's not far to walk up – you can see for miles from there – if you've got binoculars.'

We conduct a small but pleasant conversation, whilst his sons (probably) look on boggle-eyed, before he drives on and turns down into a field. Sadly I have no binoculars, and with equal regret, before I realise it, I've passed the point at which I could have made the ascent of Crow Hill.

This is County Tipperary, my third walking county, and I whistle 'It's a Long Way to Tipperary' – an infectious tune which once started is difficult to stop.

The song was written by two friends Jack Judge and Harry Williams, and most probably started life as 'It's a Long Way to Connemara'. Jack's father, from Carrow Beg in County Mayo, came to live in Oldbury in the West Midlands of England in 1870. His mother was born in Oldbury but was also of Irish stock. Jack ran a fish stall and was an amateur singer and performer who created songs but, as he couldn't read music, couldn't write his songs down. Things came together when he met Harry Williams. Harry was disabled and in a wheelchair, but played piano and was able put Jack's songs onto paper. Jack took on a challenge for a five-shilling bet that he could compose and perform a song within 24 hours. Rumour had it that he just regurgitated a song devised a few years back and simply changed 'Connemara' to 'Tipperary' to win his bet. The performance of the song was a great hit and was noticed by a London impresario who wanted it for one of his leading music hall artists; a royalty agreement was thus signed with Jack and Harry as co-authors. The song soon became famous and was heard in Dublin by a contingent of the Irish Connaught Rangers who sang it as they marched. They brought it with them to the Western Front in 1914, where it was adopted as a favourite by the troops. Jack took all the credit for the song's fame because he was the first to sing it, but he owed Harry gambling debts and as payment sold him the sole royalty rights to the song. It's sold around seven million copies worldwide to date and Harry's descendants still receive the not insignificant royalties.

After passing a forest I'm up onto moorland populated by sheep, gorse, bracken and heather, walking a narrow stony path with a clear blue sky above. The sun is shielded from my eyes by a baseball cap that I'm glad I brought along today. A plane flying south trails vapour; I stop to listen, but it's *so* high its engines are silent here – there's only the sound of flying insects.

I descend steeply through tufted long grass towards the edge of a forest on an indistinct trail marked by fingerposts to which fluorescent rectangular orange strips of plastic have been screwed; this being essential way marking in bad visibility here. The Way reaches a road at a low point and, before the climb up into the Knockmealdown Mountains, a sign warns walkers to take the road diversion in bad weather. But today is perfect. Sandwiches are taken on a grassy bank high above the Lismore to Clogheen road that carves its way through a forest to reach a narrow valley between Knockmealdown, appropriately named 'The Gap'. From this point the Way turns north to Clogheen. There's plenty of time to stroll the remaining five miles, all seemingly downhill – or so I think.

Immediately after moving off from the lunch spot I follow a well-beaten path looking for the next fingerpost. The path becomes more like a rut of compressed grass and begins to descend. I keep faith with the expectancy that at any moment a fingerpost will appear, but the rut begins to run more steeply downhill and eventually disappears. I've descended a long way towards the road, which I now realise can't be the right way. But I don't fancy the climb back up, retracing my steps, so I decide (mistakenly as it turns out) to traverse through the rough ground, keeping parallel with the road. This I do with difficulty for a considerable time: I scramble across a fissure. I'm attacked by gorse that endeavours to do me grievous bodily harm. Ferns flow above my waist. I sweat and fret. Eventually I see a car park below, which, on the map, is shown to be on or near the Way. So I try to pick my way on a steep drop towards it. But things get even more difficult: I'm ankle high in a bog. A tree breaks my downhill stumble. I scramble down a scree, cling to a ledge and lower myself down backwards. I fight my way through or around every form of natural obstacle that nature can throw at me. Then I see what I think is a mirage below – a civilised, nicely gravelled track. I leap down to the mirage and hit firm ground.

The track slopes gently downhill and, reading Paddy Dillon's book backwards, some semblance of accord can be identified. I pass the reedy, beach-like shore of tranquil Bay Lough, and further on the track is indeed 'flanked by pines and dense rhododendron' as he describes. Here I see the first person since the cowboy farmer five and a half hours ago. The time is 3.45pm as I begin the straightforward walk into Clogheen.

In town I unchain the bike and cycle back to Araglin (and the camper) via Ballyporeen. I don't fancy the look of the hills I'd meet if I were to take the direct route from there, so I continue on to Mountain Barracks. But I still get caught with a tough ride over the edge of the Kilworth Mountains before dropping down to the Araglin River valley and doubling back to Araglin. Foolishly (in hindsight) I cycle over 17 miles. Back in Clogheen I park the camper on Barrack Hill and stop off to shop. The lady serving puts my bottle of wine in a long brown paper bag.

'Is that the law then?' I ask.

'No, I think it's just that people don't want people to know what they've been buying,' she says. That's because they might think they're alcoholics, I think to myself – but the long brown bag is anyway a certain give-away.

'There are too many laws here anyway,' she continues, 'the cigarettes you can't display – look, they're there.' She points to a closed metal cabinet behind which I suppose they're hidden. 'When I was young, if you couldn't have something, you wanted it all the more,' she concludes. I nod, smile and leave.

Parsons Green caravan and camping park is a little way out of Clogheen over the River Tar. I book in for three nights and a girl walks ahead of the van and directs me to a spot at the far end of the site. The site is almost full – the start of the school holidays I discover, so it's crammed with Irish families. To get to the toilet I pass through an indoor playground teeming with noisy kids, their parents having deposited them there whilst they fire up the barbecues. Everybody's very friendly, they nod and wave – somebody directs me to the nearest water point when they see me looking vaguely around. There's a real happy holiday feeling to the place. It's a far cry from the feelings in Clogheen during those desperate days of late 1920.

Thomas Ryan was born in Ballylooby, about four miles north of Clogheen in September 1897. He was raised into a middle-class farming family who'd farmed in the area for eight generations. The family had a history of involvement in nationalist struggles over the years which had resulted in many of them having to emigrate. As a boy Ryan was taught that he should raise his hat when he passed the local landlord as a mark of respect; he was caned for not adhering to this order which probably helped to raise the rebel in him still further.

But by no means did everyone in the area feel rebellious. Ryan reflected in his BMH statement that at the time of the 1914–18 war the people in the garrison towns and villages in this area were 100% pro-British. By 1920, although sentiments had changed somewhat, there were still mixed loyalties amongst the population. Clogheen was a military centre with seven RIC personnel located in the barracks there.

But long before 1920 Ryan's nationalistic views had been consolidated, and by May of that year, at the age of 23, he was Officer Commanding the 6th Battalion, 3rd Tipperary Brigade of the IRA. His area covered the valley between the Galtee and Knockmealdown Mountains – County Tipperary then being under the overall leadership of Seán Treacy. Ryan recorded at that time he felt: 'the might of the British Empire had been massed and prepared for one great blow to wipe out the Irish Republican Army. I had visions that this fight might last for 10 years'.

The might of the British Empire in Ireland comprised not only the regular troops but also the Black and Tans, named primarily because of their usual khaki army trousers and their dark green

RIC tunics (and perhaps because they behaved a bit like the dogs so named). These forces combined with those of the Auxiliary Cadets – a Winston Churchill brainchild – comprising mostly of ex-officers of the British army, were recruited on a temporary basis. Churchill saw them becoming a branch of the RIC, which they eventually did – though they tended to operate almost independently in rural areas. These two organisations spearheaded reprisals for actions taken by the IRA. They were given free rein. By autumn 1920 the British government were well aware that reprisal murders were being carried out by these combined forces; it had been reported by General Hugh Tudor, who was, in practice, the Chief of Police as well as being a personal friend of Winston Churchill, the Secretary of State for War. Churchill now certainly had a war, not only with the IRA, but also with the world's press, but it didn't seem to deter him or the British government much – who were, at this point, sure they were winning the war. Michael Collins, however, had other ideas.

Seán Treacy, the Tipperary leader, was encouraged by Collins to spend some time around Dublin to assist on various jobs Collins had lined-up. This quite suited Treacy anyway because he had a girlfriend in tow there. But in October, together with Dan Breen, another Tipperary man, he narrowly escaped from a safe house that was raided by a police unit. During the incident two senior British officers were killed and Collins decided that a few more such officers could be bumped off at their funeral. The assigned squad assembled at a safe house for the purpose, but Collins meanwhile cancelled the attack. Treacy was the last to leave and, unknown to him he'd been followed to the house by a British surveillance team who perhaps thought they were closing in on Collins himself. In the gunfight that followed Treacy shot and killed two of the team before receiving a fatal shot himself.

Sean Treacy's death had a profound effect upon Thomas Ryan back in Tipperary. He'd been looking forward to working under Treacy, but his death caused Ryan to realise the seriousness of the organisation's undertakings – it also had wider consequences. For the IRA it was certainly a factor that persuaded their leadership to approve a plan submitted by Collins for the mass assassination of those secret service agents known as 'The Cairo Gang'. The attacks took place in the morning of Sunday 21st November, as Dubliners were going to Mass. Ten locations across Dublin were targeted, timed to coincide with a Gaelic football match so that the assassins could make good their escape by mingling with the crowds. A good many of 'The Cairo Gang' were killed (accounts vary as to the exact number, but probably 11 or 12). Two court martial officers were also assassinated and one civilian informant. Two Auxiliary Cadets who went to the scene of one of the attacks were also shot and killed. Around six British officers eluded the attacks, but Collins had severely damaged the British operation.

On the Sunday afternoon revenge was quickly to be taken at the Gaelic football match between Dublin and Tipperary played at Croke Park.

Thomas Ryan had begun playing Gaelic football at the age of 20, and was selected to play for the Tipperary side that Sunday. He'd travelled with the rest of the team by train on the Saturday, where he and another player had managed to get into a scrap with soldiers from the Lincolnshire Regiment which resulted in two of the soldiers leaving the train unexpectedly and unwillingly via a carriage window. Perhaps it was a report of this incident which made the team and their appearance at Croke Park an ideal reprisal target? Ryan at any rate stated that the press reported on the Monday that: 'A band of assassins had come up from Tipperary to carry out the shootings in Dublin on the Sunday'. Ryan and Michael Hogan, the team's captain, were, in fact, both Volunteers. They'd found out about the planned assassinations on the Saturday evening, and immediately after the shootings Ryan received a message from Dan Breen advising him not to appear at Croke Park – Collins had had a premonition of what was likely to occur.

Ryan ignored the warning and recorded that an aeroplane had flown over Croke Park and had fired a red flare after about 10 minutes of play in the game; his report continued: 'A penalty had been awarded against the Dublin team and I was about to take the free kick when a burst of machine-gun and rifle fire occurred. The crowd of spectators immediately stampeded. The players also fled from the field in amongst the sideline spectators, except six of us who threw ourselves down on the ground – Hogan, I and four of the Dublin team'. The players each made a dash for the paling that surrounded the pitch and during Hogan's run he got hit by a bullet, Ryan continued: 'Going across to Hogan, I tried to lift him but the blood was spurting from a wound in his back and I knew he was badly injured. He made the exclamation when I lifted him, 'Jesus, Mary and Joseph! I am done!', and died on the spot'. Ryan managed to reach the paling, got off the pitch and into the crowd – his statement goes on: 'I was the only member of the Tipperary team who wore the national tricolour in my stockings and knickers and I realised that this fact alone made me conspicuous'.

Ryan, however, managed to get out of the ground over a wall and made it to what he thought to be a safe house nearby, which was, however, soon surrounded by the Black and Tans and Auxiliaries... 'They forced their way into the door of the house. An old man who had made some remark to them in the hall was knocked down with a blow from the butt of a revolver. One of them, seeing me, said, 'There is one of the Tipperary assassins! Take him out and shoot him!' Two of them had bayonets drawn and I was knocked down and the stockings and knickers ripped off me with bayonets, leaving me naked...' But an officer instead ordered that Ryan be marched back to the ground. '...I found myself eventually back at the railway wall inside Croke Park where I was placed in company with the remainder of the team. I was still in my nakedness... I and the remainder of the team were lined up against the railway embankment wall and a firing party stood in front of us. There we remained until all the people in the grounds had been searched. We fully expected to be shot as the Auxiliaries had promised us, but later a military officer informed us that, if any shooting or resistance took place during the searching of the crowd, he had orders to shoot two of us for every such incident'.

A crowd of around 10,000 attended the game; 14 people lost their lives and around 80 were injured. Later that night things were 'rounded-off' in Dublin Castle. Two captured IRA officers and a captured young Gaelic scholar were 'shot while attempting to escape' by Auxiliaries. The day came to be known as 'Bloody Sunday'. A total of 31 people had died.

Tomorrow I will pass, on the East Munster Way, the Liam Lynch Monument. I'm looking forward to seeing it. For tonight though I head for the Curry House Chinese restaurant in Clogheen. I'm the only customer. The Irish waitress is chatty which is nice as, apart from the farmer, I've spoken to nobody all day. She asks where I'm staying and I tell her I'm at the campsite.

'I bet it's full,' she says, 'the kids have just started their holidays; the seniors get 12 weeks and the primary get eight weeks.'

'Good for the teachers,' I say.

I intend to give her a tip, but whilst I'm drinking my coffee she goes off for the night.

Ten
Tipperary Tribulations

'I joined the Flying Column in 1916
In Cork with Seán Moylan, In Tipperary with Dan Breen
Arrested by Free Staters and sentenced to die
Farewell to Tipperary said the Galtee Mountain Boy.'
From: *The Galtee Mountain Boy* by Patsy Halloran

Saturday 6th July – Clogheen to Newcastle
The camper's engine booms into early life this morning disturbing most of the campsite. The road to Newcastle is thankfully flat, along the River Tar valley, which bodes well for the return bike ride later in the day. By the time I return the camper to its pitch later this morning some holidaymakers have no doubt been roused from their slumbers for the second time.

I get an early start and am looking forward to a stress-free 13½-mile walk, which according to Paddy Dillon's book will first take me to some fine views at a sharp bend called 'The Vee'. Paddy has written at least 15 walking books, but if he intends to write another I'd like to suggest that at the end of his walk he considers turning around, walking back and describing the return trek. I say this because once again I get lost.

So here I am trying to puzzle my way out of Clogheen to pick up both the route from the book (reading in reverse) and the map, which *do* actually agree. But the only East Munster Way sign I see points *back* to Clogheen. At the road junction that Paddy describes as 'bristling with signposts' the only East Munster Way sign leads *back into* Clogheen. The road going east is actually the one I've driven already this morning. I take it, and carefully look out for where the map and book both say I should take a right turn off the road onto a footpath. Nothing appears.

I feel at this juncture I should mention I'm not exactly a novice walker. The first long distance footpath I completed was 30 years past. I lived in Berkshire, England at the time and went up one day onto a path called the Ridgeway and *did* then actually get myself lost. Relating the story to our milkman who was a walker, he next morning presented me with a book entitled *Discovering the Ridgeway*, written by a lady called Vera Burden – but he'd crossed out the word 'Discovering' and had substituted to words 'How not to get lost on'. The book prompted me to walk the whole 85-mile length of the Ridgeway which goes east from the village of Avebury in Wiltshire and finishes on Ivinghoe Beacon in Buckinghamshire. I did it with my then young son, both camping and staying in bed and breakfasts. Since then I've managed to complete 18 long distance paths in the UK – sometimes alone, sometimes with human company, and sometimes with canine company. Of course I've gotten lost on a few occasions, but nothing like as on this walk – it can only be my age!

In the future, getting lost will perhaps be something unheard of. I read recently that someone with too much time on their hands has come up with the idea of having satellite navigation in your shoes. What you do apparently is to download an 'app' which connects to a microchip in your shoe. Then you programme your destination into the thing and if you go wrong it emits a load buzz. I would be buzzing along all the time if I had one now. But I suppose it wouldn't be much good on a scenic trip like this because it'd take you by the most direct route – probably by road.

I walk on to a crossroads, take a right and head up, according to the map, towards 'The Vee'. But on the way, a sign for the East Munster Way mysteriously appears on a footpath running from the west (that I somehow should have taken) and leads east across my road. I take it and am now officially on the Way. I've been walking for an hour. I expect the path to now turn south towards 'The Vee' with Paddy's promised 'fine view of the broad and verdant vale between the Knockmealdown and Galty Mountains...', but it continues east bearing no relationship to either the map (which shows the Way running parallel to the R668 road) or to the book. After about another half an hour I realise the path is not going to turn south and somehow I've missed those fine views. Somebody has changed the route.

There is, however, good views to be had over a valley, where the trout filled River Tar runs east to meet the River Suir. I cross the pretty and rock-strewn Glenmoylan Stream, flanked by gorse, ferns and rhododendrons that runs down from Lough Moylan and is fed by the run-off from the Knockmealdown Mountains.

Soon I'm on a forest track and a red squirrel appears on the path. It's the first I can recall seeing in my life. There are plenty of grey squirrels in Britain; they were introduced from North America and carry a disease which doesn't affect them, but which kills the red squirrels.

At shortly after midday I arrive at a clearing and car park which doesn't seem to appear on either the map or in the book. I take my sandwiches early here at Glengalla, close to the village of Goatenbridge which on my map is marked as 'Goats Bridge' – under which you might find (if you key it into a search engine – and according to the fairy tale) a hungry troll. There are a couple of cars in the car park. Another pulls in, and a young couple and (I suppose) their daughter aged about eight emerge and gather together rucksacks for a trek. They head off in the direction I'm about to take and are probably about to do the Liam Lynch trailhead as indicated on a brown sign. It says that 3½ hours should be allowed for the complete loop, which somehow must lead them back to this spot. I hang around for a few minutes to give them a head-start then set off on the wide stony track that climbs up into the Knockmealdown Mountains. I'm heading for the Liam Lynch Monument.

The War of Independence officially came to a close on 11 July 1921 with a truce, the terms of which had been agreed two days before at a meeting in Dublin's Mansion House. The war had cost the lives of between 1,500 and 2,000 people.

Liam Lynch received an official visit from de Valera in August. Together, they and other officers spent three days inspecting the IRA companies, columns, and various ambush positions used during the war. The columns were congratulated by de Valera and there was a general feeling of elation and national unity. His visit was part of a country-wide tour he made reviewing parades, visiting training camps and whipping up enthusiasm, such that there was a huge influx of those joining the Volunteers. The organisation rose from a few thousand at the start of the truce to around 70,000.

De Valera had recently returned from a conference, held in

London, with the British government. He'd headed the Irish delegation of six that met with Lloyd George at Downing Street. Michael Collins was, despite his protests, reluctantly obliged (by de Valera) to remain in Dublin.

The British proposals that emerged on 20th July was the offer of the 26 counties receiving Dominion status, including the counties of Donegal, Monagahn and Cavan in Ulster, with the remaining six counties of Ulster partitioned for so long as they wished. An Irish army would be allowed but not a navy. The Royal Navy would control designated ports. De Valera had completely rejected the proposals and said that he wouldn't recommend them to the Cabinet or the Dáil, to which Lloyd George raised the threat of the resumption of war. The British were still trying to hold together the threads of the Empire and saw a republic in the south – which is what the delegation of course sought – as threatening it.

Correspondence continued between de Valera and Lloyd George through August, and a letter sent by the former on the 30th concluded with the line that he was 'ready at once to appoint plenipotentiaries'. Lloyd George was, however, taking a quiet break at the time on the west coast of Scotland where he received the letter. The 'Welsh Wizard' had somehow managed to wave his magic wand and had accompanying him both his wife *and* mistress. Instead of hastening back to London for a meeting with his Cabinet and, perhaps at the behest of the ladies, he instead summoned everyone from London up to Inverness – which, to put it politely, pleased none of them very much. It was the first full British Cabinet meeting to be held outside of London. The outcome of the meeting, held in Inverness town hall, was that a letter was sent to de Valera revealing that Lloyd George had perhaps developed writer's cramp, or had in some other way damaged his wrist. It began: 'You will agree that this correspondence has lasted long enough' and it ended by inviting the Irish to a conference to be held in Inverness on 20th September.

But de Valera, whilst accepting the principle of a conference, also made further statements that were somewhat contentious to the British – which caused Lloyd George to suffer further in his wrist. Finally a new invitation was made to the Irish for a conference in London to commence on 11th October – exactly three months after the truce had come into force.

The mood in the country was positive; Liam Lynch wrote to his brother Tom from Lombardstown on 26th September: 'You may rest assured that our Government as well as the army is out for the Republic and nothing less'. But his real thoughts were that it would probably come back down to the army and the resumption of war.

Éamon de Valera now dropped a bombshell on Michael Collins; he'd left him out of the delegation that accompanied him to London in July, but now, having found out what a tough stance was likely to be taken by the British at the conference, he manoeuvred Collins to go in his place. He needed a scapegoat in case the outcome was not an Irish republic and the man who'd helped him escape from prison and who'd arranged for him to be ferried back and forth across the Atlantic fitted the bill. The phrase 'With friends like these who needs enemies' springs to mind. De Valera had though acquired allies in his Cabinet and cast the deciding vote himself. Although Collins strongly protested that he was a soldier and that de Valera was the politician, Collins was finally pressured to go. De Valera also felt that as 'Head of State' he should remain aloof from whatever transpired.

At the conference the nitty-gritty issues of Ulster's unity with the south and the Oath of Allegiance to a British monarch were the major stumbling blocks. The British stuck to their guns with their offer of Dominion status.

At a critical point in the negotiations Lloyd George pulled off one of his typical crafty manoeuvres; he produced a memo that he'd previously shown privately to Arthur Griffith and to which the latter had assented, which tied the acceptance of Dominion status to the setting up of a boundary commission. Lloyd George hinted that this would reduce Ulster and make it unworkable such that it would need to join a proposed 'free state' (as it was decided the southern counties would be collectively called). Collins took the view that Dominion status was a 'stepping stone' to complete independence, knowing that if Dominion status was not accepted and war was resumed by the British, his force would be really up against it because they were low on ammunition. He also knew that as his identity was no longer a secret he would personally be a marked man.

Arthur Griffith was now prepared to sign the treaty and it was thought that Collins and another member of the Irish delegation would also sign, but Lloyd George also needed the remaining two members to sign. Dramatically now Lloyd George pulled off another stunt by holding up two envelopes that he said were addressed to James Craig in Belfast (who had succeeded Carson as leader of the Ulster Unionists). One envelope Lloyd George claimed said that agreement had been reached, the other that it had not. If the latter was sent, he said, it would mean war within three days. Lloyd George stated that he needed their answer by 10 o'clock that night. Under this threat the Treaty was eventually signed by all five delegates and the headlines on Wednesday 7th December read: IRISH OFFERED FREE STATE. That same day King George V ordered the release of all Sinn Féin prisoners.

But in Dublin de Valera was livid. After an acrimonious meeting though the Irish Cabinet voted narrowly to accept the Treaty. To those who'd supported the old Irish Parliamentary Party, the Treaty offered more than they'd hoped for under home rule; it gave fiscal autonomy, an Irish Parliament that stood alone with an army, civil service and police force all responsible to it. More than that the British would leave Ireland and there would be peace. They saw the Treaty as a victory. To de Valera and others though, who wanted a united republic of Ireland, it was a defeat.

The Supreme Council of the IRB who met on 10th January 1922 came out in favour of the Treaty and issued a note to divisional and county centres to that effect. It did, however, add a rider saying that 'Members of the organisation, however, who have to take public action as representatives are given freedom of action in the matter'.

Liam Lynch was a member of the IRB – he recorded his views at the time in a letter written to his brother Tom on the 12th: 'My attitude is now as always, to fight on for the recognition of the Republic. Even if I were to stand alone I will not voluntarily accept being part of the British Empire. Whatever will happen here on this week of destiny we must and will show a united front. Thank God that we can agree to differ. Minority of the Dáil will stand by majority no matter what side; the same will apply to the army'. Lynch's thoughts regarding solidarity were sadly to be proved incorrect. If his predictions had been correct there wouldn't now be a 60-foot-high round tower monument to him on Knockmealdown Mountain.

Large brown signs, spaced at fairly frequent intervals, point the way to the Lynch Monument. It's quite a slog up the wide, gravelled, stony track that winds its way onto the mountainside. I suppose some motorists could avoid the sweat and drive up – but no cars pass me. I've given the young couple and their daughter a good head-start but dawdle so I don't catch them up. From the map, it seems like about a four-kilometre walk to the monument. After a brown sign tells me there's one and a half kilometres to go, I make an estimate that I should be there in about 20 minutes. So I go, frequently stopping to check the map and ascertain where I might be. It seems like the monument must be around here somewhere – I can't possibly miss such a prominent structure. I pull out the map again, glance to my right and catch sight of the trio who left the car park ahead of me – they're sitting eating a packed lunch. I check the map again and go on. It must be around here somewhere. Paddy's book read backwards says I should continue up a clear forest track bending left and right 'with views of the Comeragh Mountains and Galty Mountains from the clear-felled slopes'. I walk on. The forest track leads to a narrow footpath that climbs to a stile then turns right, which from Paddy's book rings untrue in relation to the location of the monument – but I can't possibly have missed it. So I carry on – the path takes a right turn. After another 10 minutes and another stile or two the path starts to descend steeply on a grassy footpath between two hedges. I'm sure now that somehow I've missed the thing. I don't like mysteries, but it seems I've overshot the monument by about two kilometres. Back up the footpath I go in annoyed haste. There's not a cloud in the sky, it's scorching hot and I'm sweating. I stop to take a long slug from my water bottle. Back on the wide gravelled track again now – Paddy's book tells me I should find the monument. After five minutes or so I come across a barrier pole painted yellow behind which is an obvious path, bordered by dwarf walls either side. It leads a short distance to the elusive monument. Then I realise that the family who'd been sitting eating their lunch had been obscuring the yellow barrier. It'd all been a subconscious Republican plot to thwart a stupid old English pensioner from finding the spot where Liam had been shot.

Three men in their late 30s or early 40s are at the monument. I nod to them and then walk slowly around it, passing the four bronze wolfhounds that guard each of its corners – and so I return to the front of the monument and climb a couple of steps to look up at two plaques inset between the stones of its structure. The inscriptions (disappointingly for me) are carved in Irish.

Irish is one of six 'living' Celtic languages. The Irish call the language Irish, whist foreigners like me tend to call it Gaelic – but this can cause confusion with Scottish Gaelic, which was brought to the west coast of Scotland by Irish settlers in around the 4th century. Irish has constitutional status in Ireland and is one of 24 official languages of the European Union. But only around 3% of the Irish population speak it as a household language, not least because it was discouraged by the English in 1831, when Chief Secretary Edward Smith-Stanley introduced a system of national education where instruction was given only in English. Gaelic (or Irish) suffered another sharp decline following the potato famine in the mid-19th century.

The plaque at the top looks like it was part of the original monument – erected in 1935, which I knew replaced the simple cross that had stood there before. The bottom plaque I can see has been added later to commemorate the 50th anniversary of his death. His name is there in Gaelic (or Irish): LIAM O'LOINGSIGH.

I stand back and take a photo – the three men watch me.

'It's all in Gaelic then!' I say, stating the obvious.

'Sure, we can't even read it,' replies one of the guys.

'We passed you on the road,' the other guy adds I try to think where this might have been.

'I had some difficulty finding it,' I say. 'They put these big brown signs up all the way up the track and then when you get here there's nothing.' They agree and we chat for a while. Then one guy fires me a testing question.

'Is this where he got shot then?' Now, I'd done a wee bit of homework, but still felt nervous in my reply.

'Yes, I know a bit about the history,' I say. 'He fought in the Anglo-Irish War but was killed by an Irishman in the Civil War,' – perhaps not too diplomatic an answer – I should have said the War of Independence and perhaps *not* mentioned that he'd been shot by an Irishman.

On 16th December 1921 the British House of Commons ratified the Anglo-Irish Treaty. The Dáil voted on the Treaty on 7th January and approved it by 64 votes to 57. Two days later de Valera resigned – then optimistically stood again for re-election as President. But on the 10th he lost that vote too by 60 votes to 58 and, being not too good as a loser, walked out of the chamber in protest – followed by his supporters. There ensued much acrimony between the pro and anti-Treaty sides.

On 14th January a provisional government was formed, with Michael Collins as chairman, whilst Griffith remained president of the Dáil. Two days later Collins received the handover of Dublin Castle from the British – and their troops left the country.

Liam Lynch's initial optimism remained with him during those early days of 1922. He'd just returned from a visit to Dublin when on 16th January he wrote to brother Tom that: 'You can rest satisfied that the IRA will save the situation. Time will tell whether L, George (sic) has got the best of the Irish nation or made a big mess of himself'. Lynch hit the nail on the head with regards to Lloyd George; Ireland ruined him, as it had Robert Peel and Gladstone: the Liberals and Labour blamed him for bringing in the Black and Tans, whilst the Conservatives were angry because he'd foisted on them a treaty which had made them face up to the reality of Ulster. In October of 1922 Conservative peers and MPs met at the Carlton Club and voted to end the coalition government; they disowned their leader Austen Chamberlain and thus an isolated Lloyd George was forced to resign. The King asked Bonar Law to form a new government.

The two opposing wings of the IRA met on 18th January. They were led by Richard Mulcahy for the Collins camp and Rory O'Connor for the anti-Treaty supporters. The outcome was a 'watching council' which was created to prevent clashes between the two sides. Politically Collins was hoping to produce a constitution which would be acceptable to both the British and the republicans.

Lynch and other senior army officers decided that they would revert to being a volunteer force responsible not to the Dáil but to their own executive though he still held out hopes for unity within the army and wrote to his brother Tom on 6th March: 'If we can force the Treaty party to draw up a Republican constitution we are all A1 again, this I consider quite possible'.

But during March the country edged slowly towards civil war. Both pro and anti-Treaty army forces were now building up arms; the pro-Treaty supporters were supplied with large quantities of grenades, rifles, revolvers and machine guns by the British, whilst the Cork IRA intercepted a British naval vessel off the coast of Cork and also obtained a large quantity of arms. On 14th April an anti-Treaty force of around 200 led by Rory O'Connor took over the Four Courts and other premises (including Kilmainham Gaol) in Dublin. They set up the Four Courts as their headquarters, with the objective of inciting the British to attack it and so reunite the two factions of the Irish army.

On 22nd June two members of the IRA bumped off the die-hard Ulster Unionist, Field Marshal Sir Henry Wilson outside his home in London. Wilson had played a pivotal role during the Curragh Mutiny in 1914, had pressed for conscription in Ireland in 1918, had opposed the truce and as military advisor to the six counties Ulster administration, he was judged by nationalists as being culpable for the pogrom carried out against the Catholics there.

The British thought that those in the Four Courts were to blame for Wilson's assassination and Lloyd George, after examining documents found on the assassins following their capture, got Churchill to draft a letter which was sent by special messenger to Michael Collins impelling him to oust Rory O'Connor from the Four Courts. When Collins took no immediate action, General Macready, who commanded the remaining British troops in Dublin, was ordered by Lloyd George's government to attack the Four Courts. Sensibly Macready resisted on the grounds that such an attack would draw the two factions of the IRA together. On 28th June Collins finally succumbed to British pressure and issued an ultimatum to the Four Courts garrison to surrender. No reply was received.

Liam Lynch and some of his officers had been woken by gunfire in the Clarence Hotel, across the River Liffey from the Four Courts when the attack had started. They decided that their best action was to return to their commands. Lynch travelled to Mallow and began to make plans for war against the Free State army. His thoughts were to establish a 'Munster republic' that would be defended on a line stretching from Waterford to Limerick, the latter of which was recognised by both sides as being of critical strategic importance.

On 13th July Michael Collins took up duty as Commander in Chief of the Free State army who made speedy territorial gains – landing in Waterford on 23rd July, taking Tralee the next day, Tipperary town on the 30th, Carrick-on-Suir on 2nd August and, after stiff resistance, taking Kilmallock on the 5th. The battle for Cork lasted less than three days but at around 5pm on Thursday 10th August the Republicans withdrew from the city.

Lynch now decided that they should fight on in another way; they would do so as they had against the Brits – but this time they would not have the support of the populace. On 11th August Lynch evacuated Fermoy Barracks and burned it. His guerrilla war was about to commence. On 22nd August Michael Collins set off for a tour of west Cork, the area in which he'd spent his childhood – and in a little valley (translated from Irish to mean 'the mouth of flowers') he was ambushed in one such guerrilla attack and shot dead.

The New Year of 1923 saw further setbacks for the Republicans. Lynch had moved his headquarters to Dublin to facilitate improved communications but, relying perhaps on optimistic reports. He failed to see that public sympathy for the cause was on the wane once his men began acts of sabotage such as damaging the railway network utilised by Free State troops.

Things got progressively worse such that a meeting of the 'Executive', which many had been pressing Lynch for some time to hold, was finally held on 16th March. It lasted over a week. Some of the members, including General Lynch, held the view that the army was not yet defeated and that the war should go on. Others were of the opinion that further resistance was useless. The meeting was adjourned until 10th April, when it was hoped that some of those who'd not been present would be able to attend. But that meeting would never be held.

Someone had tipped off the Free State forces that the Republicans would be in the area and Major General John Prout, C/O of the National Army in Waterford, based at Clonmel, ordered a search to start in the early hours of Tuesday 10th April. The Republicans were being hunted like foxes; they went to ground each night in safe houses. That night Liam Lynch and his six comrades were billeted just to the south-east of Goatenbridge in farmhouses on one of three minor roads that led off southward from the Clogheen to Newcastle road onto the slopes of the Knockmealdown Mountains. Six guards were posted at three possible approaches to the farmhouses and at 5am a party of about 60 Free State troops were seen approaching from the direction of Clogheen. Liam's party, who carried only side arms and had not a rifle amongst them, knew that they were no match for the rifles carried by their hunters. They moved to a house higher up the mountainside and at daybreak saw, further down and to the north, three columns of Free State troops. They were, however, unperturbed, as they were planning to go up and over the mountain. But at 8am, just as they were about to have a cup of tea, a scout ran in to tell them that another column was approaching across the mountains to cut them off. Liam's party, numbering seven, set off through gorse up a glen towards the mountain. Two scouts located to the west were known to have a sub-machine gun and a rifle, and word was sent for them to join Liam's party who stopped to wait for them at the head of the glen. But instead of the scouts appearing, a column of Free State troops led by Lieutenant Clancy appeared over a rise and opened fire on them. The Republicans continued scrambling up a sunken, almost dry, stream bed that gave them some cover, but after 250 yards and with no option but to keep climbing, they were forced to scale the bare shoulder of the mountain. Liam and a companion were at the rear of the party. Bullets whizzed around them as they climbed, splattering bog and splintering off pieces of rock. They kept going; turning occasionally to fire off a few shots from their revolvers which they knew didn't have the range to do any damage. Liam was being helped along by Seán Hyde, who had him by the hand, as they staggered on upwards, hoping to make it over the mountain. Suddenly the firing stopped for a period of perhaps 20 seconds. There was a strange and complete silence. Then a single shot was heard.

'My God I'm hit, lads,' Liam managed to say as he slumped to the ground.

The guy who'd fired me the question to test my knowledge or, as he probably thought, lack of knowledge about Liam Lynch seems to pay no regard to my answer; he just kind of grunts and smiles. His colleagues pass no comment either on the subject – but I'm very conscious of my Englishness and that they're all Irish and might hold against me the 700 years of turmoil between our lands. I also know that one of the principles for which Lynch and many like him had died – that of a non-partitioned Ireland – has still not come to pass.

But we chat some more. I tell them about my walk and that I shall finish this year at Clonmel. We say our goodbyes and I leave them there at the monument whilst I trek off over ground I've trodden twice already today. I rattle along, passing once more familiar little landmarks remembered from two previous traverses of this ground, until I start to descend on the grassy footpath between two hedges. I remember the exact spot, an hour or so ago now where I made the correct decision to turn back. Then I'm into new territory on a winding footpath that dives down to meet a road in the Glenboy River valley. Turning left then on the road, I follow it for about three miles into Newcastle.

I know that Lynch was carried down to a pub in Newcastle called Nugents, but I don't know if it's still there. I walk on past my chained up bike looking for it and am pleasantly surprised. Its cream-walled, grey-slated roof gives it a cottage feeling that looks welcoming enough. A group of people are seated outside at a wooden picnic table. Inside, a couple of men at the bar are deep in conversation about local issues. They ignore me, but I don't think they're being impolite – I have the feeling that if I went into a pub in any one of the villages around about things would be the same. Nobody's behind the bar and there's no bell to ring. It seems like it might be self-service, in which, in my dire state of thirst, I'm sorely tempted to indulge. One of the men, maybe sensing my desperate impatience, says:

'She'll be out in a minute.' I wait the minute and a good few more before she appears – but the first gulp of the wet stuff (not Guinness, but lager) is worth the wait. I noticed as soon as I entered, that hung on the wall at the far end of the bar was a familiar photograph of the uniformed, bespectacled Liam Lynch (as I'd seen on a website). Below it is a framed poem, so I saunter over to get a closer look. This I decide, I must photograph, but don't feel easy about doing so without perhaps being drawn into a contentious discussion with the men at the bar. So I take my pint and sit on a tattered couch, that looks as if it might have been here since 1923, and change out of walking gear and into cycling kit. I finish both changing and the

pint in fairly swift time and now psyche myself up to take the photo.
I check that the two men are paying no attention and quickly snap
it – but I have difficulty keeping light reflections out of the frame.

The poem is in fact a song as it has a chorus; it's been written and
arranged by Rose Condon and Paul Devaney and eloquently tells the
story of Lynch's death. It's titled: General Liam Lynch, R.I.P. 1923:

'As I gaze out of my window, and see the mist come down
I think of that April day on the slopes of Knockmealdown.
A shot rang out across the hill, his comrades gathered round
Everything seemed so still, as Liam fell to the ground'.

Chorus
'For I never will forget the day in 1923
When Liam and comrades the staters had to flee
And I never will forget the day that General Liam fell
For if truth be known a little part of all of us died as well'.

'They made a stretcher with their guns, and brought him down the
track
He was one of Ireland's bravest sons, they would not turn their back.
A jennet and realthan was got, and they carried him nice and slow
But the bleeding had proved too much when they got him down
below'.

''Twas in the local public house that on the couch he lay
He was anointed by Father Bradley, and his friends began to pray.
It's with sorrow that I have to say he died in old Clonmel
And history has proven that part of Ireland died as well'.

'Well general Liam you are gone but your memory is held so dear
And we gather to remember you in April of each year,
And we think of all of Erin's brave who died so selflessly,
And we hope that maybe some day that our island will be free'.

Frank Aiken took over from Liam Lynch on 24th May. He ordered
the Republican fighters to 'dump their arms' and return home,
calling an end to the painful Civil War.

Eleven
Sally Power's Honey Meadow

'Lonely shades, and murm'ring founts;
Limpid streams, and azure mounts;
Rocks and caverns, ocean's roar;
Waves whose surges lash the shore.'
From: *Stock in Trade of Modern Poetesses*, from *The Keepsake* by
The Countess of Blessington.

Sunday 7th July – Newcastle to Clonmel

The thunder of the van's diesel engine wakes the happy campers again early this morning. I fancy I hear a few mumbling curses as I reverse off the pitch. Joyous thoughts of an early morning walk on the East Munster Way soon dissolve as I do my usual trick of getting lost – this time in the van, by turning the wrong way at a junction and, after a few miles, then trying to work out how it appears I'm heading south towards Dungarvan instead of north.

But the Sunday newspapers have still not yet alighted on doormats (if this still happens) as I drive into sleepy Clonmel. There's nobody about in Irishtown, except for a lone lady sitting in a car (for what reason at this hour I'm not sure, unless she's meeting somebody to go to Mass); she watches me with gathering suspicion as I unload the bike and chain it to a bollard – I just hope she doesn't phone the Gardai.

I drive back to Newcastle, park up the camper and follow a Munster Way sign without consulting either map or compass. It's the second error of the morning; again I head south instead of east and lose another 45 minutes before being reunited sooner than expected with the van.

The remainder of the morning's walk comprises a series of pleasant country lanes as I enter my fourth county – Waterford. Crossing the slow flowing River Nire bordered by overhanging trees and blossom I pass through the village of Fourmilewater where departing churchgoers chat in little huddles. After crossing the main Clonmel to Youghal Bay road it's a long drag up to the forested Curraheenavoher Hill. The last bit of road before the forest track is very steep and has been recently laid with tarmac. It's a hot and humid day and I have to stop several times and wipe the sweat from my face and neck with my tee shirt. The tarmac is melting and the smell of it brings back a sweet boyhood memory of playing with the treacly stuff and being scrubbed down by my gran.

An hour or so later, I lose account of where I am; neither the book nor map seems to make sense, but I continue to follow the fingerposts hoping that something will soon make sense. The forest track changes to a footpath. On a downhill stretch, a father and young daughter pedal past me struggling uphill. Just before I reach a lane the pair passes me again biking downhill. As they reach a lane, I catch them up and ask the father if he knows where we are. My first thought is that either I've somehow gone wrong or the route has been changed because he tells me we are at Glenabbey car park near Caherbaun. I've been in the process of tracing my way from Discovery map 74 to map 75, and now realise that the car park must be located in the top left-hand corner of *map 82* which I don't have. I press on, east along the lane to a T-junction where the fingerposts point uphill. Skirting a farm I keep climbing, passing sheep pens and crossing a ladder stile into wild deserted moorland – which at this late hour is disconcerting because I'm tired and expected instead to be on the outskirts of Clonmel.

Then suddenly the town appears below me like Lilliput from Johnathan Swift's novel; I feel like Gulliver towering above it. Below the steep tree slopes lies the flatlands, with Clonmel's buildings set in the foreground fanning out in an inverted 'T' shape. It's a large town. The footpath meets a road and descends down into Clonmel; this must be the road described in Paddy's book as 'the punishingly steep Roaring Spring Road' – but going downhill in the opposite direction it's OK. Now it seems I'm back in County Tipperary at the end of the day's 13-mile walk.

At the first pub I come across I partake of a beautiful cool pint, watch Wimbledon tennis on the TV and change into cycling gear ready for the unappealing 18-mile bike ride back to Newcastle.

From the pub I walk in trainers that feel light and cool after the hot and heavy walking boots, into the centre of Clonmel across Suir Island where the River Suir splits to flow either side of it. But first I stop to take a photograph of the weir known as Lady Blessington's Bath, very near where she lived between the age of eight and 17. It's said that the beautiful young girl, known then as Sally Power, used to swim here in the early 19th century, perhaps spied upon by approving men and disapproving women.

Lady Blessington had not always been beautiful – and her early life promised nothing of her colourful life that would follow. She was born in 1789 in the village of Knockbrit, two miles from Cashel. She was christened as Margaret, but was known as Sally Power, and as a young child not only was she plain, but she suffered from ill health, was frail, white faced, peaky and was not much loved by her parents. Though feeling isolated from the rest of her family Sally, however, loved the lanes and fields of Knockbrit. She dreamed her days away and soon formed a close relationship with a spinster called Anne Dwyer who mothered her, took pity on her and guided her towards the joy of reading.

When Sally was eight her father, who was a corn merchant and butter buyer, decided that the family would move from rural Knockbrit to bustling Clonmel town where he'd joined a firm of corn-chandlers. It broke Sally's heart to leave the village not least because she would lose her friend and mentor Anne. On the day the family left she picked a bunch of wild flowers to hold in memory, clutching them close to her in a coat pocket during the journey and trying unsuccessfully to hold back her tears. But her mother couldn't take her nonsense and alternately pinched, scolded and slapped her to try and stop her whimpering. At their new house in Clonmel her mother, already incensed by Sally's performance, discovered the squashed posy in her coat pocket and threw it out of the window. Her siblings added to Sally's misery by laughing mockingly at her for her weakness.

Sally's father Edmund Power was the buck of the area, swanking around in white cravats, frills, ruffles and leather breeches so that he acquired the title of Beau Power. He was an extraverted, swaggering boozer who gambled and who'd also been known to fight the odd duel. His life changed dramatically when he came to the notice of Lord

Donoughmore following a session where they each endeavoured to drink each under the table. Lord Donoughmore, otherwise known as Richard Hely-Hutchinson, ostensibly a general in the British army, who occasionally sat in the House of Lords, had recently arranged the construction nearby of a mansion for himself. He'd also become the chief representative of the Castle Party thereabouts. Donoughmore talked Power into his service on the promise that if successful he'd land himself a cushy little number which may even result in a title. The position offered and accepted was that of a magistracy upon which Beau Power acquired a troop of dragoons but no money. Although a Catholic himself, his task, which he took on with much gusto, was to put down Catholic rebels and agitators throughout counties Tipperary and Waterford, capturing and beating them – some of whom had previously been his friends. The problem for him was that the Catholics, who of course hated the Castle's rule, carried out revenge attacks by burning his grain stores, maiming his cattle and destroying his plantations.

What effect all this had on Sally can only be guessed. She was maturing into a beautiful young girl and together with her younger sister Ellen they were exposed to the rowdy drinking sessions conducted by officer friends of her father who rendezvoused daily in their small, uncomfortable house by the river. Sally's mother's maiden name was Ellen Sheehy, a descendent of the Earls of Desmond, from a well known Catholic family. She'd been attracted to the handsome young Edmund, but he'd perhaps only been attracted to her by Ellen's heritage and standing. To escape the house and its drunken carousels Mrs Power got out as much as possible and didn't much bother about her young daughters doing so also.

But when Sally was about 14 Beau noticed that his daughters, particularly Sally, who was well formed for her age, were getting lustful looks from some of the officers and that the girls' presence in the house ensured that his friends called more regularly. One such regular visitor was Captain Maurice St Leger Farmer who was both rich and ruthless, as well as, by today's standards, being a paedophile. He made no bones about wanting Sally and had no difficulty purchasing her from Beau.

Sally was forced to live with the Captain as Mrs Margaret Farmer. He turned out to be an even worse deal than her father; a sadistic sod, subject to fits of insanity, he forced himself upon her, beat her with his fists, pinched her and, when he left the house, kept her locked up – sometimes without food. After three months of this treatment the Captain received orders to report to the barracks at Curragh near Dublin, but Margaret, still not yet turned 15, refused to go, and he was forced to leave her behind – but not before giving her one last vicious thrashing for good luck. She had little option but to return to her parents' house.

Good luck was, however, to come Margaret's way eventually, but not before a lot more strife. First, Beau was about to bring bad luck upon himself: Lord Donoughmore talked him into launching a pro-British newspaper, *The Clonmel Gazette and Munster Mercury*, which was subsequently sued successfully for a libellous article – written in fact by Donoughmore himself, who when it went to court craftily left Beau to foot the bill.

Beau's debts and worsening reputation brought the house to a state of debauchery, iniquity and squalor; the only visitors were those soldiers who fancied having it away with Margaret or her sister Ellen. Then a further disaster struck Mr Power: whilst out one night trying to track down rebels, he accidently (or not) shot a boy who'd attempted to flee from questioning for no other reason than he was scared shitless. Power brought him into Clonmel Gaol where he died and Beau was subsequently tried for murder. Although acquitted, his character had been called into question and he was debarred from further service as a magistrate. Donoughmore dumped him faster than an unwanted Christmas present. Power was ruined and, looking around for someone to blame, he took out his frustration and anger upon Margaret because she'd left Farmer and the financial security that the union might perhaps have brought the family.

By this time Margaret had spent three years living back in the family home, although she escaped the house as much as possible, and with her sister they usually visited neighbours. She was now 17. During one of these visits she struck up an intimacy with a Captain Thomas Jenkins who had an estate in Hampshire, England. Jenkins had been a regular guest at the Powers' dinner table prior to Beau's murder trial and now, when Margaret began to suffer wrath and violence from her father, and there was an added threat from a rumour that Farmer was on his way back to Clonmel to claim her back, Jenkins came to her rescue. He took her away with him – it's thought to Dublin or maybe to England. At any rate by 1809, at the age of 20 it's known that she was ensconced in his house in Hampshire. She lived with him there for about five years, during which time she came to meet a gentleman called Charles John Gardiner, 2nd Viscount Mountjoy and 1st Earl of Blessington.

Charles Gardiner was a widower with four children, two with his wife before they'd married, and two after. He was seven years older than Margaret and was a supporter of the cause of the Catholics; his great-grandfather Luke had generated the family's wealth as a banker and property developer in Dublin and had married into the aristocracy and gained the Blessington name. Charles had been educated at Eton and at Christ Church, Oxford and was elected representative peer for Ireland in 1809. Much taken by Margaret's beauty, he effectively purchased her from Jenkins by the payment of the sum of £10,000 as a reimbursement for the jewels and clothing Jenkins had bought for her.

As it happened Captain Farmer, who'd been cashiered out of the army, had not long died, having fallen out of a window in the debtor's King's Bench prison in Southwark, London, whilst pissed. This left Margaret free to marry Charles, which she did in February 1818 at the age of 28. It was then that she changed her name again to Marguerite, Countess of Blessington. I suppose Marguerite somehow sounded more mystique than Margaret. It was no secret that she married Charles for his title and position, while he married her for prestige and for her beauty.

Marguerite unfortunately had no idea of the value of money and must have thought Charles had a money orchard somewhere where he grew the stuff. Together they lived a fashionable life in London, opening and lavishly decorating houses there whilst throwing many parties for the nobility and the numerous artists, actors and writers that the Lady 'collected'. One such guest was Alfred Grimod d'Orsay, known as Count d'Orsay. Twelve years Marguerite's junior, d'Orsay was a French amateur artist and also most probably a randy dandy, who formed a close relationship with them both which was later rumoured to have developed into a ménage à trois.

Charles and Marguerite travelled extensively for the next 11 years to Paris, Switzerland and the south of France. In 1823 they invited the Count d'Orsay to join them on a trip around Italy, first travelling to Genoa where Marguerite met Lord Byron. She saw him frequently afterwards and made a copious record of their interviews which she published almost a decade later, entitled *Conversations with Lord Byron*. When the book was serialised, as was common in those days, it became an instant sensation. The couple continued their European travels to Naples, where they stayed for about three years, before returning via Florence and Rome to Paris, arriving in June 1826.

Charles died in Paris in 1829, aged 46 leaving Marguerite an income of £2,000 per year, along with considerable debts. The Countess moved back to London in 1831 where she lived for the next 18 years, accompanied by her toy-boy – the Count d'Orsay. But her extravagant lifestyle caught up with her eventually and she was forced to auction the contents of her home in order to satisfy her creditors. Count d'Orsay went to Paris, and Marguerite followed him to escape ruin – renting an apartment close to the Champs-Élysées. Six weeks later, on 4th June 1849,having dined with the Duchess of Grammont, she returned home and died, aged 59 – it doesn't say much for the Duchess's cook!

Marguerite's literary works totalled 13 novels written over a period of about 14 years, the first published in 1822; she also wrote memoir/travel writing books, poems, and edited annuals (a fad of the time, presented usually at Christmas to middle-class ladies). She wrote from financial necessity and perhaps is remembered not so much for her writing as for the wonderful literary hostess she was.

It's strange that most of us know our place of birth, yet may never be sure of where we will die. I'll bet wan little Sally Power from the village of Knockbrit in County Tipperary, weeping as her wild flowers were tossed out of the window from the house near the weir by Suir Island, never thought she'd die as a Countess in Paris. She surely never forgot her childhood roots as one of her famous quotations was 'happiness consists not in having much, but in being content with little' – perhaps she was thinking of the time she'd spent in Knockbrit with Anne Dwyer.

From Suir Island I walk along Bridge Street and turn left into Irishtown to retrieve my bike. The ride back to Newcastle is no more strenuous than I imagine. But I'm a wee bit wary every time a car passes me having read that the Gardai stopped a man near Clonmel who was driving erratically and found he was steering with a pair of pliers because his steering wheel had come off.

Back in Clogheen in the evening I go for sit-down fish and chips, which seems to be the 'in place' for every teenage girl (and a few boys) in the area to congregate. I eat quickly and escape for some peace and quiet across the road in Nedeen's bar.

Here I'm served by Brendon and, when I order a second pint, he has a problem with the Heineken and disappears to change a barrel – but it seems there's a problem with the carbon dioxide bottle and he has to phone the brewery. He apologises and manages to squeeze out three-quarters of a pint which he gives me for free – nice man.

I feel at ease in the pub and ask Brendon about the advertisement displayed in his off-licence for a certain brand of dark rum that happens to be my favoured tipple. I ask him if it's spiced rum, which is not to my taste and he confirms it is. In Ireland it appears that normal dark rum is unobtainable, certainly I've not seen it anywhere. So sadly I return to the campsite empty handed. If I were to spend much more time in Ireland I'd have to acquire a taste for Jameson's.

Monday 8th July – Clonmel

Clonmel, or *Cluain Meala* in Irish – which means 'honey meadow'– conjures up a charming image. I find a quiet parking place just up from the river which I note as a potential wild-camp spot for next year. Then I stroll into the town centre, lively with tourists, street musicians, locals and business people.

In an establishment called Span Tierney they get the lunch orders mixed up, and I get chicken in some sort of a sauce when I should have been served Cajun chicken. I'm so lost in thought that I don't notice and begin to eat it. The waitress discovers her mistake too late – I finish the meal without complaint, and imagine that the waitress has to explain away the delay to another customer, the manager frets and sweats, the cook has a paddy (no pun intended), and that somebody else an hour later gets my warmed up Cajun chicken.

I make my way back to Suir Island and saunter east along Riverside Walk to the Gashouse Bridge, where I've parked the camper and where the walk will restart in just under a year's time on this slow progress along the E8. For this year though the walk is over.

Twelve
Folk of the East Munster Way

'The yellow bittern that never broke out
In a drinking bout, might as well have drunk;
His bones are thrown on a naked stone
Where he lived alone like a hermit monk.'
From: *The Yellow Bittern* by Thomas MacDonagh

Monday 16th June 2014 – Clonmel to Carrick-on-Suir
Three hundred and forty-two days have passed quickly enough –
and though I'll be glad to be back on the path, another year of my
life has slipped by as quickly as a broken branch on the waters of
the River Suir floats under Gashouse Bridge. I've spent the night
in the camper van in a car park overlooked by riverside flats a
few metres from the bridge. I've had an untroubled night. All year
I'd pictured myself camping in the road outside the greyhound
stadium but hadn't reckoned on the appearance of double white
lines (perhaps they'd always been there and I just not noticed or
had forgotten them).

Clonmel, apart from that, seems to have changed little. Not too
much has changed in my life either, but a lot of things had happened
in the world. There was a natural disaster in the Philippines when
typhoon Haiyan claimed around 6,240 victims. Man made plenty
of his own disasters as well, with wars, terrorism, repression,
human rights violations, ethnic cleansing and killings. There's a long
list of places where one or more of these happenings took place:
Afghanistan, the Democratic Republic of Congo, Egypt, Iraq, Israel,
Kashmir, Mali, Nigeria, Palestine, Somalia, South Sudan, Syria,
Turkey, Uganda, Ukraine and Venezuela – and probably some more
I've missed. During 2013 in excess of 120,000 people lost their lives
in these conflicts, not to mention whatever may have happened
behind closed doors in countries such as Burma, China, Iran, North
Korea, Russia and Zimbabwe.

I feel quite safe in the Republic of Ireland; their issues are not life threatening. There was a referendum which questioned whether the Seanad (the upper house of the Oireachtas – the Irish legislator) should be abolished. In the debate leading up to it, Senator David Norris who was obviously in favour of its retention, said of Regina Doherty, who was for its abolition, that she was 'talking through her fanny' – an entertaining turn of phrase, I thought. He later withdrew the remark and regretted if any offence had been caused. What I think he might have meant to say that she was talking through her ass – a less sexist remark that he may have gotten away with. In any event 51.7% of the 39.2% of people who bothered to vote wished to retain the upper house, in the main on the grounds that the Dáil would be held more accountable for its actions and decisions.

I have three weeks of fresh air to look forward to and at 9am take just a few steps from the camper van to the spot where I trod the path last July. There's a bus service between Carrick and Clonmel, so I can avoid a drive and bike ride today, and the camper can stay where it is.

The path is paved and civilised as I stroll the first couple of miles along the banks of the Suir, savouring being back on the E8 on a pleasant sunny morning. Life doesn't get much better than this. But it does seem to be taking a while to reach Sir Thomas Bridge at Ferryhouse, so I ask two men I see chatting over a hedge how far it is.

'It's about a moil,' one, who's about my age, tells me. Interestingly, he didn't give me the answer in kilometres, which is surprising as all Ireland's road signs are in that unit of measure; perhaps it was because of our ages.

Sir Thomas Bridge is reached after the 1.6093 kilometres predicted, although it feels more like a mile to me. I turn sharp right to cross the River Suir into County Waterford – my fourth walking county, although the sign for the Way (and for some unknown reason) points in the exact opposite direction. There follows a humid, stiff four-kilometre road climb up to Harney's Cross Roads at which point my tee shirt looks as if it's taken itself for a swim in the river. I'm high up now and turn off onto a forest track. The consolation is a slow, gentle and cooling decent, with views of the Glasha River valley and the mountains beyond opening up to the south.

Trackside, a fuchsia rhododendron stands out bright and bold amongst the green, and later a large reddish-purple mass of it appears below in the distance, wedged between the forest and mountains. These shrubs were brought from the Black Sea to Ireland by Victorian and Edwardian landlords for them to hide behind whilst they popped away at pheasant and the like. In Killarney National Park the shrub has completely taken over and is threatening native oak trees and wild flowers, so much so that a cull is being called for.

Some time passes in the forest. The fingerposts tell me I'm correctly on the East Munster Way, but when I check the map I can't recall taking the twists and turns shown. A village appears mysteriously down to my right – I check the map again but no village is shown (unless one has been built since the map was printed four years ago). The only village shown is Kilsheelan – my destination, but the last sign I saw pointed onward, so onward I go. At a Y-junction of the tracks, the top track climbs slightly whilst the lower one descends more steeply – but neither is signposted. I've missed a sign – so back I go for 15 minutes until I reach the last one I'd seen. It points the way I went (correctly), so 15 minutes later I'm back at the Y-junction. In such situations my principle is always to take the higher track, so I do – onward. After another 10 minutes and at a further junction of tracks there are again no signs, so I double back to the last Y-junction and this time take the descending track. In another 10 minutes I reach still another track junction with no signs. I've been too lazy to get the compass out of the backpack, but now, as instinct tells me I'm heading west and the wrong way – I check it. Yes, west I'm going. By now I'm confused and fed up, *as you probably are* reading this account. I've given up on the map long ago. The track I now take also deceivingly starts off going west before gradually swinging to the desired east. I walk on for about 15 minutes and then it encouragingly begins to descend fairly steeply, whence I come across a notice pinned to a tree.

The notice is headed 'COILLTE' (which I later discover is a company that was formed in 1988 to replace the Forestry Commission). It reads that, in keeping with open forest policy, walkers are welcome, but warns that tree felling is taking place. It then makes what I interpret to be a convoluted apology: 'To ensure your safety, necessary diversions or closures have been put in place for the duration of these operations'. It's a pity a similar notice wasn't prominently displayed at the end of the forest I'd entered – at least then I'd have known *why* I was about to get lost. Thanks a lot, Coillte.

I've spent around three hours in Kilsheelan woods (mostly lost) and take a very late packed sandwich lunch at Kilsheelan Bridge, sitting on a bench by the Suir, back in County Tipperary. My feet are sore from the stone forest tracks and I'm glad that the remaining 12km will be on a towpath along the banks of the river.

I'm meeting an old friend for a drink in Tipperary tonight and to make it on time I need to catch the 17.10 bus from Carrick; there should be enough time to complete the walk comfortably. The grassy path has recently been mown and I figure it'll be an easy walk to Carrick – but then the manicured lawn ends and the path is, as Paddy Dillon describes, 'rougher and covered with nettles and brambles'. What he doesn't say is that I should have packed a machete. I'm just glad I'd decided against wearing shorts. Sometimes I'm obliged to walk with arms extended above my head to avoid the stingers. The ground beneath the undergrowth is rutted and I have difficulty staying upright, then – as I try to round a fallen tree encroaching the path – I stumble, fall, twist my left ankle and cut my arm. I plough on painfully, tentatively and more carefully through the long grass, coming to a dilapidated hut. Inside is a poster headed 'NO HYDRO ON GLASHA'. It's an appeal to the fishermen of Clonmel and Carrick-on-Suir angling clubs to oppose the construction of a proposed hydro-electric scheme on the River Glasha, a tributary of the Suir that joins it just to the east of Kilsheelan, by Glen Bridge.

Planning permission for the scheme was granted in 2011, and Fine Gael's Minister of State at the Department of the Environment, Community and Local Government – Paudie Coffey – stated in June 2013 that: 'no objections had been lodged and fisheries bodies and others have all expressed support'. Paudie claimed that the scheme is all part of the plan to help Ireland reach renewable energy targets that it must achieve by 2020, but clearly he's not hacked his way through the undergrowth on the banks of the Suir to hear the fishermen's concerns. These include claims that salmon stocks will be reduced due to the loss of spawning pools, that the scheme's proposed weir will increase oxygen levels in the water and adversely affect the river's ecology and that the associated tree felling will destabilise the embankments and cause siltation and damage to the spawning beds.

I take off my tee shirt for a time as it's so hot now and is sticking to my back under the rucksack.

This stretch of river was, during the potato famine, one of the most dangerous in the country. Grain was regularly taken by barge from Clonmel to Carrick for export and during this journey the barges were susceptible to ambush. Thereafter they were escorted by a convoy of warships accompanied by cavalry and infantry.

Closer to Carrick the long grass turns again to the short mowed variety on reaching the fishing beats. A beat is a measured stretch of river within which an angler is given a set amount of time to fish before he must move on along the river to the next beat. Some beats are better than others – the ones having deep pools in which the salmon rest – and anglers sometimes linger in these. A sign stapled to a tree requests that beats are fished straight through at a reasonable pace to give everyone a sporting chance of making a catch. Atlantic salmon are the main catch here, although the brown trout is also abundant.

The salmon (known as 'king of fish') remains in the river or stream of its birth for the first three years of its life, firstly as an egg laid in a nest created in the gravel by the female. In early summer the baby salmon emerge as a fry; in its second year it develops into a parr with a spotted skin for river camouflage. In its third year it turns into a smolt and becomes bluish along the upper half of its body and silvery along its sides. When it finds a mirror and realises it's made this spectacular change to enable it to blend into the background of an ocean, it scoots off down the Suir to find one – namely the North Atlantic. It stays up in the cold waters of Greenland, Iceland and the Faroe Islands for between one and four years before returning to its original river or stream to spawn. After this, the poor old fish is so knackered that it pegs out soon after – unless that is it's already been caught by an Irish angler.

A couple of wader-clad anglers appear in mid-river as I make the last mile (I mean 1.6093km) to Carrick and the Old Bridge comes into view. The eight-arched bridge appeared in William Petty's Down Survey of 1656, so it was built before then – it's thought in around 1447. It's the end point of today's walk for me, but not quite the end of the East Munster Way which starts or finishes in Castle Park opposite Ormonde Castle. From the bridge I walk into the centre of town and make my way back to Park Side in good time to sip an ice-cold can of drink whilst I sit and wait for the bus. It arrives promptly at 17.10.

Tuesday 17th June – Carrick-on-Suir

Today, there is no walking for me – all because of two Carrick-born brothers Tom and Paddy.

They bought an old banger in Cleveland, Ohio and set out to drive to California but, soon after they'd started, the car broke down. So, being more or less broke, instead of taking the long drive west, they decided to make their way east and finished up in Greenwich Village, New York City. They were joined there later by their brother Bobby who returned to Ireland in 1955 to run his father's insurance business. His place was taken by the youngest of the four brothers – Liam. They were all aspiring actors, but were to become unexpectedly famous as singers.

A decade passed by before they made the big time when, billed as The Clancy Brothers and Tommy Makem, brothers Tom, Paddy, and Liam became part of the folk music revival of the early 1960s. A young kid called Bob Dylan followed them around the Village, pestered them for advice, studied their singing style and was inspired by their songs of Irish rebellion.

I became a Dylan fan when I first heard him in 1963. I bought Dylan's *The Freewheelin' Bob Dylan* album when it was first issued in 1963 together with his eponymous album released the previous year. Like many other teenagers I was completely hooked and purchased *The Times They Are A Changin'* album as soon as it came out, in 1964. I still have them. They would probably be quite valuable now if I hadn't worn them out with constant plays trying to learn the words. So this is why today there is no walking for me – the link between Dylan and the Clancy Brothers is the reason I'm stopping over the day in Carrick. I'm meeting Bobby Clancy's son, Finbarr, who's a member of an Irish folk group The High Kings.

When I discovered that the Clancys originated from Carrick-on-Suir and their links with Dylan it connected so sharply with my past that I knew I *had* to try to meet one of the family. I made several unsuccessful attempts on the Internet then, in almost a last throw of the dice, emailed Carrick Heritage Centre (but without much hope). It turned out that I'd rolled a six – Patsy, the manager, would arrange to introduce me to Finbarr.

Two ladies are standing behind the counter in the heritage centre and I ask if one of them is Patsy. This gets a laugh from both of them – which I don't quite understand – until I meet Patsy, who turns out to be a bloke. Finbarr Clancy shakes my hand and smiles warmly and some of my nervousness disappears. We go for a coffee and cross Main Street to the Carraig Hotel. Patsy buys the coffees and tells me that he's indebted to the Clancys because in 1994 the heritage centre was in some financial trouble and the brothers performed a concert and donated all the money raised to the centre. I confess to him that I'd pictured in my mind during our email correspondence that he was a woman, and Patsy tells me that some Canadians he'd met found his name absolutely incredulous and said that he'd have had some very strange looks and encounters in Canada with a name like that. In Ireland it's a common abbreviation for Patrick.

I have a short list of questions for Finbarr scribbled on a piece of paper and pull it from my rucksack, at which point Patsy leaves us to chat by ourselves. Finbarr tells me that he was an electrician by profession but had originally always wanted to become a rock musician. His dad, Bobby, who played five-string banjo, used to practise in a bedroom each day after dinner and Finbarr, at the age of nine, and being a bit curious, peeked around the door one day. Bobby asked if he'd like to learn a bit and that started him playing.

I ask him about his dad, who'd taken the place of Tommy Makem in the Clancy group when Tommy Makem left in 1969. He tells me that Bobby was supposed to do a farewell tour of the United States with the rest of the Clancy brothers in 1996 but was scheduled to have a quadruple heart operation. So because, like his dad, Finbarr also played five-string banjo, Bobby asked him if he'd take his place. It was during this tour that Finbarr decided to have a go at singing, taking the third verse of the song 'Finnegan's Wake'.

Finbarr tells me that he was very worried about his singing role and was advised to make sure that he delivered clearly and well by opening his mouth really wide.

'I was so nervous,' he admits, 'that I began to stutter.'

'Do you have any interesting stories about your dad?' I ask.

'Yes,' says Finbarr. 'He played at Bob Dylan's concert to celebrate Dylan's 30 years with Columbia in Manhattan and he shared a dressing room with Rolling Stones' Ronnie Wood, and Stevie Wonder. He got on really well with Ronnie; they had a similar sense of humour. He had a place over here near Kildare and one day shortly after the concert the phone rings, I pick it up, and it's Ron. He's having a party at his place and wants Bobby to come.' Finbarr takes a sip of coffee.

'I would have given my right arm to have gone,' he says, smiling, 'but Dad declined the invitation because he said he had a gig on. The gig was something he did just down the road every week and he could easily have missed it – I couldn't believe he'd done that!' I don't believe it either!

I check my list and ask Finbarr how Irish folk songs are generally acquired.

'Many are passed down orally through the family,' he says, 'or passed around in a particular locality. Dad used to collect songs – he had one of the first reel-to-reel tape recorders in the country that he'd lug around.' I recall then having read in Liam Clancy's autobiographical book *Memoirs of an Irish Troubadour* that he and Bobby went on a momentous collecting trip in 1955.

Bobby had returned to Carrick, having travelled extensively in Europe and had spent some time in New York with older brothers Tom and Paddy – singing in Saturday night concerts. Liam had also recently returned home from a not too brilliant job with an insurance company in Dublin. They were both helping out in their father's insurance business. Paddy and Tom, who were both still in New York, suggested to two American women who were about to visit Ireland, that Bobby's mother had some wonderful children's songs. The pair turned up at the Clancy household in Carrick out of the blue one summer's day and what transpired was to sow the seeds from which sprang The Clancy Brothers and Tommy Makem. The four – Diane Hamilton (a rather rich lady), Catherine Write (a rather large lady), Liam and Bobby set off in a rented car to tour Ireland and gather songs.

In County Kerry they met the legendary fiddle player Pádraig

O'Keefe who unfortunately had drunk himself into debt and had been forced to pawn his fiddle. Although the quartet paid the ransom to get his instrument back he was apparently a bit rusty – until that is he'd had a few whiskys, when the fiddle suddenly began to purr like a kitten that'd just got the cream.

In Letterkenny, County Donegal the group met and recorded Paddy Tunney who was himself a collector of songs, many of which have now become folk standards. Amongst other labels given to Paddy was that of political activist (he spent time in gaol), poet, songwriter, author and diddler – a word that has several meanings, none of which are very complementary. In Gaelic folk terms though a diddler is another term for one who lilts – a tune from the mouth, usually with undefined lyrics, practiced by those who unfortunately and for whatever reason, are without an instrument.

Over the Northern Ireland border in Keady, County Armagh they visited Sarah Makem's house, gathering and recording some of her large collection of songs. Sarah was a singer married to fiddle player Peter, and Liam struck up a close friendship with their youngest son Tommy, who was planning to go off to America to pursue an acting career. The pair stayed in touch, and many years later the friendship forged during this visit would change both their fortunes in ways they couldn't then guess. Many of the songs gathered in Ireland were later incorporated in the Clancys' repertoire

During the trip it soon became apparent that Diane Hamilton had taken a shine to Liam Clancy. She talked him into joining Catherine and her on an extension of their collecting tour to Scotland. There Liam, Diane and Catherine Write met poet and folk song collector Hamish Henderson in Edinburgh who took them over to Barra in the Outer Hebrides and acted as their musical guide – a role he'd once played for Alan Lomax.

Lomax was a renowned American collector of folk music who spent most of his life promoting its growth and appreciation. As far back as 1937 he'd been appointed Assistant in Charge of the Archive of American Folk Song, and had set about actively expanding its holdings by undertaking many field trips throughout the world. From Ireland, England and Scotland alone he collected a three-volume, six-disc series of field recordings for Columbia Records. He also produced concerts and radio shows and introduced the general public to such artists as Woody Guthrie, Lead Belly, Josh White, Burl Ives and Pete Seeger. It was Lomax too who was one of the first to introduce Bob Dylan to folk music.

Dylan in his pre-fame days (and after), like many others, 'adapted' songs from older versions (some people say borrowed, others say stole). What I didn't realise then was that one of my favourite tracks: 'Restless Farewell' was, let's say – adapted, from 'The Parting Glass' that had been recorded by The Clancy Brothers and Tommy Makem on their 1959 album release *Come Fill Your Glass With Us*.

Finbarr and I talk of course about the Clancy Brothers.

'They were just in the right place at the right time,' Finbarr affirms, 'they didn't know they were in the middle of a folk revival. Paddy was amazed when they referred to him as a folk singer,' he chuckles. 'They were actors really, but found they could get $80 from singing when they only made $10 from acting – it was a no-brainer.'

The rise to fame of The Clancy Brothers and Tommy Makem is well documented. Diane Hamilton had fallen for Liam 11 years her junior and wanted him to become her third husband (she was divorced from the first two). Her maiden name was Guggenheim and she was the daughter of millionaire Harry, who'd made his money in mining. She was loaded, and she knew that one of Liam's ambitions was to learn about film-making, so she paid for his passage to New York. He arrived there in January 1956.

Diane had started Tradition Records and Paddy ran the company, becoming its president and director. Their first release, the album *The Lark in the Morning*, contained the material from the field trip recorded on the portable recording kit that Bobby and Liam had lugged in and out of the rented car. Tommy Makem had also migrated to the US and in 1956 went to New York to see a St Patrick's Day parade – and stayed there, where he met up with Tom, Paddy and Liam (again). Here, at the suggestion of a professor of folklore from Columbia University, they recorded and released *The Rising of the Moon*, an album of Irish rebel songs.

In March 1958 Tommy moved to New York permanently to join Tom and Liam in their acting career endeavours. They were still sometimes acting, but also sang at The White Horse Tavern in Greenwich Village. It was where it all happened, and had been the hangout of amongst others, Jack Kerouac – who'd been thrown out a few times, and Dylan Thomas, who had, it's claimed, committed alcoholic suicide there. The group (as they would to become), made a second album – *Come Fill Your Glass with Us* which got the acclaimed attention of the music press and which started their rise to fame.

So, by the beginning of 1961, the group were being booked for exclusive nightclubs like The Blue Angel in Manhattan, with its red-carpeted entrance and rich clientele. A review in *The Village Voice* dated 23rd February 1961 headlined: 'Clancys Break for Uptown, Blast into Blue Angel'. It was reported that whisperings of disapproval were heard at first amongst the elegant audience because the group apparently hadn't been able to afford the purchase of tuxedos to replace their Aran sweaters their mother had sent them from Carrick. But the boys soon won over most of the audience. It was at one of these appearances at The Blue Angel that they got scouted for *The Ed Sullivan Show*.

They appeared in the American television show in front of an audience of 80 million for a record-breaking 16 minutes because the evening's star performer had bowed out. Those who'd previously appeared on the show included Elvis Presley and Buddy Holly; those soon to appear would include the Beatles, the Rolling Stones and Bob Dylan.

William of Orange had camped the night with his army outside the walls of Carrick-on-Suir prior to marching on Limerick in 1690. William Street was named after the Dutchman. It's where Finbarr and I are now heading. On the way, I tell him about my interest in Dylan. He tells me a story:

'Dylan played Dublin,' he says, 'I think in about 1995 and a lady from Limerick was a huge Dylan fan. She hung around outside his hotel trying to get to speak to him. So she's thinking of an original line that will get his attention. He of course had his bodyguards with him. So she said that *she* was a poet too and wrote songs.'

We cross Main Street and walk along New Lane. Finbarr continues: 'Dylan stopped and asked her to sing the start of one of her compositions, which she did, and they walked around Dublin together for a couple of hours chatting. He asked her if she knew 'The Fox Went Out on a Chilly Night' – which she didn't. If she'd have known it, he'd have asked her to join him to sing it as the opening number in his concert that night.'

We arrive at 4 William Street.

'She knows it now!' Finbarr adds with a smile.

He tells me some history of the terraced house and how it's been altered since the brothers had lived there as boys. On the wall, a plaque confirms it was the family home of the four famous brothers. A few doors along, on the wall of the end terrace house a large mural depict the Clancys in a pub. Either side of the group portrait appear the words and music of 'The Parting Glass' – the very song that for me linked the Clancys with Dylan; it's a perfect conclusion.

We go our separate ways with a handshake and my thanks, at the back of the heritage centre. Inside I spend a long time looking at the comprehensive display of Clancy memorabilia, together with other local history collections. The morning has vanished quickly. I take lunch at a pub on Main Street and the friendly barman, who's possibly also the landlord, asks if I've visited Ormonde Castle. He tells me that entry is free, which clinches it.

Thomas Butler, the 10th Earl of Ormonde was the cousin of Queen Elizabeth I through the marriage of Margaret Butler to William Boleyn (father of ill-fated Anne). They had become friends in childhood and thereafter always remained close. Thomas had a Tudor manor house added to the original castle, furnishing it expensively, so that Elizabeth would have a comfortable place to stay when she visited him in Ireland. She never came. Thomas died there in 1614, 11 years after her death.

The receptionist asks me to wait for the commencement of the guided tour of the castle. I don't have to wait long because it soon becomes apparent I'm likely to be the only taker. Robert is my guide; he hails originally from London and tells me he's only been doing the job for three weeks. I opt for the shortened tour and am led around the rooms, some of which contain beautiful decorative plasterwork. We pause in each room whilst he delivers a polished elucidation. One room extends the whole length of the building and Robert informs me that it was an exercise room used by the gentry.

'Why didn't they use the grounds outside?' I ask.

'That would have meant they'd have had to mix with the peasants,' he explains. 'The gentry always exercised indoors so that they'd remain pale. Only the common folk had tans in those days.' We enter a bedroom, and Robert reveals that the four-poster bed, which is very high off the ground, was that height to prevent rats from nesting underneath. The nobility, he adds, always slept sitting up because lying down was something you only did when you were dead. They would be watched over by a servant who'd sit up all night – making sure that a rat didn't climb up a bedpost. As the tour ends and I leave, Robert – perhaps slightly homesick – calls out:

'Give my regards to England.'

Thirteen
The South Leinster Way

'O then, tell me Seán O'Farrell, tell me why you hurry so'
'Hush, me Buachall hush and listen'. And his cheeks were all aglow.
I bear orders from the captain get you ready quick and soon
For the pikes must be together at the rising of the moon'.
From: *The Rising of the Moon* by J.K. Casey

Wednesday 18th June – Carrick-on-Suir to Mullinavat
I leave the campsite at 8.15am and plan to get back by catching a
bus from Mullinavat and another from Waterford, thus avoiding
a long and complicated bike ride. I start out a second time 20
minutes later having initially forgotten to pack the most essential
item – water. The local radio this morning said the temperature
would reach 26 degrees.

The South Leinster Way meets the East Munster Way in Castle
Park, Carrick, opposite Ormonde Castle. The River Suir runs south-
east from there to reach Waterford and flow on into the Celtic Sea.
There are no signs for the Way as I leave Carrick, so I rely upon book
and map. The map shows the Way shooting off north on a boreen
in a loop for two kilometres to pass the tiny settlement of Tinvane
before returning to the N24. A cyclist sees me puzzling over the map
and asks:

'Are you alright?'

'I would be if I knew where I was going,' I say.

It seems I've missed the turning. No surprise there then. I walk
on to where the boreen rejoins the main road and then double
back for about a kilometre to do the bit I've missed. A narrow
grassy path up an embankment links the N24 with the boreen;
it's the only off-tarmac walking I shall see all day. I'm now in
County Kilkenny, the fifth county I shall walk in. Returning to the
N24, I cross the road onto an arboured lane, following a sign for
Tybroughney (which – on what is perhaps my *Irish* map – is shown

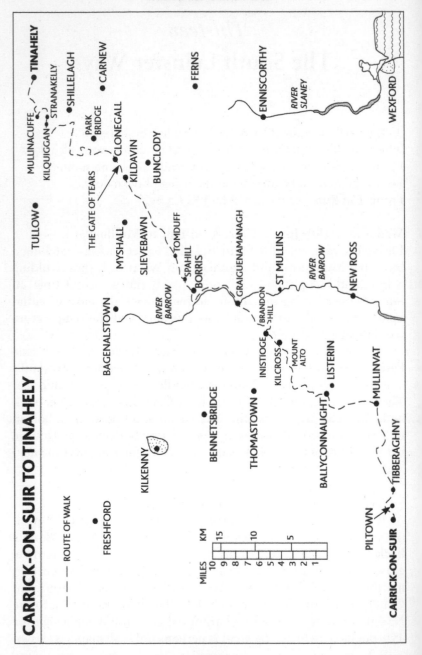

CARRICK-ON-SUIR TO TINAHELY

as Tibberaghny). It's a pleasant enough walk, the sun dappling through the grove onto the lane and flickering across my eyes. A notice pinned to a tree confirms my arrival at the once thriving village, not much of which I can find; it reads 'Tybroughney – Graveyard & Church Ruin – 6th century monastery of St Modomnoc who brought the first bees to Ireland'.

My grandmother used to say that talking to oneself was the first sign of silliness that would eventually get you sent to an asylum. St Modomnoc, then should have been well on his way to a funny-farm instead of a monastery. Because although not exactly talking to himself, he *did* talk to his bees. The story goes that he'd gone to Menevia in Wales to train for the priesthood under St David and had been hived-off to a corner of the monastery to take care of bees. Bees were kept by the monks for their honey, for beeswax from which was made candles and to make mead, which the monks consumed in liberal quantities during their less spiritual moments. Modomnoc kept the bees lovingly in wickerwork baskets called skeps. There he talked to them, asking them which flowers they liked the best. Then he buzzed about planting their favourite ones. The bees became fond of Modomnoc's soft words and never stung him; they became very much attached to him in fact. At the end of his studies Modomnoc went to the bees and told them sadly that he'd have to leave them. Twice he boarded a ship to sail back to Ireland and on both occasions the bees swarmed aboard the vessel so that it was forced to turn back. The Abbot by now was becoming fed up with this and told the ship's captain to sail on to Ireland if they came aboard a third time. This they did – and that's how Modomnoc is said to have brought bees to Ireland.

On reaching a T-junction at the village of Piltown a sign for the South Leister Way points right. At a sharp bend in the road a car swerves and narrowly misses hitting me – his window is open – he swears. I pass a graveyard; many of those buried beneath the gravestones were younger than I am now when they died and that, together with the close encounter on the bend, makes me ponder my mortality. In this gloomy mood I walk on for three kilometres, carefully checking for South Leinster Way signs. There seems little accord between the surroundings and features on the map. It's when I cross new road workings of what will become a bypass that I have grave doubts that I'm going in the right direction; the compass confirms I'm incorrectly walking south.

At a petrol station a man is filling a plastic container with petrol. I show him the map and incredibly it seems I'm in Fiddown, three kilometres in the wrong direction. He offers me a lift back to Piltown. I decline and walk away – then, remembering the uninteresting slog I've just made, I rush back and accept, just as he's about to pull away. I tell him that I'm heading for Mullinavat and he drops me back at the T-junction in Piltown almost an hour after I've left it. I should have taken a left turn a few metres after the junction, but there's no South Leinster Way sign, and neither the book nor map is very clear.

I climb over a gate to take lunch in a field of tall grass and buttercups with a good view over the river valley to the distant peak of Tower Hill. The remainder of the day's walk is uneventful. It's hot and humid road walking and I use up my last supply of water. There's no sign of human life until just before Mullinavat, where a yokel is trying to persuade a limping and reluctant cow to progress along the road by shouting and wildly waving his stick in the air.

I arrive in Mullinavat earlier than expected at around 2.15pm having just missed the bus. The next one is in almost two hours' time. In the local grocery shop I ask where the bus stop is.

'There's no actual stop,' the assistant says dubiously, 'if you can see one coming, just wave him down.' I do just that.

Thursday 19th June – Mullinavat to Mount Alto
Last night I checked Paddy's book; the next section to Inistioge is 30km. I'm not worried by the walking, but there's no direct or easy cycle route back to Mullinavat. The South Leinster Way goes north and east to a crossroads near the hamlet of Ballyconnaught before winding its way north again to Inistioge. I decide to break the walk at Ballyconnaught simply because I want to catch a World Cup football match on TV in which England play Uruguay. The decision will mean I'll have to walk further than planned tomorrow in order to make a tentative appointment with members of the Graiguenamanagh Historical Society on Saturday.

I drive the camper to a crossroads on the R704 a kilometre

south-east of Ballyconnaught (at a place that I later learn is Listerin), chain up the bike, buy sandwiches at the general store and drive back to Mullinavat, parking in the car park of The Rising Sun pub. By 10.30am I'm on the E8, Irish Coast to Coast Walk and South Leinster Way (all the same path).

The boreen becomes a track and then enters an area of deforestation before the unfettered forest closes in. A red squirrel barrels along towards me. I freeze. A few metres before it gets to me it freezes too and turns sideways to get a good view of the strange creature standing in its path – it's a wonderfully warm reddish-brown colour. Then, having ascertained that I must be a threat, it suddenly darts off the track into woodland.

Bees are busy pollinating red clover. I try to photograph one, but it's away too quickly to the next plant. Apparently there are around 100 native bee species in Ireland – somebody has obviously made a closer study of them than I'm attempting now; the number of species rather jeopardises the St Modomnoc theory, unless they have since somehow mutated. I watch intently as my bee of indeterminate species is first out and then in the clover – one plant after another. They're useful little insects, bees – helping to sustain fruit and vegetables as well as plants like red clover. It's an interesting herb; claimed to be useful in treating anything from sexually transmitted diseases to hot flushes, whooping cough and cancer, as well as being utilised as a green manure to increase soil fertility. The value of a bee's pollination is said to be worth 10 times that of its honey production (a sweet enough statistic in itself). Somebody has also obscurely calculated that it takes 30,000 bees to pollinate an acre of fruit trees. But the bee population is worryingly in decline, threatened by climate change, habitat loss and pesticides. Over half the species have declined over the last 35 years; 42 species by more than 50%. And bees are not yet protected by law in the Republic.

I arrive at Ballyconnaught at 2.15pm, far too early to finish for the day and decide to press on until around five o'clock, by which time I must turn around (in order to see the game) and walk back to collect the bike. I'm hoping to make it past Mount Alto to meet a road and return to Listerin by it via a different route.

Quickening the pace, I'm hindered only by forced detours over and around fallen trees in the forest. I've seen nobody again all day, but in a remote clearing come across the charred remains of rubbish and a half-burnt wooden pallet. How and why anybody would want to manoeuvre a vehicle here for that purpose is a mystery.

By 4.45pm I meet the road, where a sign indicates it's only 3km to Inistioge (although it's longer walking along the South-Leinster Way). From Listerin I bike the R704 back to Mullinavat to arrive at just after six o'clock, leaving me just enough time to change, eat a plate of fish and chips in The Rising Sun and see England kick off at eight o'clock against Uruguay. I don't know why I bother; they lose 2-1 to 'nipper' Suarez goals.

Friday 20th June – Mount Alto to Graiguenamanagh

I've driven to Graiguenamanagh where there's a steep and persistently uphill climb out of it. It's a long time before I attempt to pedal. I don't know which is worse, pushing the bike uphill or attempting to brake on the downhill stretch into Inistioge. I say 'attempting to brake' because the brakes obviously need some attention, and to slow down I have to resort to trawling my feet along the ground, like an anchor attempting to gain purchase in a sandbank.

I turn left at Inistioge to bike the 3km to yesterday's finish point. It's a gradual uphill haul and third gear is the highest I can manage. But the brown South Leinster Way signpost I'm expecting to see fails to appear. The road sign to New Ross I'd seen yesterday at the end of the walk indicated it was 13km so, when I see an 11km signpost, I know I've somehow gone wrong. So I dismount and pull out the map. With the aid of a lady motorist, I establish that though heading towards New Ross, I'm stupidly on the wrong side of the River Nore. I've misread the map – again!

'Never mind,' the lady says, reassuringly, 'it's all downhill into Inistioge.' This I know. The problem is: it's all steeply uphill again out of the village on the *correct* road (the establishment of which takes a bit of head scratching in Inistioge Square). By the time I start to walk on the South Leinster Way it's gone 11 and I've been with the bike (but not always on it) for over two hours.

I make the leafy walk through Woodstock Park and along the hidden banks of the River Nore back to Inistioge in just over an hour – in time for a pint of lager shandy taken outside O'Donnell's pub in the Square.

After crossing the Nore there's a stiff climb up a road to Kilcross; then on up a stony path and rutted cart track before I reach a wider track and Brandon Hill comes into view. No chance of getting lost, although the odd fingerpost is unhelpfully buried within a sea of fern. I eat my sandwiches at a cross-track clearing and wind my way up through a forest.

The faint sound of machinery gradually increases in volume until I glimpse through the trees its source – a dinosaur monster of a tree demolition device known as a harvester. On the end of its long articulated hydraulic neck a greedy felling head ambushes a tree trunk and hugs it at its base before severing it rudely from its roots, stripping it of its branches and slicing it into precisely measured portions. It does all this in just seconds. Further along, another tyrannosaur is immersed in the sunlight it's just created from denuding another section of the forest. These machines were developed in Scandinavia (Finland in the main) and are used there extensively; they're the finale of a progression that began with an axe, progressed to a two-man crosscut saw and then to a chainsaw.

How many traditional lumberjacks have harvesters replaced? I don't know but, according to statistics produced by CareerCast, a US jobs agency, lumberjacks are no longer in tune with Monty Python's lumberjack song – they are no longer it seems 'OK' (even if they don't now put on women's clothing and hang around in bars). CareerCast put them bottom of their 2014 jobs list at number 200. The list is created based upon the criteria of stress, income levels and job opportunities. The latter is declining it seems because of a reduction in wood pulping for paper manufacture due to digitisation. Safety is another issue: to be a lumberjack is still listed (by listverse.com) as the fourth most fatal occupation after cell phone tower workers, commercial fishermen and dust crop pilots.

But the forestry industry in Ireland confounds this negative feel. Forests had, by 1903, been depleted over the years by both industrialisation and the creation of agricultural land, and stood at a low of 1.5% of the total land area; today it stands at around 11%. Forestry is an important contributor to the Irish economy and has been forecast to grow by a factor of 2.6 between 2011 and 2028. Financial assistance from the European Union, providing grants to private landowners, has assisted in this growth, whilst its climate and soil means that Ireland can grow many tree species faster than other European countries – so lumberjacking probably is 'OK' in Ireland (Michael Palin will be glad to know).

I come out of the forest to a wonderful view down across a profusion of foxgloves to the town of Graiguenamanagh. But then an incorrectly selected or planted fingerpost confuses me as it points towards dense undergrowth and trees that disappear down a steep slope. After an attempt to negotiate a way through I retreat and continue on the stony track which does indeed eventually swing sharply left in the direction indicated by the dodgy fingerpost – after about 100 metres. The track drops down steeply to a house at a place called Deerpark. Here, an elderly man with his lady in a car asks me if it's possible to drive uphill and be able to turn the car around.

'I wouldn't advise it,' I say.

'Is there anything to see?' he asks.

'Good views, but you'll need to walk,' I tell him.

'I think I'll give it a miss then,' he says, smiling – but drives off up around the bend anyway. Ten minutes later he's up behind and then alongside me.

'Do you want a lift to the end of the road?' he asks. By this time of the day it's a tempting offer, as the walk into Graiguenamanagh will be pretty uninspiring, but it will break one of my ground rules.

'No thanks – I'm walking.' Neither of them quite understand. The car roars off.

Saturday 21st June – Graiguenamanagh

I'm standing outside Doran's Super Valu, the only supermarket in town according to David Flynn, whom I'm waiting to meet. He's secretary of the town's Historical Society. I made contact with him via Graiguenamanagh library and then by email because I became intrigued by the rebellion of 1798 and by a certain General Thomas Cloney who took part in it and who lived in Graiguenamanagh for 48 of his 76 years.

David is a few minutes late and, as I have no idea what he

looks like, I speak to several likely but incorrect and bemused candidates before the bearded, bespectacled real David makes himself known. A moment later he introduces me to Owen Doyle, an elderly gent and chairman of the Society. We stroll off together to General Cloney's house, the first stop on a planned guided tour around the town. When arrangements had been made for my visit, Cloney's house had been occupied for many years by John Joyce, a renowned local historian and author of books about both Graiguenamanagh and Cloney. I'm looking forward to meeting him. Unfortunately John has died a month ago and his son, who would have shown us around the house, has gone off on holiday early this very morning. We reach the house and look up at a plaque on the wall that reads:

General Thomas Cloncy
1774–1850
United Irishman, Rebel Leader
And lifelong labourer in Ireland's Cause
Lived here

John Joyce made a detailed study of Cloney and was convinced that, although subsequently denying any premeditated participation in the rebellion, as recorded in his 'succinctly' titled record: *A narrative of those transactions in the county of Wexford in which the Author was engaged in the awful year of 1798*, Cloney was indeed a colonel in the underground United Irishman organisation *prior* to 1798.

Cloney was born into an affluent family and lived with his father at Moneyhore, a few miles west of Enniscorthy. His father had connections with Wexford's landed proprietors; he was a middleman, who rented land from them to farm and graze cattle and sheep. Although a Catholic, Thomas socialised equally well with his Protestant neighbours, but during the events of 1798 he associated very much with members of families similar to himself – Catholic middlemen and farmers.

The Society of United Irishmen was founded in 1791, a century after the Treaty of Limerick which ended the Williamite War in

Ireland and saw the disbandment of the Jacobite army. During that century Protestant domination of Irish affairs was at first absolute, enforced by the passing of the Penal Laws that stopped Catholics, who comprised 70% of the population (and also Presbyterians), from having any sort of power in running the country. They were prevented not only from attending parliament and voting, but also from entering the legal profession, the navy, any public bodies and Trinity College, Dublin. They were also not allowed to purchase, inherit or be gifted land and could only hold short-term leases. There was even a restriction on the quality of horse they could own, limited to a value of £5. So if a Protestant fancied a Catholic's horse he could force its sale for that amount. If he fancied a Catholic lady though, he would have to convince her to become a Protestant in order to marry her – there was no chance of him becoming a Catholic because it was a capital offence for anyone found to be involved in such a conversion. Senior Catholic clergy were banished and could be hanged, drawn and quartered if they returned to Ireland – a good enough incentive I would say not to do so.

Things got no better for the Catholics when William of Orange died in 1702 and Queen Anne began her brief reign.

Gradual change began around 1745 with the suspension of some of the Penal Laws (which actually remained on the statute book until 1829). These laws were primarily designed to ensure Protestants retained lands and goods obtained from Catholics, but they were also a defensive strategy against the potential rising of the Jacobeans – a threat that was largely quashed in 1746 on bleak Culloden Moor near Inverness in Scotland with the crushing defeat of Bonny Prince Charlie.

There was, also around this time, a change in the fortunes of the country, which saw increased economic, agricultural and population growth. This remained a purely theoretical prosperity for the peasantry though, whose woes increased as pastoral land expanded and poor tenant farmers were squeezed onto diminishing plots. The Enclosure Acts which were created so that landowners could charge higher tithes to tenant farmers and peasants reinforced their grievances and resulted in the formation of agrarian protest movements.

In 1761, one such group in County Tipperary called the Whiteboys (because they wore linen smocks) retaliated by going out nightly to rip down fences, dig up crops and maim animals. The authorities called them 'Levellers' for obvious reasons. They were an enterprising bunch who had on occasion extended their activities to pulling people out of their beds and forcing them naked into a pit they'd previously filled with water and briers. The Whiteboys were active in the parish of Graiguenamanagh between 1770 and 1832.

Events from elsewhere in the world began to be felt in Ireland too. In 1775, what would later be known as the American War of Independence kicked off, leading eight years later to King George III finally throwing in the towel and recognising the new republic. During this war the French and Spanish sided with the Americans and their ships became ever more evident around the Irish coastline, raising the threat of invasion.

The French Revolution too became the catalyst for a change of thought and attitude in Ireland; France was the leading Catholic power in Europe and her people had overthrown the aristocracy! Its potential with regard to Ireland was not lost on Wolfe Tone, who quickly saw the light, describing the Revolution in 1791 as 'the morning star of liberty to Ireland'.

Theobald Wolfe Tone was an Anglican, born in 1763 and descended from an affluent French family. As a youth he'd wanted to join the British army in America, but respect for his father's views curtailed this idea. Instead he attended for a short time a Bachelor of Arts course at Dublin University before quitting, travelling to London and becoming a law student – a profession for which he had no appetite. It was whilst there in 1788, aged 24, that he, along with his brother, devised a plan to form a military colony on one of the British Sandwich Islands (now Hawaii). Having researched the possibility extensively, he wrote first a memorandum and then a letter to Pitt, with his recommendations. Pitt, it seems, completely ignored both. Tone recorded in his autobiography: 'In my anger I made something like a vow, that, if ever I had an opportunity, I would make Mr Pitt sorry'. If Tone's proposals had been taken up there's no doubt there would not now be a huge statue of him standing at a corner of St Stephen's Green in Dublin.

As it was, Tone turned his energies and attention to his native country and there he came to prominence following the publication in 1791 of a pamphlet entitled *An Argument on behalf of the Catholics of Ireland*. In this he proposed a radical union of Protestants, Presbyterians and Catholics, an idea that didn't go down too well with the British. His pamphlet led to his being elected an honorary member of the Volunteers of Belfast and in his assisting in framing the first club of United Irishmen – he in fact wrote their declaration.

Things began to get tough for the United Irishmen following the appointment in 1795 of the Earl of Camden as Lord Lieutenant. Camden was an opponent of Roman Catholic emancipation who brought with him to Ireland a tough counter-revolution policy. Members of the United Irishmen soon found themselves in some trouble. The organisation now became a secret society and some of their leaders fled to France and America. Wolfe Tone himself left in May, his aristocratic friends having gained agreement with the government that if he were to leave Ireland he'd not be pursued. He left for Philadelphia and took with him only his wife, family, a sum of money and 600 books. In Belfast, before sailing, he met up with other United Irishmen and together they swore an oath to destroy Britain's rule in Ireland and ensure its independence.

Whilst Tone was in America, sectarian violence flared up in County Armagh between rival agrarian groups – the Protestant Peep o' Day Boys and the Catholic Defenders. The victorious former, who had the magistracy on their side, subsequently formed the Orange Order – and Orange societies began to spring up all over the country. A large number of the Defenders joined the United Irishmen. A friend wrote to Tone that the United Irish organisation was nearly complete and ripe for a rising and urged him to go to France to gain her assistance.

Tone duly sailed from New York on 1st January 1796, leaving his family in America. His discussions in France were protracted (he whiled away time between meetings by writing his autobiography), but Tone eventually got the approval of Lazare Carnot, the director responsible for war. The French angle was to split Ireland from England and so diminish her maritime supremacy.

So it was that in December 1796 Tone sailed from Brest for

Ireland with a French fleet of 17 ships of the line, 26 other vessels and almost 15,000 troops. They headed for Bantry Bay with a view to marching to and occupying Cork, but here Tone's fortunes and that of the French went speedily downhill. A dense fog separated the fleet so that a third of the invasion force, together with General Hoche its commander, became detached and drifted away somewhere out into the Atlantic. On 23rd December the weather changed and a heavy gale blew up; on the 24th the gale turned to a storm. General Grouchy, second-in-command and now in charge was, due to the weather, unable to land, and delayed, whilst supplies began to run low and people chucked up over the side. Tone also felt none too well and languished in his hammock. Perhaps Grouchy's reluctance to land also had something to do with the fact that there were not thousands or even hundreds of Irish revolutionaries on shore, as Tone had promised, waiting to support them but just a few peasants busily boiling up potatoes for English regiments. On 29th December, and after spending seven days battered by the storms in Bantry Bay, Grouchy gave the signal to steer for France. Wolfe Tone's Christmas trip had not been too good.

Following this failed invasion the Earl of Camden appointed General Gerald Lake (who'd seen active service in the American and French Revolutionary wars), to clamp down on any possible insurrection. He carried it out his task ruthlessly. Under the semi-guise of recovering weapons, the campaign terrorised the population; it included house burnings, floggings, arrests and executions. Lake's manpower consisted of the Irish Militia, established in 1793, the Fencibles (mostly of Scottish origin) and yeomanry, a voluntary force of part-timers, trained, paid, armed and equipped by the government. Lake got results; informers were prevalent and large quantities of pikes and muskets were gathered up, together with senior members of the United Irish organisation.

United Irishmen meanwhile bided their time and looked with interest at events elsewhere: at the Nore and Spithead in the spring of 1797, the British navy mutinied; the many pressed United Irishmen amongst them were perhaps pivotally involved. Assistance from France was still expected, which would be the signal for an Irish rebellion. All now seemed to rest with Napoléon Bonaparte; having subdued Austria in March, by the end of the year he began to turn his attention to an invasion of Britain, perhaps via Ireland.

In Ireland, United Irishmen now began to recognise the Defenders as their allies and a merger effectively took place. Contact was also made with Paris. By the end of the year the new organisation of United Irishmen had spread the movement as far south as Cork. But only in Wexford were these arrangements unknown to the authorities.

Prime Minister William Pitt was under some pressure in London not only trying to contain radical parliamentary reformists but also worrying about an invasion, following reports that ships and troops were massing at French ports. Reports also reached him from Camden that insurgents were now regularly carrying out robberies for money and arms, which made him fret that the country would be converted into a Jacobite republic controlled by France. A rebellion coupled with a French invasion seemed a real possibility. Things were evidently on the boil and Pitt decided on 30th March that martial law should be declared throughout the land.

On 23rd May the rising began in Dublin under the leadership of Samuel Neilson; areas of Dublin were allocated to colonels as rendezvous points and orders were given to stop mail coaches as a signal to the rest of the country that the rebellion should commence country wide. But the rough plan had been discovered following the seizure of papers, and the Dublin Castle authorities, now sure of an imminent rising, sent out their spies and placed a large body of the yeomanry at each rendezvous point – which somewhat deterred the rebels and sent them home to their beds. Neilson himself was arrested trying to case Newgate Gaol for an attack. In short, the plan had 'come a cropper'; only some of the mail coaches had been stopped, and those rebel armies that *had* mobilised, in the counties surrounding Dublin, to assist in the rising waited in vain for it to happen.

In County Wexford the United Irishmen were unaware that 23rd May had been nominated as the day of the Rebellion. People there were still exchanging weapons to assure they were protected from the unwelcome attention of the yeomanry. But news of rebellions in the counties of Kildare and Carlow filtered through to Wexford some days later, as did the mass murders of prisoners in County

Wicklow. Because the United Irishman movement in Wexford had been kept relatively secret it had been overlooked as a source of rebellion and had up until then escaped the worst of Lake's terrorising measures. But by May 1798 fear and turmoil reigned. The yeomanry had by now been sent out by the magistrates to intimidate the county and perhaps force the people into rebellion before its leaders were ready and the French could arrive. Thomas Cloney claimed in his *Personal Narrative* that he'd known nothing of a gathering of insurgents at Oulart Hill, six miles north of Enniscorthy on Sunday 26th, but that instead some neighbours had asked him to accompany them to Wilton so they could take the Oath of Allegiance and obtain protections. He claimed that it was not until Tuesday 29th that he'd found out what was afoot... right... OK!

We peer through the window of Cloney's house at the dining table, the original one, Owen assures me, that he'd used up until his death and upon which he probably wrote his memoirs. He's buried a few miles from here at St Mullins, and David and Owen tell me they'll drive me there later today.

We stroll off down Barrow Lane towards the river, passing the site of the fever hospital that endeavoured to cope with epidemics suffered by the area during the first half of the 19th century. We walk along the quay to Graiguenamanagh Bridge – the border between counties Carlow and Kilkenny. The Historical Society have erected a plaque on the bridge to record that part of it which was blown up by crown forces on 13th June 1798 to prevent the insurgents from crossing into Kilkenny and thus entering the town.

Adjacent to the bridge we scramble down by the reedy riverbank to the site of the graving dock. Here in 1821 the Barrow Navigation Company reconstructed the dock that had until then been used by the Norfolk Broads based boat building Washington family. For the next 56 years the BNC used the dock to build horse-drawn barges, utilised amongst other things to transport beet to the sugar factory in Carlow and malting barley to the Guinness factory in Dublin. The barges were constructed with very long rudders to enable them to negotiate the sometime fast flowing waters of the river. They became famously known as 'the long-tailed Barrow boats'. The last one continued in service under various ownerships until about 1955 when she was wrecked on the weir close to here.

The tour continues via Peg Washington's Lane, reputed to be the narrowest lane in the world (more of an alleyway really). It was constructed by a kindly landlord so that widow Peg could get to the waters of the Duiske to do her washing. He made it just 'the width of herself' and no more.

We walk on to the Market House, the scene in 1830 of the first meeting of the anti-tithe campaign which led to the first shots being fired in a conflict later to be known as the Tithe War – which was to spread throughout Ireland. Those working on the land were required to make considerable payments (usually in the form of cattle or similar assets) for the upkeep of the clergy and maintenance of the Protestant Church of Ireland, whilst the Catholic majority also made voluntary payments to their own clergy. Resistance to tithe collections resulted in clashes with yeomen and the Irish Constabulary who tried to enforce them. The issue was taken up by Daniel O'Connell in Parliament and was eventually resolved in 1838 by an act that both reduced the amount payable directly and ruled that the remainder should be converted to a one-time rent charge to create a general fund for clerical costs.

David's car is parked near the Market House and he drives us to the library where he tells the librarian that it's because my request was passed on by them that we're here today. He's anxious to show me the Historical Society's most prized possession: a book of pencil sketches. Obtaining keys and donning white gloves, he opens a glass cabinet and carefully takes out the book. The sketches, produced between 1840 and 1870, are of local scenes drawn by Mary Burchaell of Brandondale House. The wealthy landowning Burchaell family came to the area from Hereford in England in the late 17th century. They became respected leaders of the Protestant community in the town and Chief Magistrates. David explains that John Joyce had discovered that the sketchbook had somehow found its way to Canada and contacted his son there to purchase it for the Society.

We head next to perhaps Graiguenamanagh's most famous landmark – Duiske Abbey. A wedding has just taken place and about half the population of 'Graig' seems to have turned out for it. David tells me that this is normal in Ireland and that there's one other occasion upon which this happens – a funeral. The abbey was founded in 1204 and was first colonised by monks from Wiltshire. Thereafter it endured a chequered history; after being suppressed by Henry VIII it fell into ruin, was partly re-roofed by the Church of Ireland and was finally returned to the Roman Catholic community in 1812. Restoration work continued into the 1980s. As the remaining members of the wedding party leave the abbey, we sneak in and enter a Romanesque processional doorway used originally by the monks, but hidden for years until being discovered by accident in 1916. We descend stone steps into a somewhat creepy vault. Here lies the 13th century stone effigy of a knight in armour. His legs are crossed, not because he's desperate for the loo, but to signify his participation in and survival of crusades. Owen tells me that unfortunately the knight didn't survive too well when being moved down here, as his leg was broken on the way. Another abbey occupant catches my eye as we are about to leave – because he's holding what appears to be a watering can. It turns out that this is indeed the case as he's St Fiacre, who lived for a time in a hermitage nearby and who'd acquired a certain skill with herbs. He is in fact the patron saint of gardeners. It seems that St Fiacre must have been quite an endearing sort of a multitasking chap as he's also claimed by both taxi drivers and VD sufferers as their patron saint.

Across Main Street we stand outside the Assembly Rooms. History is all around us here. It *is* wherever you are, but the Graiguenamanagh Historical Society has brought it to life through their research and their initiation of the heritage trail, which we're still on. David tells me that the Assembly Rooms gained notoriety in 1779 when, following their attendance at a play held there, two heiresses aged 14 and 15 were abducted, this being a common occurrence in Ireland at the time. The men responsible – minor landowners and gentlemen – forced the girls into marriage before they were eventually rescued. The men were pursued, caught, tried in Kilkenny and hanged. Their execution was the last to take place in Ireland for the crime of abduction, and much sympathy for the men was engendered amongst the people of the county.

The River Duiske is a tributary of the Barrow, and we follow it upstream a short distance to the clapper bridge. The bridge was probably first constructed in medieval times and consists of long stone slabs partly supported by stone plinths, a bit like a mini Stonehenge. It once crossed the river by the shortest route to connect Duiske Abbey and the Lady Chapel. Owen says that a fallen tree had destroyed it, and that it had taken the Society 10 years to get approval for its restoration. Then, one week after it was finally restored, a tree fell on it again and returned it to its previous state. I photograph the two amateur historians posing on the near shore in front of the unfortunate bridge, its far shore plinths again strewn around – 'slab-less'.

For lunch they take me to The Duiske Inn, where they refuse to let me pay a cent.

'That's the way we do things here,' says David firmly.

After lunch and as we leave, the man sitting opposite wishes that God be with me, which is a nice Irish way of saying farewell.

As promised, I'm driven out to the village of St Mullins named after Saint Moling, who founded a monastery and who was buried here in 697. The site has been a place of pilgrimage since the Middle Ages; the Sunday before St James's Day on 25th July, known as Pattern Sunday, the blessed well and graveyard is visited by a large gathering of people. *My* pilgrimage is to see the grave of Thomas Cloney.

The graveyard we walk through is sprinkled with staked green 'shields' upon each of which is painted a pike head. This indicates that buried beneath is the remains of a participant of the 1798 rebellion. One 'shield' in particular catches my eye – that of Henry Hammond from Aclare, a blacksmith, hanged (so the 'shield' tells) at Kilkenny for making pikes. After he was found guilty, a Miss Eleanor Doyle, a member of the landed gentry, intervened on his behalf and he was released. Unfortunately on his way home he met with a few friends and repaired to Murphy's ale house in Thomastown where he foolishly sang a few rebel songs and slagged off the yeomen. They were less than amused when they found out and Henry was brought back to Kilkenny Gaol and publicly hanged. To round things off the yeomen then proceeded to burn his forge and house.

Hammond's grave sits beside the penal altar. Owen points out the rectangular spy hole at the rear of the altar, which the priest would face with his back to his congregation. This enabled him to warn the congregation to disperse instantly should he see the authorities approaching.

We make our way to Cloney's grave. The inscription chiselled into the flat stone slab is illegible and spotted with white lichen. The staked green 'shield' does, however, record the role he played in one of the battles of the Rebellion, it reads:

General Thomas Cloney
Who at the age of 24
Led the charge on the
Three Bullet Gate.

On Tuesday 29th May, Cloney later claimed, a large body of men came to his father's house and pressed him to proceed to Enniscorthy. He wrote that he put them off, but that more came: 'Louder and more peremptory in their demands', so that eventually he joined them.

At Enniscorthy, Cloney must have learned of the successes of the rebel forces. Of note was the success of Father John Murphy at Oulart Hill and at Scarawalsh Bridge, two miles north of Enniscorthy.

When Cloney arrived at Enniscorthy on 29th May, he found it already burned. His unit was one of many from all over the county that had mustered at the camp on Vinegar Hill near the town during that day. Trials were in progress of captives and those convicted of complicity with the yeomanry or harbouring loyalist sympathies were duly shot or piked. The rebels' sights were now set upon Wexford – thought to be a possible landing place for the French. That evening Cloney and most of the rebel force marched and made camp high upon a rocky outcrop, at a junction of five roads. The place was known locally as The Three Rocks.

On Wednesday 30th May the Wexford garrison felt reasonably secure having recently been reinforced by the Donegal Militia. They spent the day making thorough preparations for the defence of the town. Also, they learned that a General Fawcett was on his way to their aid from Duncannon Fort with regular troops and some new-fangled high trajectory guns called howitzers. The howitzer party lagged somewhat behind the General, who waited for them to catch

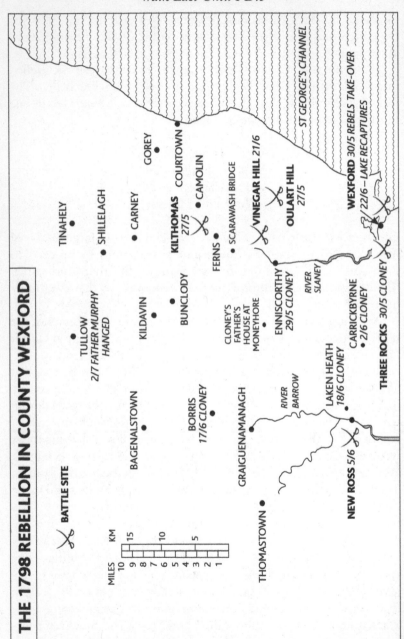

THE 1798 REBELLION IN COUNTY WEXFORD

up. But somehow they passed him unseen and ploughed on to where the road passed below The Three Rocks.

Cloney sprung the ambush here, rushing down on them; the encounter lasted no more than 15 minutes, after which all but a lieutenant and a couple of soldiers from the 90 strong troop lay dead. Cloney received the sword of surrender from the lieutenant who scuttled back to Fawcett with news of the ambush.

Cloney's rebels were then left to figure out how to operate their newly gained howitzer toys ready for an attack upon Wexford. They never got to use them though because by the evening of the 30th it became apparent that the entire garrison of the town had scooted off, leaving the loyalist townspeople at the mercy of the rebel force. Many tried to escape (most unsuccessfully) on fishing boats bound for Waterford or Wales. The rebels meanwhile ran riot in the town firing off shots in the air like drunken cowboys in a western, and doing a spot of looting, the green cockades in their hatbands being the only visible indication of their true rebel cause. They swarmed around the narrow streets celebrating the establishment of the First Irish Republic.

For the past week Bagenal Harvey, a Protestant barrister, together with two United Irish colonels, had been held in Wexford Gaol. They'd been implicated, along with around 20 other United Irishmen, by Anthony Perry, who'd been arrested and brought to the garrison town of Gorey. To be fair to Perry, if somebody had rubbed a mixture of pitch and gunpowder on my head and set fire to it, I'd probably have spilled the beans rather quickly as well. Anyway, Bagenal Harvey and the colonels were now set free by the rebels whilst Captain Matthew Keogh, a retired British officer who'd risen through the ranks, was made military governor of the newly declared Republic of Wexford.

At a camp established next morning on 31st May outside the town, Harvey was made Commander-in-Chief for the County and it was decided to split the force into three divisions; one would head to County Carlow, another to County Wicklow, whilst the largest division under Harvey would march west towards the garrison at New Ross in order to open up the road across the river to Counties Kilkenny and Waterford, which would unlock the whole of the south of Ireland for the rebels. Colonels John Kelly, Henry Colclough and

Thomas Cloney amongst others were to accompany Harvey.

Cloney joined the force at Carrickbyrne on 2nd June, but by 5th June the rebels were still on Corbet Hill about a mile from New Ross. Their delay in making an attack was to prove costly. At daybreak on 6th June, Harvey, knowing that his rebel force was vastly superior, sent a rider into town carrying the white flag of truce and a letter urging the garrison to surrender. The guards promptly shot him. This enraged the rebels somewhat, who then abandoned their previously rational plans for the simultaneous strategic attack on three gates around the walled town in favour of the all-out storming of Three Bullet Gate. Led by Colonels Kelly, Cloney and Colclough, three battalions advanced, fired by a mixture of valour, whisky and religious zeal; the battalion led by Colclough soon got cold feet as the first shots were fired and retreated back up the hill, leaving the remaining two columns to battle into the town. According to some accounts Kelly's company was the first into the town (Kelly being seriously wounded in the thigh during the encounter). He was followed by the company led by Thomas Cloney.

By midday, with heavy casualties on both sides and much of the town in flames, a large part of the garrison had retreated over the bridge into County Kilkenny. Having thought perhaps that they'd won the battle, the rebels took a break – some took a kip, others took a nip (or two) and still others hunted around for food. There was no back-up force to relieve them; many of Colclough's battalion and a large portion of the huge army of rebels who'd stayed up on Corbet Hill had disappeared back to their homes. Harvey remained at Three Bullet Gate – it apparently didn't occur to him to burn down the bridge and so prevent a counter attack – which is exactly what was to happen.

It took the dragoons and mounted yeomanry about an hour to drive the main body of the rebels back to Three Bullet Gate (they had a bit of trouble with the rebel's long pikes). Many of the rebels were stranded in the buildings, set alight by the Crown forces, where they suffocated or otherwise were later captured – and the next day hanged. According to Cloney's account, by four o'clock the battle was over and by six o'clock the survivors were back at Corbet Hill. Cloney was *so* tired on the ride back that he fell asleep on his horse for about an hour.

Cloney was involved in two more actions, neither of which was a great success. Some 12 days after the Battle of New Ross, he was directed to attack a house in Borris with the aim of obtaining arms and ammunition. He failed. Two days later, on Monday 20th June, at a place called Goff's Bridge, 15 kilometres south-west of Wexford, and after about a four-hour battle, with ammunition short and Crown reinforcements imminent, the rebels retreated. It was Cloney's last battle of the Rebellion.

Defeats for the insurgents followed a day later at Vinegar Hill – which effectively ended the rebellion in the south-east.

In Wexford, knowing that they'd soon be overwhelmed, the insurgents decided to offer their terms of capitulation and Cloney agreed to act as an envoy and accompany a captain of the King's forces (who'd been held captive in Wexford), to convey the terms to General Lake in Enniscorthy. These were that they were prepared to surrender provided persons and property were safeguarded. Cloney's mission was by no means easy, given that the red-coated captain had firstly to pass through the ranks of the defeated insurgent army – many of whom wanted to kill him. Secondly, and more dangerous for Cloney, they then had to pass the King's troop who were busy slaughtering everyone they might come across hiding in ditches and hedges. In the event the letter was delivered to Lake who promptly refused it, although he did agree safe passage for Cloney to return to Wexford while he marched to the town on 22nd June.

Whilst the battle at Vinegar Hill was being played out 20 miles to the north-west, Captain Matthew Keogh in Wexford had been unable to restrain the more militant of the rebels who'd contrived to deal with their loyalist captives in their own brutal way. Around 90 prisoners were taken from the prison given a summary trial, marched to the bridge for all to see and piked to death. It was perhaps no surprise then that, encouraged by Lake, when they entered Wexford, his troops carried out many indiscriminate reprisals around the town including murder and rape.

Before Lake's army had reached Wexford, however, Cloney somehow managed to escape and was luckily harboured by a loyalist friend. Whilst a search for him was underway he cheekily hid under the bed of a lady in labour. He may perhaps have asked her to make some appropriate noises too because out of embarrassment the room was not searched. Cloney followed this escapade by disguising himself as a yeoman in order to get out of town; as he passed a guard at the town's exit he admonished the guard in authoritarian tone and manner for flirting with a milkmaid, claiming she was his – then he walked with her out of town. 'Houdini' then made it across country to his father's house in Moneyhore where he hid up for the next six weeks.

Other rebel leaders were not so lucky. Father John Murphy was captured and brought to Tullow, County Carlow, where he was charged with committing treason against the British Crown and sentenced to death. He was then stripped, flogged, hanged, decapitated and his body burnt in a barrel of tar whilst his head was impaled on a spike that was deliberately staked opposite the local Catholic church. Mathew Keogh, who'd tried to establish order in the Wexford Republic and pleaded that he'd never been a United Irishman, was tried and nevertheless found guilty. He was hanged and afterwards decapitated whilst his torso was thrown into the River Slaney (the name of which ironically means 'river of health' – it was not so healthy then). His head was stuck on a spike over the courthouse. Bagenal Harvey and Henry Colclough fled to the Saltee Islands off the Wexford coast but were discovered and arrested a few days after Lake entered Wexford. Early on 28th June Harvey was also hanged on Wexford Bridge followed just before sundown by Colclough. The other rebel combatant leader at the battle of New Ross, John Kelly (subject of the Irish ballad 'Kelly the boy from Killane') who was wounded in the thigh and taken to Wexford to recover, was dragged from his bed when the town was retaken. He too suffered the same fate as Harvey and Colclough; his body was also then decapitated and his head used in a grotesque game of football played through the streets before, like the others, it was mounted on a spike.

Anthony Perry, who'd grassed up Bagenal Harvey and others at Gorey whilst being pitch-cap tortured, managed to escape from Vinegar Hill with his men but was finally captured in Kildare and hanged at Edenderry a couple of days later.

Hanged with Perry was Father Mogue Kearns, a friend of Cloney's who had hid with him near his father's house. They'd received word that a fragmented group of Wexford insurgents wanted and expected them to join them in woods near Scollagh for the march north. But Cloney's father was dying and his sisters implored him not to go. He reluctantly agreed to comply with their requests – otherwise he would have undoubtedly swung with Perry and Kearns at Edenderry.

Cloney's next Houdini trick wasn't too clever. He accidently shot himself in the thigh (maybe metaphorically as close to the foot as is possible). The wound bled so much that he had to seek out a doctor and his whereabouts then became known to the military commander at Enniscorthy, who had him taken to the town and put under guard.

Luckily again for Cloney on 17th July an Act of Amnesty was passed by the Irish parliament. It led to thousands of rebels surrendering and obtaining 'protection' documents. By the end of August most of Leinster was in peace.

Towards the end of August 1798 Cloney took the Oath of Allegiance that in effect meant he'd surrendered to the government.

The French landed at Killala, north of Mayo with 1,000 men on 22nd August 1798. A month later the last land battle of the 1798 rebellion took place at Killala when it was retaken for the government by the forces of General Trench.

On 12th October the remaining French armada from Brest had finally made it to the coast of Donegal. Their numbers were still not as Tone would have hoped, consisting of nine ships and 3,000 French troops. He sailed with them with his usual optimism – which was soon to be dashed. After a 10-hour battle they were defeated by the British and most of their ships and troops were captured. Amongst them was Adjutant-General Smith, better known as Theobald Wolfe Tone.

On 8th November Tone was brought to a military trial in Dublin dressed in an impressive French uniform, charged with treason. He was found guilty and, despite an appeal put before Lord Cornwallis, the Lord Lieutenant of Ireland, that he wished to die by firing squad, was condemned to death by hanging. But Tone cheated the hangman by cutting his own throat and a week later died of his wounds. Although his death effectively brought an end to the United Irish movement, his vision of Irish liberty lived on and inspired others to take up the cause. The course of history might have been different had his scheme for the British Sandwich Islands been accepted.

Cloney remained during this time in Enniscorthy; he was without doubt a survivor, having been attacked by a yeoman with a bayonet and slashed in the face, he at least escaped again with his life. His father died in October and it was not until the following March that he returned to his father's house at Moneyhore. Two months later Cloney was in trouble again when a tenant with whom he'd had some dispute made accusations against him with regards to the Rebellion, and he was arrested and marched three miles to Enniscorthy and from there taken to Wexford Gaol.

Here he was court-martialled on two counts. The first was for (and they weren't at all sure about his rank) 'being a General, Colonel, Major, or Captain in the rebel army'. He could hardly deny that he had been at least one of these. The second was 'for being present at the murder of John Gill on Vinegar Hill, on 29th May 1798'. Despite many credible character witnesses giving evidence in his favour and very dodgy evidence against him, he was nonetheless found guilty and sentenced to death. After six weeks in Wexford Gaol Cloney learnt that his death sentence had been commuted by Cornwallis to life, to be served in the penal colony of New South Wales.

But influential strings were again pulled, and when he left the filth of Geneva Barracks at Waterford it was not, as he'd expected, to board a convict ship, but to be returned to Wexford Gaol. More strings were pulled, and after 21 months in gaol he was released on 12th February 1801 on condition that he left Ireland for two years. His exile was spent in Liverpool, which he possibly disliked more than he might have done New South Wales. But his time there was short, and by spring 1803 he was back in Dublin –although he realised that he was now being kept under surveillance by the authorities. They rightly guessed that his rebellious ideals were still intact.

On 23rd July 1803 Robert Emmet organised a rising in Dublin and it was suspected that Cloney was involved in the conspiracy. Cloney was shopped to the authorities by Valentine Gill, the brother of John Gill, murdered at Vinegar Hill; not content with Cloney's court martial sentence, it seems he sought further revenge. In the event, Cloney was arrested again and imprisoned in the tower of Dublin Castle where he was interrogated about alleged financial dealings with one of the conspirators in Emmet's rising, Thomas

Russell. The rising was not a success and both Russell and Emmet were caught, hanged and afterwards beheaded. Cloney, imprisoned in the castle, wrote later that he was hard done by because he was allowed no wine, and merely got a bottle of porter and a glass of whisky every day with which to make punch. Things were soon to get 'slightly' worse for him when he was transferred to Kilmainham Gaol in Dublin. Here, living in a dungeon, his physical and mental health soon deteriorated. His sisters and several influential people, however, campaigned and managed to get his case reviewed and he was released in November 1804 after spending about 16 months in prison. 'Houdini' the survivor returned and settled down with his sisters in Graiguenamanagh – he was still only 28 years old. His survival during the past six tumultuous years was due in part to debts repaid by those he'd helped, and partly due to luck – which all survivors luckily possess – except that in the end nobody survives.

I'd visited the house Cloney lived in for 48 years and now I'm standing above his bones that have resided here for the past 164 years. After 1804 he turned his attentions from rebellion to political agitation, working with Daniel O'Connell for the repeal of the Act of Union between England and Ireland that William Pitt had devised. Cloney died in 1850 at the age of 76. John Joyce relates in his biographical tribute to him that on 25th July each year, or the Sunday before, known as Pattern Sunday, a pike is gently laid on his grave.

'He was luckier than most,' says Owen, mirroring my thoughts.

We stroll through the graveyard to the monastic ruins. David points to the remains of an elevated room (possibly the chapel) where he tells me James Freney, a highwayman, used to climb to. It seems that he'd buried some gold somewhere on Brandon Hill and from this viewpoint he knew exactly where he'd buried it, but when he'd climb the hill he couldn't find the burial spot. Freney was a member of an 11-man gang known as the Kelly Mount. Nine of the gang were eventually hanged, the tenth was sent to prison, whilst Freney, who was from a respectable family and who had connections, worked out a deal with the chief justices and finished up as a Customs official in New Ross until his death in 1788.

Before driving back and dropping me off in Graiguenamanagh we stop off at the Mullichain Café, a restored 18th century mill and grain store situated beside the River Barrow. The place is doing a roaring trade this sunny Saturday. I'm bought a coffee and scones accompanied by heaps of butter, jam and cream which again I'm not allowed to pay for. Martin the proprietor tells us that the place once belonged to Odlums Millers and claims that it has the largest millstone in Ireland.

Graiguenamanagh has been good to me today – and so has the Historical Society. I thank David and Owen. It's been a pleasant interlude from walking, but tomorrow I'll cross the bridge into County Carlow on the twentieth day of the trek to Dublin.

Fourteen
The Gate of Tears

'Take it from us, every grain,
We were made for you to drain;
Black starvation let us feel,
England must not want a meal!'
From: *Famine and Exportation*, by John O'Hagan

Sunday 22nd June – Graiguenamanagh to Tomduff
On the map, Tomduff village is shown sitting below the 400-metre-high Tomduff Hill, so I don't fancy biking up to it – and there's the added problem of parking the camper in the narrow lanes. My solution is to drive up there, drop the bike, drive back to Graiguenamanagh and start the walk. It's what I do.

But finding Tomduff proves none too easy. I park in a lay-by by a school in Borris, not sure whether I'm taking the correct road out of the village. It's still early – around nine in the morning. I walk into the village and enquire in a newsagent's shop. The shopkeeper doesn't get a chance to answer.

'Is that your camper parked by the school?' asks a customer. I'm amazed that already I've been spotted. I affirm it is.

'You're on the right road sure enough – it's well signposted,' he assures me.

But I see only a single sign for TOMDUFF FIELD 1798; a rebel campsite – then nothing. I reach a crossroads with a signpost, stop the camper, get out the map and spread it over the bonnet. None of the names on the signpost appear on my map. I'm aware that the camper is virtually blocking the crossroads but don't know which road to take. I've not seen a soul since leaving Borris.

A car purrs down the road and the driver stops to help.

'Can't see well without my specs,' he says. I offer him mine – but then notice he's already wearing a pair. But he takes mine, puts them on and studies the map. The right lens of my specs is very thick because the vision in my right eye leaves a lot to be desired after an accident I had in my youth. But he tells me he also has a bad right eye – so my glasses actually suit him.

'What's the time?' he asks; then checks his watch. 'I'm on my way to Mass,' he says. 'Follow me to the crossroads, there's a sign there.' He hands me back the map and starts the car. I've forgotten he has my glasses and so has he (almost).

'Better give you back your lookers,' he says, handing them back. His breath smells of whisky.

Then we're off. At the crossroads he signals me to carry on and swings back the way we've come. Just up the lane is another crossroads and this I suppose must be Tomduff itself. It's hardly a village; just a few scattered houses. I block the crossroads again, offload the bike and chain it to a sign pointing to MOUNT LEINSTER HERITAGE DRIVE. Next to it is a huge red-lettered sign indicating this is a TEXT ALERT AREA. I hope nobody texts about my bike.

By just after 10.30am I've crossed the River Barrow at Graiguenamanagh into my sixth walking county – Carlow. I've been looking forward to a gentle stroll along the towpath to Borris and it doesn't disappoint. Accompanied by blue skies, bonhomous white clouds and sunshine I follow, at a distance, a couple, out for a Sunday morning stroll. Canoeists and joggers are out in force too. A rowing coach on a bike shouts words of encouragement at a quartet of lads gliding past – but struggles to keep up himself. Another quartet of ladies follows a short time later, accompanied by a cox. At the approach to Ballykeenan lock a sign directs craft (except crazy white-water canoeists) away from the weir and into a section of canal.

Construction of the canal was commenced by the Barrow Navigation Company in 1760. The 114km long Barrow Way follows the course of the river north, with canal diversions from St Mullins up to the village of Robertston where it joins the Grand Canal which goes west to the Shannon and east to Dublin. I'm walking a short section of the Barrow Way now.

On the stump of a tree a yellow wagtail watches me pass without flying off and I manage to get a good close up photograph of him. The morning passes just as peacefully. At Ballingrane Lock the couple I've been tracking all morning have stopped for a drink. I pass them – she's wearing a flowing white dress and he a baseball cap and shorts. They catch me up at Borris Lock when I stop for a sandwich lunch. We chat, and it seems they've left one car at Graiguenamanagh and have another waiting at Borris. I ask them to take my photograph – the only one of the walk.

The route leaves the Barrow at Ballyteigelea Bridge and follows the main road through Borris. I'd been looking forward to a pint here at one of the (reputed) seven pubs, but there's nothing open. Passing under the 16-arch railway viaduct (which I think would make a good wild-camp spot) I follow the route I'd driven already this morning to Spahill Cross Roads where it turns left and begins to climb. It's lane-walking all the way now, with views to the east of the distant the Blackstairs Mountains, until I come across my unmolested bike safely chained next to the TEXT ALERT AREA sign.

By 4.30pm I'm back in Graiguenamanagh.

I get a good evening meal in an establishment called The Railway House, and then drive towards Kildavin on the R734 to wild-camp precariously at the entrance to a huge multi-chimneyed, pillared porch, manor house. I keep clear of the gates. The long driveway up to the house will rend the house sufficiently distant from me for the camper not to be spotted by the occupants (I hope), but I'm still anxious that someone might come out from the house and ask me to move on.

As it gets dusk I watch two horses in the field adjacent to the driveway engaging in a curious simultaneous and vigorous back-licking which seems to be a form of mutual grooming; apparently it's a way of showing affection only performed between relatives or very close friends.

After last year's experience I've brought my own supply of dark rum with me and decide, as darkness descends, that it's unlikely I'm going to be disturbed for the night. So I lower the level in the bottle a little – maybe it was a lot?

Monday 23rd June – Tomduff to Kildavin

The plan today is to walk a modest 19km (11.5 miles) to Clonegal – to complete the South Leinster Way.

I'm up early, anxious to leave before the residents of the manor house emerge to find a six-metre-long camper van outside their gates. After a week in the camper my morning routine is slick, and by eight o'clock I'm ready to roll, the plan being to drive to Clonegal and bike back to Tomduff.

I turn the ignition key – click. My first thought is the battery. But then I remember that the alternator had been hanging on by one bolt before I'd left home and I'd asked the local garage to sort it – maybe they hadn't done it? I fiddle with the battery connections and try again – click. I scramble underneath. There *is* a bolt missing, but the connections are tight and the belt seems OK. So now I don't know. What I *do* know is that the problem has to be fixed. If not, firstly there will undoubtedly be a confrontation with the residents of the manor house and secondly I'll lose at least a day's walking in an already tight schedule; the ferry is booked for 4th July.

So I decide I need a mechanic. On the bike I head for Bagenalstown, but after a few kilometres see a group of people chatting outside a row of terraced houses. I stop and ask if there's anywhere in Bagenalstown that could help.

'There's a place just down the road on the right, they're mechanics – do tractors and fork lift trucks,' says the man.

'Thanks,' I say and start to cycle off.

'But they won't be open until nine o'clock,' he calls out after me.

I wait outside the iron gates half an hour until three dogs appear and cross the yard towards me. They're followed by a man who unlocks the gates. I tell him that I think the problem is electrical.

'Igor's yer man,' he says. 'He has all the electronic gear – he's a Pole.' He calls him on his mobile and within 10 minutes Igor pulls up by the gates in a van. I follow the van back to the camper – and don't dilly-dally either.

But I'm not too impressed by Igor when he asks me if I've got a spanner and a piece of wire. I tip out a selection of spanners and he finds one he seems to like – but I have no wire. He fishes around on the ground around the camper and comes up with some wire, but it's no good. I'm beginning to suspect his mechanical abilities and wonder what I've let myself in for, so ask if he has a workshop.

'Two!' he says indignantly. 'I can sort it out tomorrow.'

This, I think, will mean I'll lose at least a complete day's walking. He fiddles around underneath for five minutes, then asks me to switch on the ignition – and the engine roars.

'Follow me and don't switch off,' he orders. I do so, but after a few metres he stops.

'Your bike!' he calls back. Shit! – I almost forgot it. So now I reverse and almost run over it.

When I've loaded the bike, the Pole drives off as if he's in pole position at Silverstone; he overtakes a tractor approaching a bend and I'm forced to coax the van desperately past it in order not to lose him – it's a hair-raising ride into Bagenalstown. I park up in his yard, where it looks like I'm going to spend the night. He tells me that the yard is not locked up until late, so I console myself with the thought that at least tonight I'll get a good meal again in The Railway House.

By now the morning is half gone, but I'm determined not to lose a complete day's walk and figure I'll bike out to Tomduff, walk to Clonegal and then worry about how I'm going to get back. I offload the bike and ride into town to get my bearings in order to find the correct road out to Tomduff. There are a number of Polish shops, so it seems that the town might have quite a high population of Poles.

An information board tells me that it was the advent of the railway in 1846 that put Bagenalstown on the map. Its station, on the main line between Dublin and Waterford, was opened in 1848 and is interestingly constructed in an Italianate villa style. Its design has been attributed to the architect William Deane Butler – although it's a wonder he had time to fit in such an endeavour given that he'd been married three times, had 13 children and was given to telling slang stories and singing funny songs. Unfortunately the information board's map and 'YOU ARE HERE' tag just tells me I'm in Bagenalstown (which I know already) and that it's located at the junction of the R705 and R724 roads.

I bike southbound on the R705, which I think is the right way; then turn left towards Corries Cross. I'm some way along this road before I realise that in my impatience to get on the walk I've forgotten to buy lunch and have to bike back into Bagenalstown. It's a long bike ride to Tomduff and the last bit is all uphill. So I abandon the bike just before it and continue on foot, making it back onto the South Leinster Way by 11.40am.

The lane climbs for some while around the lower slopes of Tomduff Hill, with forest below, until it emerges into the open at a place known as The Nine Stones. There are a few cars parked here. A well worn track leads to the top of the hill known as Slievebawn. Sheep graze its lower reaches. A red and white windsock is billowed out by a fresh northerly breeze that the paraglider, whose about to launch from the summit of Slievebawn, will probably appreciate. The road rolls away into the distance across the hillside and I keep glancing back to catch the progress of the paraglider. He stays up there for a good while, frequently changing direction by catching the thermals. The high ground continues; I leave the road and climb still higher on a track that leads through a forest and passes below some wind turbines before dropping down to cross the N80 into Kildavin. The walk has taken me just over four hours.

I consider walking on to Clonegal, but have no means of getting back to Tomduff or Bagenalstown apart from walking or by taxi. Parents are waiting in cars for their kids to come out of school, so I ask a lady:

'Is Clonegal a bigger place than Kildavin? I need a taxi.'

'No,' she says. 'Bunclody is bigger, but you probably won't get one there either.'

'It doesn't sound good,' I say.

'Ah! I know a local taxi lady,' she says, and tries her on her mobile, but gets no reply.

'Wait a minute,' she says thoughtfully. 'I know where she lives – she's just around the corner.' The lady drives off; she's back within five minutes.

'No – sorry,' she says. 'She has several runs to do today.'

So now there's nothing for it but to start to walk; by road Tomduff is about 10 miles and Bagenalstown is even further, perhaps 15 miles away. I trudge off along the R724 towards Myshall in a very poor frame of mind. I haven't hitch-hiked for perhaps 25 years but, though I'm walking facing the oncoming traffic, I stick out a hopeful thumb and start to count the cars that pass. I walk about a kilometre and count four cars – then a lorry stops.

Anthony, the driver, is based in Dublin and tells me that these days he doesn't do overnights trips; only daily runs out and back. He's been doing the job all his life. He's going to Bagenalstown and I decide against being dropped off halfway and making my way across country to Tomduff – it would still be a long hike, and the bike should be alright left overnight. By fortunate coincidence the company he's visiting is on the same industrial estate as Igor's workshop.

Igor tells me that he can maybe look at the camper in half an hour's time, so I wander off into town, have a pint, watch some football on TV and come back. He's not ready. By now I'm feeling quite hungry, so I sit in the camper's passenger seat snacking on Bombay-mix and playing a CD when I notice a small red light flashing.

At this point something also flashes in my mind: the security fob has long since broken off from the rest of the camper keys. This fob has to be inserted in its slot in order for the engine to be started (unless you are an Igor and know what to do underneath); when the fob is not in its slot, the red light flashes. Now I remember – last night outside the manor house, when I imbibed a good measure of the contents of the dark rum bottle, I worried that the Gardai might breathalyse me for attempting to drive, so I took out the fob to immobilise the camper – it's still out now! What an idiot. But WORSE: I have to admit my foolishness to Igor.

I go to his office. Igor's on the phone for ages haggling over the price of a part that he wants. He tries to screw the seller down, so I know what's going to transpire. When I tell him what I've done, he doesn't laugh – at least not until later. But, after he disconnects his magic start-up override device from underneath and I check that she fires up OK, he tries to charge me an extortionate amount.

'How much do you charge an hour?' I ask with genuine indignation.

'I had to drive out to you,' he argues. We compromise on a 20% reduction, but to get the last laugh (which he will have anyway, later down at the pub) he watches me struggle trying to manoeuvre the camper out of his yard without hitting anything. Eventually, and with one hand clamping his mobile phone to his ear – doing another deal – he reluctantly guides me back.

I round off an eventful day with another cracking meal at The Railway House, and then drive back west to wild-camp the night parked under the 16-arch railway viaduct in Borris that I'd earmarked during yesterday's walk.

Tuesday 24th June – Kildavin to the Gate of Tears

At eight in the morning I drive and pick up the bike from its overnight sleep in Tomduff, then drive on east to Shillelagh and park in a large gravel car park adjacent to the general store. It's an easy level bike ride following the Derry River valley back to Clonegal. Here the hills begin and I'm forced to dismount and push the bike up a hill at the village of Watch House, where a man constructing a stone wall nods good morning. I imagine he'll be repeating the greeting when I return later this way minus the bike (at the time I don't realise I've taken a wrong turning and so won't come back this way). I'm surprised when I emerge on a main road with a signpost to Bunclody.

The 2.7-mile walk along the little road from Kildavin to Clonegal bridges the gap between the South Leinster Way and the Wicklow Way. I start the walk at Kildavin by 11 o'clock and make Clonegal within the hour. This little walk takes me briefly into my seventh county – Wexford. The River Derry runs pleasantly alongside for much of the way. Fishing is closely guarded here; a sign on a gate says that a bailiff is on duty, and warns that bubble fishing (which apparently means fishing with a float) is strictly prohibited. I cross the Derry, back into County Carlow near Watch House. This was where during the 1798 rebellion permits were issued by yeomen to those wishing to bring animals across to the fair at Carnew. Over the bridge (known as Young's Bridge) I pass a stone plaque imbedded in the ground which marks the place where the river was once crossed by means of a ford. The plaque tells that this is THE GATE OF TEARS or in Irish is *GEATA NA nDEOR*. The inscription on it is a poignant reminder of where, around the time of the potato famine, emigrants from Clonegal got their last look at their homeland and said goodbye to their relatives before setting off into the unknown.

During the potato famine of 1845 to 1849 it's estimated that around one million people perished, whilst a further one million people emigrated during the 1840s.

Many of those who emigrated were more or less forced to do so by landlords who'd become bankrupt because their tenants couldn't pay the rent. The landlords realised that better profit could be had by turning their lands over to pasture for cattle and sheep to be sold to Britain than from acquiring tenant rents. Landlords carried out ruthless evictions; peasants were dragged from their cabins that were then demolished with battering rams to prevent re-habitation.

On the ferry coming across, a group of English who belonged to a motorhome fraternity were chatting loudly within my earshot and that of an Irish couple.

'How is it that the Arabs have oil and the Irish have potatoes?' asks the talkative one of the group. Everyone is silent, awaiting the punchline answer. A smile creeps over his face.

'Because the Irish had first pick,' he quips. A derogatory racist's joke, I thought – but the Irish couple smiled and didn't seem to take offence.

But it wasn't such a bad pick. Frequently potatoes were combined with buttermilk – a diet which provided all the proteins, calories and minerals the labourer needed. It certainly seemed to have been something of a fertility food. Over 60% of Ireland's potato crop was consumed by labourers and their families. And all that was needed was a spade and some moist ground – there was, and is, plenty of the latter in Ireland. The only snags were that the crop had to be grown each year and potatoes didn't keep well. The reliance of the Irish peasants upon the potato as their sole food source was, in today's clichéd health and safety vernacular, an accident waiting to happen. And it did.

An airborne fungus came across the Atlantic in the holds of ships. It attacked the potato crop in Belgium, Holland, France and Germany leaving fields a stinking, rotting black mess. The blight was first reported to have arrived in England on the Isle of Wight in August 1845. Spread by the wind, it reached Ireland in September where it first appeared in the countryside around Dublin.

By October, as the crop was dug up and the destruction discovered, Robert Peel learned of the seriousness of the situation. He was no lover of Ireland or of the Irish, but realised that famine was a real possibility.

Assistant Secretary to the Treasury Charles Edward Trevelyan was the man responsible for the famine relief. This included fund-raising schemes, a public works programme designed to enable the peasant to earn money to buy food and the opening of food depots that, it was proposed, stock Indian corn. Trevelyan was a moralist who believed that the Irish should help themselves and not rely upon the government. It was perhaps not quite what Trevelyan was thinking, but by March 1846 the peasants had their own ideas of how to help themselves. They sacked food shops, stole livestock and attacked food convoys; tens of thousands applied for employment on the public works. Those without work pawned their clothes for food money and walked miles to purchase it. When it wasn't available they boiled seaweed, ate grass and their infected potatoes that upset their stomachs and bowels.

At first they didn't much like the Indian corn either and complained that it gave them diarrhoea; there was even a riot when it was first introduced. Nonetheless by the end of March starving stomachs began to acquire a taste for it and in Cork people rioted *to get* a share. There was always an insufficient supply of grain stocked to feed everyone. Trevelyan's intention had never been to feed all those in need but just to distribute enough of the corn on the market to keep the price reasonably low. Also, he saw the operation as a 'one-off' – once the present stock was gone, it was gone and that was to be the end of the relief. His idea was that just enough food was to be provided to prevent famine. It more or less just managed to work out that way over the winter of 1845/46.

Peel had long since come to the conclusion that an Irish diet of grain would be a suitable substitute for the potato, and at the Cabinet meeting on 31st October 1845 he'd set off on an old hobbyhorse of his whilst at the same time managing to open a whole can of worms. He urged that the Corn Laws be repealed in order to allow for the import of cheap grain. The Corn Laws were sacrosanct to many members of Peel's Tory Party as they protected the profit of English farmers and landowners. His proposals were of course vigorously opposed by many in the party, notably by a young ambitious Benjamin Disraeli, and although the Corn Law Reform Bill finally struggled its way through the approval of both houses by the end of June 1846, the issue had split the Tory Party and led to Peel's demise as prime minister. It would be another 28 years before the Tories were returned to power. Peel was succeeded as prime minister by the Whig, Lord John Russell.

Trevelyan's views fell nicely into line with the laissez-faire approach that Russell now took. They both felt that Peel had overreacted to the famine situation and Russell resolved to take a far more 'wait and see' approach.

Things began to look worse for the majority of the Irish people as the spring of 1846 turned into summer. In July little brown dots began to appear on the leaves of the potato crop and it became apparent that the blight had returned for a second year; this was just about the time that the relief programmes were shut down on Trevelyan's orders.

The Whig administration appointed Lord Bessborough as Lord-Lieutenant in August and, following unrest at the closing of public works projects, he ordered that all uncompleted works should be restarted. Getting on a public works scheme became for many a desperate matter of survival. Applications went through the roof: public works employment rose from 12,000 in September to 300,000 by the end of the year. None of this was anticipated by the government, so initially there were not enough tools for the labourers and not enough money to pay them. Because public opinion in England had it that Irish public works' labourers had the previous year largely been a skiving lot, Trevelyan introduced a piecework system; not too good if you're knackered, half-starved and standing in the cold rain. And then you have to wait up to four weeks whilst the bureaucratic wheels turn slowly around to deliver you your bonus. A pay clerk's job was somewhat dangerous given these circumstances and, under the threat of violence from angry workers, many resigned. When wages *were* paid they were not enough anyway if there was a large family to feed and rent to be paid to avoid eviction. There was fierce competition for employment and many Board of Works officers were assaulted. There were also anti-piecework and anti-export food riots, which resulted in troops being deployed.

Very little food was coming into the country. The government had decided that no orders for food were to be placed abroad for fear that prices would be raised against British buyers; everything was left to private enterprise and Russell's non-interference approach. But much of Europe was also suffering famine and most of the corn from Britain had been sold, so Trevelyan was eventually forced to place orders for Indian corn to be obtained again from America. But by the time these deliberations had taken place it became apparent that shipments would not arrive in Britain until the spring of 1847.

By November people were dying of starvation. Sir Randolph

Routh, the Commissary General of the relief programme urged Trevelyan to send food over immediately. Trevelyan refused. There were by now no nettles or blackberries left to forage. Food depots were not opened as in the previous year because there was insufficient food in them to be had. And now the snow began to fall, roads were blocked and the public works had to stop. Half naked women and children shivered whilst they scratched around in fields looking for *anything* to eat. Famine had now arrived with a vengeance

Desperation drove many Irish peasants to an erstwhile feared and hated institution: the workhouse. Established after the passing of the Poor Law Act in 1838, the previously under-occupied workhouses were rapidly filling up and by Christmas 1846 over 50% of them were full. The attraction of the workhouse system was that it guaranteed the provision of food (in exchange for work). However, distasteful features for the inmates were multifarious. Inmates were just that – they had to stay and live within the confines of the workhouse; there were many strict rules such as having to wear a uniform and remaining silent; family members were split into separate quarters; the work was both arduous and boring – for men it was typically breaking stones for use in road building and for women cleaning and other domestic work. But frequently there was no work to be had, and the staff were often insulting and cruel to the paupers. To complete their list of woes, the food itself was often of very poor quality – generally consisting of milk and stirabout (the same weak porridge of oatmeal and cornmeal boiled in water and stirred that was fed to prisoners). Despite those conditions, before Christmas a member of a relief committee reported that police had been stationed outside a workhouse to prevent paupers from breaking *in*.

As the horrors of 1846 crept into the new year the government did a U-turn. John Russell at last acknowledged in the House of Commons that the relief committees were not working and the public works projects were too expensive. The relief plan, he admitted, had failed. All effort was to be put into the establishment of soup kitchens to feed those made redundant from public works. The Destitute Poor (Ireland) Act, popularly known as the Soup Kitchen Act, was passed which, it was thought, would have several benefits. It would give relief *outside* the workhouse system at a low price –

providing the workhouse was full, and it would also enable men to return and tend their plots ready for next year's harvest.

A cheap soup recipe was accordingly created by a famous French chef (at a cost of three-farthings a quart – and you couldn't get much cheaper than that). He claimed that it, combined with a biscuit, would keep a person strong and healthy! It was first dished out to some of the London poor (whose comments are not recorded), whilst at the same time it was tasted by the gentry who gave glowing reports that it was good and nourishing (but they of course didn't have to live on it). It was, however, not so good and nourishing if you were used to consuming a large quantity of potatoes each day.

But the introduction of the soup kitchens were slow to get underway and fell behind the government's target, whilst, despite desperate appeals, the closure of the public works schemes proceeded on schedule, making those on them instantly redundant. For those poor devils there were little prospects for the future – except to wait for death. They were told, and many believed it, that it was the will of God.

God must of course love all creatures – even the common louse, or they wouldn't have been created (or he does indeed work in mysterious ways). But in 1847 lice spread an epidemic of typhus and relapsing fever across Ireland.

The typhus bacteria were spread to humans via the louse's excrement, after it had bitten its human host to feed upon blood. Other lice-free persons were also infected as the excrement could enter through the eyes or be inhaled as a dust. In Ireland typhus was known as black fever because in its latter stages the person would turn a shade of that colour. Its early symptoms included headache, chills, coughing, muscular pain and high fever. Victims frequently became delirious and burnt up with the fever and some were known to have thrown themselves into a river to cool down. The stench given off from a victim was apparently also pretty horrendous; sufferers inside a cabin could be smelt from the outside.

Relapsing fever was caused by another type of bacteria being transmitted from the damaged body or limbs of a louse entering a victim's bloodstream via the skin; if you splatted one or scratched at it the bacteria would be released and enter the bloodstream by way of a cut or scratch. Upon infection, high fever and vomiting began quickly, and after a few days this was followed by sweating and exhaustion. This pattern would repeat itself after six or seven days in a relapse and the victim instead of turning black, as with typhus, would turn yellow as jaundice set in; the Irish called this 'yellow fever'.

These diseases together with scurvy (named 'black leg' by the Irish), dysentery and famine dropsy (usually evident by swelling in the feet and ankles) caused thousands of deaths each week. Mortality figures are unreliable, but there were undoubtedly more deaths from these diseases than from actual starvation. It was both the starvation and then the fever that finally drove around one million Irish people to leave their native land.

The emigrants from Clonegal would have hugged and kissed those loved ones who'd decided to stick it out and stay. Then they might have looked back across the valley to the Wicklow Hills beyond for the last time before dropping down from Drumderry Hill along the little lane and crossing the ford that was then the only way to get across the River Derry. They were on their way to New Ross and a new life in a new land.

I too have to push on from 'The Gate of Tears' on my way to Istanbul via Dublin.

Fifteen
The Wicklow Way to America

I'm a dacint boy, just landed from the town of Ballyfad;
I want a situation: yis, I want it mighty bad.
I saw a place advertised. It's the thing for me, says I;
But the dirty spalpeen ended with: No Irish need apply.
From: *No Irish Need Apply* by John F. Poole

Tuesday 24th June – The Gate of Tears to Shillelagh
As I cross the 14th century bridge into Clonegal a dad and his young daughter, sitting on a wall, are throwing a stick across the river for their golden retriever to fetch. Without hesitation the dog splashes through the shallow weed-clogged waters and then dives into the deep clear water beyond. I worry that he won't make it out, but he's obviously done this trick before and at first swims, then churns his way back to them.

All thoughts of a swift pint soon evaporate; everything in Clonegal appears to be closed, yet there are cars parked everywhere. I look up the road to the village green where a crowd of people are gathered. What's happening? Is it some kind of festival or gala? Then, as I get closer I realise it's a funeral. It seems the service has just concluded at St Bigid's Catholic church and the cortège is about to follow the coffin to the graveyard on foot in traditional fashion; they trail off like a centipede behind it. There are hundreds of people and it appears that the whole population of the village are here, confirming David's point that everyone turns out for a wedding or a funeral in Ireland. The only difference, it's been said, between the two affairs, is that at a funeral there's one less drunk in attendance.

The process of sending off the deceased in Ireland begins with a wake in the home – though the tradition is sadly on the decline. A room is set aside for the coffin, in which are usually placed candles and a statue of Christ or the Virgin Mary. After the wake, the mourners follow the hearse on foot as the deceased is moved to the church for the service. I'm witness here to the final stage, and think that perhaps my route might also be the one to the graveyard and that I might have to tag onto the end of the cortège at a respectable distance. But another lane leads off from the village green – that runs alongside the River Derry. A signpost points me along it. I'm now on the famous Wicklow Way.

The Wicklow Way was created in 1980 and was the first long distance path in Ireland. It's the last of the six long-distance walks in Ireland that I shall trek, and the one that will take me the remaining 130km to Dublin's Marlay Park. As I leave Clonegal behind the church bells ring out a mournful three peals followed by a single peal. The sound fades as I go and the Way swings north away from the river.

This morning I forgot to put walking socks into the rucksack as I set off on the bike, so now my already blistered feet are beginning to feel the heat. Each step is somewhat painful.

A gravelled track with a grass centre leads off through a forest. It emerges on a lane that soon swings east. But now it starts to descend and I begin to worry that yet again I've gone astray. I ask a couple of ladies walking uphill if I'm on the Wicklow Way which they confirm. But after about two kilometres I check the compass and realise it's pointing south not east, and that they clearly didn't understand my question. I'm almost down at the village of Park Bridge before I finally decide to slog it back uphill and search for the missed fingerpost, which is hidden in the undergrowth. The air is blue with the muffled curses. My blistered tootsies are complaining. It is, or seems like, a very long walk before I meet the road – where I leave the Way and head to my destination of Shillelagh. But the views compensate – and by 5.30 I'm back at the camper.

This is oak country; Tomnafinnoge Woods to the north-east of Shillelagh is the largest remaining oak forest in Ireland. Tradition has it that it was oak taken from these woods that was originally used to make the walking sticks to which the village of Shillelagh gave its name. But Shillelaghs are usually made from blackthorn, as were, it's said, witches wands. The Irish smeared them with butter and stuck them up their chimneys to cure and to prevent the wood from cracking. If you got a crack from one though you'd know it – they were used during the 18th and 19th centuries in faction fighting – a kind of Irish mass brawl that took place at fairs, markets and such between rival gangs. They were particularly common in County Tipperary.

I drive back to Kildavin to pick up the bike, then down to Bunclody to try and get something to eat.

Everywhere appears to be closed, but a lady directs me to The Millrace Hotel and Spa – a posh-looking glass fronted place where I fear the price will make a dent in my budget. But I'm pleasantly surprised, and the waiter (who thinks I'm staying there instead of slumming it in the camper) is very friendly and attentive. I leave him a tip and then drive back to the gravel car park adjacent to the general stores in Shillelagh to camp for the night.

Wednesday 25th June – Shillelagh to Tinahely
By 9.35am I've driven from Shillelagh to Tinahely, biked back, locked the bike to a post by the general stores, changed and have walked the two miles back to the Wicklow Way. The day is overcast but there's no sign of rain.

A little way into the walk I come across the first anti-pylon sign, pinned to the trunk of a tree: PEOPLE BEFORE PYLONS it reads, with a picture of said pylon encircled, with a red line drawn through it. A little further along another sign announces: NO PYLONS HERE! What's this all about?

Apparently it's to do with the Grid Link Project. This is a huge investment proposal to link electricity stations near Cork, Waterford and Kilcullen in County Kildare in order to provide a reliable electricity supply for Leinster and Munster. In addition, the proponents claim that it will help the country meet its renewable energy target – and maybe some electricity might be able to be sold to Britain and France! A lot of consultation and debate is afoot with regards to the route corridor, where the substations might be located, and the major issue as to whether, instead of running the power lines over ground connected by 50-metre-high pylons, they could be run underground. The government say that running underground would increase the cost of electricity to the consumer; there are also, it's claimed, technical and operational difficulties. Pylon opponents claim that magnetic fields emanating from them cause cancer in children and that tourism would be affected. There's also of course the 'small issue' that house prices would be devalued. The proposed route would traverse through several areas of outstanding natural beauty and there's no doubt that pylons as they are, are not particularly attractive. It's been optimistically suggested that a design which is both functional and aesthetic might not be beyond the realms of possibility.

It will be interesting to see what develops on the pylon front. EirGrid plc who are running the project and who operate Ireland's national electricity grid, have received over 35,000 submissions as a result of the public consultations held to date. They propose to submit a planning application to an independent national body called *An Bord Pleanála* anytime from 2016 onward.

I walk through the village of Kilquiggan, which was devastated during the potato famine. It's a time still marked nearby by a road known as Union Road – constructed as one of the public works projects to create employment.

Further along the boreen a corrugated tin hut and explanatory plaque confirms I've reached a place called Stranakelly. The hut was built in 1950 as a store and fuel depot for a shop which was a further 200 yards up a narrow lane. Delivery vehicles couldn't reach the shop and would leave their goods at the roadside, so a chap called Tom Shea built the hut. It was in use for 11 years until the shop closed.

At the crossroads a little further on there used to be a pub called Tallons – but it was renamed following a visit one night from the Gardai. The story goes that they raided the pub for serving drinks out of licensing hours and the widow who ran it told them she was just serving neighbours who'd called around to help her with her dying cow. So the pub has ever since been known as The Dying Cow.

Today's walk has been entirely along lanes, but after leaving the village of Mullinacuff a sunken footpath skirts interestingly around a farm; the path descends gradually around the side of Muskeagh Hill. Sheep graze on either side of the path and I pass a ewe and her (almost as big) lamb snuggled up together in a bank under a tree. For once they don't scuttle off as usual, so I manage to get a good photograph. Wicklow sheep are descended from Cheviot sheep that came from the borders of England and Scotland and were imported here around 1850. I've read that they are usually a very alert and active sheep, but this pair believes in leading a quiet life.

I'm leading a quiet life too, having seen not a soul since leaving Shillelagh about six hours ago. But now the footpath meets a lane which soon joins the busy R747 main road. The Way turns left up the main road, but I turn right and walk down into Tinahely to re-bond again with the camper.

Thursday 26th June – Arklow and Tinahely

I meet Jim Rees as planned at the Arklow Bay Hotel, a short drive from the relative luxury of the campsite at Redcross where I've spent last night. Jim has just turned 60, and is a published author of quite a few history related books. He doesn't drive, so we head out in the camper back towards Tinahely. I'd tracked him down somehow from the Internet and had written to him about Father Thomas Hore who'd led 1,200 people over to America in 1850. Jim's written a book about it called *A Farewell to Famine*. He's also written *Surplus People*, a book that tells the story of those who were evicted from the Coolattin Estate close to nearby Shillelagh during the potato famine period. I feel I'm in good hands.

We're heading for the famine graveyard at Whitefield and to St Kevin's church in Killaveny, near Tinahely, from where, on 2nd June 1850, Father Hore had tried to convince a congregation of about 2,000 to follow him to a better life in America.

During the journey Jim tells me something about himself. He'd left school at 16 with few qualifications and over the years had worked in various jobs – but he'd always harboured a passion for history and literature. This he finally realised when, through the Open University, he obtained a BA in Humanities with Literature and later a Masters Degree in History from Maynooth in County Kildare. He now teaches the subject to youths aged between 15 and 22 whom for various reasons did not fit into the main-stream educational system.

We park just off the main road, about a kilometre from Tinahely and climb up the lane towards Whitefield but then turn right to the famine graveyard. Within this site was once the old church – burnt during the 1798 rebellion. Now the graveyard's been renovated and laid out again as an outdoor church with wooden benches and an altar, supported on four plinths, facing the benches. A limestone memorial stone on six granite pillars standing adjacent to it was uncovered during renovation work. Long strands of cut grass lay strewn around the area outside the church heaped up against the headstones. There are fewer than I expected; around 30 it seems, though many other graves are marked by a fieldstone. A lot of those who died during the famine were buried without markers and as I look out over the famine graveyard I feel a pang of guilt about being English.

Things became still more desperate for the Irish people as 1847 progressed. Throughout the country paupers poured from the countryside into the towns; Cork had around 20,000 and begging became prevalent. By July well over two million people were receiving government rations, but the government then decided to let the supplies in food depots run out. Relief employment was closed down. Deaths in the workhouses approached 3,000 a week – there were more bodies than gravediggers, and as all the seed potatoes and grain had been eaten over the winter, there was nothing to plant.

In June the British government passed the Poor Law Extension Act which nullified aid previously given to tenant farmers who owned more than a quarter of an acre of land. This meant that they were required to contribute through rates to maintaining their peasant labourers, many of whom had finished up in the workhouse or on outdoor relief. It was cheaper for them to get rid of their tenants. By September this course of action had begun to kick-in as the number of evictions began to increase. For about half the cost of keeping a peasant in the workhouse they could be exported to Canada. The governor of Nova Scotia perhaps foresaw what was about to happen when he wrote to the Colonial Secretary warning him that the prospects of employment were poor in Canada. But they were non-existent for many in Ireland and this together with the fever outbreak drove thousands to flee the country in a mad rush.

The largest estate in County Wicklow was the Coolattin Estate, which consisted of over 80,000 acres; Coolattin House near Shillelagh was at its centre. It was owned at the time of the famine by Earl Fitzwilliam, a descendant of the infamous Thomas Wentworth (known in the area by the nickname of 'Black Tom' as he rode around in black armour on a black horse – or perhaps because of his sour nature), who'd acquired the estate by coercion. Fitzwilliam was chiefly resident on his Wentworth House estate in South Yorkshire, but on his Irish estate he had more than 20,000 tenants, who by and large considered him a fair and liberal landlord. But the dire circumstances of his tenants and their sub-tenants meant that, with the responsibility of paying the rates for them and with decreasing rent revenues, he faced bankruptcy. Unlike many of his contemporaries though he took the relatively humane approach of offering them free passage and financial help to resettle overseas.

Emigrants generally sailed in sturdy cargo ships, crudely adapted for passengers, with little thought given to their comfort, but many went in ships that didn't comply with the basic standards laid down in the Passenger Vessels Act – such ships were later known as 'coffin ships'. They were overcrowded and were not provided with adequate supplies of food and water. On the Cork to Quebec run 20% died either on board or soon after landing. Quebec was the usual landing place for Canada bound emigrants who'd managed to get a cheap passage across the Atlantic. Thirty miles up'river from the city they were disembarked at an island quarantine station called Grosse Isle.

Those passengers who landed there were housed in overcrowded sheds, an attempt being made to segregate the healthy from the sick, though the incubation period of typhus made this difficult to determine. At the end of May 10,000 emigrants on board 30 vessels were waiting to be processed off Grosse Isle. By July almost 60% of the 3,500 people on the island were in hospital sheds whilst the healthy were allowed to move on to Quebec. On declaring their intention to settle in Canada emigrants then generally got free passage down the St Lawrence to Montreal – but most were aiming to cross the border into the United States. By the end of 1847 over 300 families from the Coolattin Estate had emigrated – most arriving in Quebec.

The clearances from the Coolattin Estate continued through to 1856 with in all a total of almost 900 families emigrating.

Most who left the shores of their native land for the new life carried with them a hatred of Britain and especially everything English.

Jim leads us now up the hill to St Kevin's church. A plaque inside records that it was built in 1843 by Father Hore and the parishioners to replace the church known as the Penal church (erected in 1700 during the Penal laws) that once stood on the site we've just left.

Father Thomas Hore's family are thought to have come to Ireland with the Normans in around 1169. He was born around 1795 and was called to the priesthood at the age of 24. Dr Patrick Kelly, who'd been appointed bishop of the diocese of Richmond Virginia, favoured Thomas as his assistant and so he travelled with Dr Kelly to America. After six years there, and with deteriorating health, Father Hore returned to Ireland where he held a position as an administrator for 13 years. He was aged about 46 when he finally made it as parish priest of Killaveny and Annacurra, residing in the old parish church of the former. Three years later the new church in which he'd had a big hand in building was consecrated by the Bishop of Ferns.

I thought that it was in this church where on 2nd June 1850 Hore had preached to a large congregation trying to convince them to follow him and emigrate to America, but Jim tells me that there were so many people (an estimated 2,000) that they couldn't fit into the church, and that actually he'd addressed them in a field just across the road. We step outside to take a look.

At the time Ireland had suffered for the past five years with famine and its aftermath, and nobody knew how many more years of these conditions would have to be endured. As it happened 1850 was the last year of the famine. Hore, drawing upon his previous American experience while addressing his congregation, contrasted life in Ireland with that of 'the promised land'. He then stated that he proposed to leave for America in September and asked for the names of those who would like to go. About 100 persons gave their names.

In the autumn of that year Hore and 400 families left Counties Wexford and Wicklow and set off by horse and cart on the first stage of their long journey. They arrived in Dublin two days later. Mostly they were small farmers, better off than some as they had to cough up a fare of £5 each, which would have been about half a year's wages for those at the bottom of the pile. They took with them a good stock of agricultural implements and some pooled savings to purchase land in America – the horses and carts were sold or abandoned on the Dublin dockside.

They sailed to Liverpool on ships catering more for the comfort of valuable cattle than for human cargo. The conditions were undoubtedly overcrowded and uncomfortable. More 'adventure' awaited them at The Pool. They had first to dodge the attentions of currency converters, tailors, outfitters, confidence tricksters, pilfering hucksters, muggers, unscrupulous ticket brokers and the notorious 'Crimps', a despicable bunch of lodging-house touts who, amongst their other 'services', would guide sailors to dodgy lodging houses where they were sometimes dragged from their beds and shanghaied.

Because of the large size of his party Hore was able to avoid purchasing individual tickets from the brokers, and was instead able to charter three ships, but he was most probably still ripped off. They set sail to cross the Atlantic – two ships leaving at the end of October, whilst the remaining one sailed from the Mersey eight days later. To maximise their profit the brokers packed as many emigrants aboard as they could, turning a very deliberate blind eye to their passengers' legal entitlements. The ships' toilets (heads) were on deck and in rough weather they were out of bounds, so that chamber pots were used between decks and embarrassment, especially for the ladies, was unavoidable. Cooking was also difficult and then, when you'd eaten, there was the problem of keeping it down as the Atlantic rollers cut in. It took 40 days for the first ship, the one with Thomas Hore aboard, to reach New Orleans. She was the fastest – the slowest ship took 70 days.

Having endured this torturous crossing, some of Hore's party, having decided enough was enough, voted to stay in New Orleans. Others knew from a Wexford man, James Power, of a small town called Refugio in Texas that already had a small settlement of people from Wicklow and Wexford – and so set off west.

A thousand miles of river travel on a paddle steamer still faced the remainder of the group. They proceeded north up the Mississippi River accompanied by pickpockets, tricksters and crooks all of whom plied their trades aboard. From the swamps of Louisiana they finally made it to their planned journey's end of Little Rock in Arkansas. It seemed like a bit of an anticlimax.

Father Hore had expected houses to have been built there for his emigrants, but the priest given responsibility for making this happen had unfortunately upped and died before instigating this undertaking. They were instead offered the charitable accommodation of pews in the parish church. This was a prospect that the more affluent amongst them did not much savour and many families travelled on up to the sizable city of St Louis in north-east Missouri, which at the time had a population of over 160,000, over half of whom were immigrants. Those that remained in Little Rock did so either because of lack of funds or because members of their families were sick.

Other families told Father Hore that they wanted to go to Fort Smith, 150 miles west. After a month of scratching around unsuccessfully looking for suitable land on which those in Little Rock could settle, Father Hore accompanied this group there where he left about eight families before heading on up to St Louis to join the bulk of his flock.

Father Hore's ultimate goal had been to push on into Iowa, where he knew a new monastery, linked with one at Melleray in County Waterford, had recently been established. He intended to scout out for suitable purchasable land there. So this he did where he found a valley not far from Harper's Ferry that reminded him of home. Instinctively he splashed out the dollars and bought the land. But when he returned to St Louis to tell them the good news, many there had already settled down.

Those families who decided to share Father Hore's dream and re-embark on a steamer north were reduced to 18. They arrived at their final destination over three months after landing in America and represented only about 8% of those followers who'd set out from Ireland. The place of their settlement was named Wexford. The community prospered and grew. Towards the end of April 1851 a church was completed and by 1855 there was a school.

Father Hore had scattered his seed well in New Orleans, Refugio, Little Rock, St Louis, Fort Smith and Wexford (Iowa). Satisfied now that his crops would grow in the new land he returned to Ireland where he died in June 1864 aged 69.

We walk back down the hill to the camper and drive into Tinahely. In the centre of the square sits the old market house. Across the road is the old courthouse, now a thriving arts centre, with information plaques which tell some of the history of the village. It was totally destroyed by rebels during the 1798 rebellion as it had a reputation for supporting the yeomen. It was rebuilt afterwards, a plaque relates, as a Coollattin Estate village with support from the Fitzwilliams.

On the way back we stop off at Woodenbridge for a spot of lunch at the Woodenbridge Hotel, established in 1608 and said to be the oldest hotel in Ireland. Jim tells me that it was where Eamon de Valera stayed on his honeymoon and where John Redmond spoke to the Volunteers in August 1914 (convincing around 150,000 Irishmen to fight for Britain in the First World War).

We order drinks and check that we're not too early for lunch. Jim takes a Guinness of course, but I've not yet been fully converted – and stick to a lager. We take a table and order burger meals made (the menu states) from Irish beef, but named 'The Colorado Burger Supreme', perhaps catering for American tourists visiting here to find their Irish roots.

Jim tells me something of his work teaching history to youths who don't fit into the mainstream education profile.

'There's never any more than 12 in a class,' he says.

'Just boys?' I ask.

'No, mixed classes, it's difficult, but can sometimes be very rewarding. I start off by asking them if they like history and I get lots of bad language and abuse back. Don't forget, these youngsters have been left to one side in mainstream and learning history reminds them too much of that. Then I ask them who's interested in a good story, and they all say they are. So I write up the word *HISTORY* and cross out the *H* and *I* to leave the word *STORY*. That usually gets them on board.'

Before we drain our pints and set off for Arklow, Jim takes a call from East Coast Radio. He explains that he's started a campaign to prevent the proposed closure of the local studies services for County Wicklow which is based in Bray and is the HQ for research for the entire county.

'I put out an appeal yesterday,' he says, 'and a lady called Mary Mooty set up a website – so already 500 people have signed a petition. If they close the local studies there, we would be the only county that would have to go to Dublin to do research.'

That's just where I'm going – but I've somehow fallen one day behind my original schedule and, in order to spend the time I wanted to in Dublin and not have to change the ferry booking, I'll have to do some rethinking.

Sixteen
The Rocky Road to Dublin

'Then off to reap the corn, and leave where I was born.
I cut a stout black-thorn to banish ghost or goblin;
With a pair of brand new brogues, I rattled o'er the bogs
 Sure I frightened all the dogs on the rocky road to Dublin'.
From: *Rocky Road the Dublin*, by D.K. Gavan

Friday 27th June – Tinahely to Iron Bridge

Paddy Dillon reckoned to do Drumgoff to Tinahely (the reverse in my case) in one 36km bite. I spent some time last night considering the possibility, especially as I'm behind schedule. Close examination of Discovery maps, however, revealed that not only is the walking route hilly, but so is the bike ride back, running as it does (from the Glenmalure end) along the Military Road. This road, which crosses the spine of the Wicklow Mountains, was built by the British army following the rebellion in 1798 so they could easily flush out any rebels hiding out up there. It took them over nine years to complete the road and, judging from the contours on my map, it wouldn't have been a choice assignment.

Apart from the distance and the hills, the other problem I have is where to park the camper. There's only one 'P' shown on the map and that's at a place called Iron Bridge, which crosses the Ow River as it flows along the Ow valley. Either side of the valley the map shows tight-packed contours set in woodland. If I can't squeeze the camper in at Iron Bridge I'm in real trouble. I arrive there early, which is just as well given that the camper takes up the entire parking spot. The good news is that a brown Wicklow Way sign means there will be no 'off-route' walking today at the end of the walk. The footpath tumbles down through trees and leads straight to the camper.

It's an easy bike descent, following the Ow River valley, down into Aughrim, but from there to Tinahely is an undulating struggle. I even have to walk *down* one hill because my brakes still need, let's

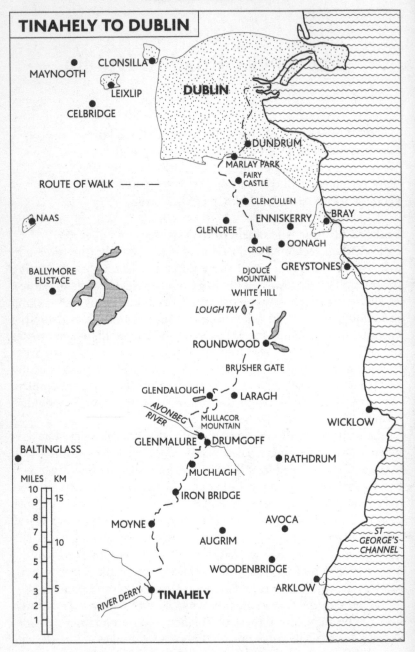

TINAHELY TO DUBLIN

MAYNOOTH
CLONSILLA
LEIXLIP
CELBRIDGE

DUBLIN

DUNDRUM
MARLAY PARK
FAIRY CASTLE

ROUTE OF WALK — — —

GLENCULLEN

NAAS

ENNISKERRY
BRAY

GLENCREE

CRONE
OONAGH

BALLYMORE EUSTACE

GREYSTONES

DJOUCE MOUNTAIN

WHITE HILL

LOUGH TAY

ROUNDWOOD

BRUSHER GATE

GLENDALOUGH
LARAGH

AVONBEG RIVER

MULLACOR MOUNTAIN

WICKLOW

GLENMALURE
DRUMGOFF

BALTINGLASS

RATHDRUM

MUCHLAGH

MILES KM

IRON BRIDGE

MOYNE

AVOCA

AUGRIM

ST GEORGE'S CHANNEL

WOODENBRIDGE

RIVER DERRY
TINAHELY

ARKLOW

say, some attention – and dragging my right foot along the floor proves not to be a suitably reliable braking technique.

When I'd left the Way to walk down into Tinahely, it went north along the main R747 road, and it seemed unlikely that there would be anywhere to park safely to pick up the bike at the end of the walk. So I leave it in Tinahely and trudge back up to the start of the path.

A late start today; it's 10.55am by the time I get going on the path. I cross the gentle flowing River Derry. Derry is the Irish name for oak, reflecting its prevalence in these parts, but here the river's banks are swathed in a white mass of giant hogweed, dangerous to man and dog alike. I follow the footpath and climb to walk back towards and above Tinahely, with last-glimpse views down over the village.

Today the clouds hang in long laminated sheets with ominous dark underbellies. The forecast is for showers – and so it proves. It goes like this: it starts to rain – I haul out mac from bottom of rucksack and put it on – rain stops – sun comes out – I take off mac and stow it at bottom of rucksack – it starts to rain again; this sequence repeats itself several times until I decide to leave the damned thing on.

After an hour I meet another walker also wearing a mac going towards Tinahely. He says:

'It can't make up its mind whether it's starting or stopping.'

'No,' I say, and we walk on in opposite directions – it's not the weather for a chat.

The day passes uneventfully. Somewhere in the distance church bells toll lonesome tunes and it's not even Sunday. A five-bar gate with teardrop rain reminds me I'm in a foreign country: *Dún an geata le do thoil* it reads; it's a good job they translated it into English as well, or I might have left it open.

I pass through the Georgian hamlet of Moyne, famous, as far as I'm concerned, for the fact that it was the southern end of the original Wicklow Way as planned by J.B. Malone.

Of Irish parentage, Malone was born and brought-up in England, moved to Ireland in 1931, joined the Irish army in 1940 and became a cartographer – which came in useful later in his life. He'd first thought of the idea of a long-distance walk through the Wicklow Hills in 1942 and proposed the concept in a series of newspaper articles in 1966. When he'd retired he put his efforts into negotiating rights of way with landowners to make his dream come true and in 1980 the first section of the Wicklow Way was opened. Ireland now boasts 40 such long distance trails. I might not be standing at this spot now if it hadn't have been for J.B. Malone.

'I CAN MAKE IT TO THE GATE IN 10 SECONDS – CAN YOU?'

This sign wins, for me, the best guard dog deterrent sign I think I've seen – and though there's no sign or sound of a canine, I still creep past.

Towards the end of the walk, on a narrow lane, a car slows up to squeeze past me; the first seen since leaving Tinahely. I give the thumbs up sign and the car stops.

'Are you waiting for me?' asks the driver. Then I realise it's a taxi.

'Oh, you're a taxi – no – I was just saying hello.' After all that hassle in Kildavin a few days ago trying to get a taxi, one turns up unrequested in the middle of nowhere!

The final forest walk back to the camper proves tricky as the previously clear signposting gives way to blue arrows and other confusing indicators painted on the ground – a final initiative test to dispel any complacency I might have. Then to add to the ferment, God plays a little joke on me and lets loose a heavy shower of rain. It begins slowly then pours down. I start a futile jog, but by the time I lunge down the slope to the parking spot near Iron Bridge I'm thoroughly soaked and my jeans are sticking to my legs like soggy chips to vinegar-soaked newspaper.

Back in Tinahely I pick up the bike and have pleasant thoughts of a nice shower back at the campsite. But... the camper won't turn over to start. My first thought is that I've foolishly taken out the immobilisation fob again. But no! My next thought is a loose battery connection. So I up the bonnet, fiddle about with it and turn the ignition key. Dead! I crawl underneath and check the alternator belt – it looks OK. So what now? I know it's not going to start, but try again anyway. Nothing...!

A man is passing; looks like he's had a few to drink, and it's only just after six. I ask if he knows of a garage. He has a foreign accent, and I don't mean Irish – possibly Polish. He scribbles down the phone number of a man called Pete. Pete is on answerphone when I call so I leave a message.

I need to eat and luckily I'm parked just over the bridge, not far from the centre of the village – but will anything be open? A few metres along the road I find O'Connor's bar in the square. I order fish and chips and tell the waitress my problem. She scoots off to fetch the barman.

'Ah,' he says, 'Paddy Brennan will be able to help you.' He makes a mobile call but nobody answers.

'He'll be open tomorrow morning,' the barman says. 'Your best bet is to stay where you are tonight and sort it out tomorrow.'

'OK, what time does he open?'

'About nine.'

'I don't seem to have much option,' I say. So he tells me that Brennan's garage is located back out along the R747. In fact I'd passed it this morning on my way to the start of the walk.

The fish and chips are of huge proportions, redolent of those sampled over a year ago at O'Neill's bar in Allihies. Pete calls me up during the meal. I thank him, but tell him I'm sorted. With nothing but the prospect of sitting in the camper for the rest of the evening, I order another pint and slip into a haze of languidness trying not to worry too much about tomorrow.

Saturday 28th June – Iron Bridge to Drumgoff

Early next morning whilst I'm eating breakfast in the camper a man gets out of his car and comes over to me.

'There was a mechanic here last night looking for you,' he says. It was obviously Pete – so now not only do I feel *really* guilty, but I also hope I've not burnt my very last bridge.

I'm at Paddy Brennan's garage well before nine o'clock – but at 10-past there's still no sign of life. I think seriously about phoning the number painted above the shutter doors to ask if they're working today, but five minutes later the doors rattle open. I tell Paddy my problem.

'One of the boys will be over shortly to sort you out,' he reassures me. So I squat on a wall and wait patiently. Some boys arrive – but they're bringing a motor in to have a new ball joint fitted and get it through the National Car Test. Almost half an hour passes before Paddy comes over and says he'll drive me to the camper where one of his mechanics will meet us with some jump leads.

Back at the garage, Paul the mechanic, Paddy's son, has just slid under the camper. He tells me the alternator belt is loose and that the bolt I thought my local garage had fitted is not there. He finds and fits a bolt and adjusts the belt – but the battery still isn't charging. So now he checks the fuses (when eventually establishing where they are); they're OK. Now he is, like me, puzzled.

'When do you want to be away?' he asks. This doesn't sound good. But then he discovers that a wire that should run from the dashboard to the alternator (that apparently sends a small charge to excite it) has come off. I get excited anyway. He connects the wire – and bingo! The bill for his time is very reasonable and I'm glad to be back on the road at last.

At Aughrim I buy a sandwich lunch, then drive on through Rathdrum and turn off, just before Laragh, onto the Military Road that backtracks south-west across the mountains. The prospect of cycling across these tomorrow is a worry. I pull in and stop to let a bus pass on the narrow road and, as it goes by, notice it declares itself 'WICKLOW WAY BUS'. The thought that maybe I could catch a bus to replace a bike ride flashes across my mind – so I let out a blast on the horn – but the bus has gone – and so sadly it seems are my chances of that little luxury. I drop the bike off at Drumgoff and drive on to Iron Bridge, parking just before it.

At 12.35pm I hit the trail and walk at pace. It's a stiff uphill haul after the bridge, and it's another 'on mac – off mac' day. Reaching a hut at Mucklagh with picnic tables I suspect the climbing is over – but it's not. The tables are there for appreciation of views over the patchwork forested hills to the mountains beyond. But today dark dishwater clouds spill like ice cream over the edge of a cone, to smother the highest peak. A rocky path eventually descends steeply and then levels out to reach the military road.

At this point the weather definitely makes up its mind. I don't actually encounter any dead cats and dogs being washed along the road, but it could be raining them; a gushing torrent runs along the edge of the road. Optimistically, I hadn't packed leggings so my legs are soon again like chips glued to vinegar-soaked paper. I hate my head being enclosed in the hood of the anorak, but now I have no option. It's a miserable walk along the military road that the soldiers building it must have many times cursed. But I'm heartened to see two other fools (a young couple) walking towards me in a similar disheartened and wet state; a nice gentle weekend walk for them, they thought!

I'm glad when the Way goes left off the road and climbs up through a forest. The rain eases to a mizzle here and before starting the climb I stop and try to eat lunch, but I'm plagued by midges, so have to defer the attempt until later. I also attempt to phone Polly, hoping she'd be able to give me the phone number of Wicklow Way Buses, but I can't get a signal. This is not turning out to be a good day!

The remaining walk is straightforward enough though; apart from a steep and slippery descent that narrow-slices its way down through conifers to connect one good track with another. Here a cyclist hauls his bike over a rock, through mud up onto another rock and through more mud – he's not bargained on this little intrigue and it looks like he's already slipped over a few times. I do too.

Further on, a stone plinth marker reads that this is the halfway mark of the Wicklow Way. I've apparently walked 65.5km along it. A loud, high pitched screech startles me; this must be deer country (either that or somebody is being murdered).

I cross Drumgoff Bridge over the Avonbeg River and drop down onto a road where the Way turns left and leads a short distance to the crossroads at Drumgoff, which sits in the centre of the longest glacial valley in Ireland – Glenmalure. The place is dominated by the long white façade of Glenmalure Lodge and the sudden 'civilisation' of a crammed-full car park. In contrast, in the field below the lodge I catch sight of two chained horses grazing alongside a traditional gypsy caravan.

Glenmalure is full of history. There was a battle here in 1580 which the British, who were trying to capture a rebel chieftain, lost decisively; it was also one of the last places in which the rebellion of 1798 was suppressed. There were other things afoot too, or more specifically underground. In the 19th century the area was sprinkled with lead mines. Zinc and copper were also extracted.

Over the crossroads the road climbs steeply to where I've left the bike. I attempt to ride back down the hill, but without brakes this is frighteningly precarious. As I succumb and dismount, a gent out for a stroll from the Glenmalure Lodge, and thinking I'm staying there too, calls out:

'You're nearly there.'

No I'm not!

It's time to adjust the brakes – so I take out the little toolkit. Don't know why I didn't do this before; it's not that difficult and at least I'll be able to ride *down* the hills.

Forty minutes later I'm back with the camper at Iron Bridge.

Sunday 29th June – Drumgoff to Roundwood

To catch up on the schedule I decided last night to drive on to Roundwood Caravan and Camping Park with the aim of leaving the camper there, biking back to Drumgoff and walking back to it.

It's eight o'clock when I release the bike from the back of the camper and set off. The ride to Laragh is easy enough as it mainly follows the Avonmore River valley. The tough stuff, I know, is to come.

But first to get some breakfast and a packed lunch. I stop at Glendalough Green Café Deli. It's still only around 8.30am and the lady tells me that the bread I ask for is not yet baked and will be about 10 minutes. I sit at a table with a very large cup of piping hot black coffee and study the Discovery map while I wait. Pleasant smells abound – hot bread baking brings back childhood memories; I used to pass a bakery on my way to primary school. The baguette when it's done is both hot and nicely soft. It packs neatly into my rucksack. I'm surprised at how little I'm charged and ask if they've got it right.

'The coffee is gratis,' says the lady. It's a good start to the day.

But then to the hill climbs up the dreaded Military Road that snakes around the Cullentraghn and Carriglineen Mountains. I check my watch when I finish the transformation from reluctant sweating cyclist to cool walker – it's 9.45.

The day is cloudy but warm. A stony track cuts its way along a forested slope for about the first three kilometres of the walk, with views of the mountains off to my right. It's a Sunday, so I'm not alone; there's a couple a little way ahead. Suddenly a fingerpost points away from the level track and the Way climbs steeply up into the hills. After a rocky-path ascent through trees heading towards the slopes of Mullacor Mountain, I find the couple seated on a grassy knoll as the path emerges onto the open hillside – just the spot I would have chosen, so I'm forced to climb on. Four mountain bikers hurtle downhill past me. I say, thinking of the rocky path below,

'You'll have some fun down there!'

'It's a race to the bottom,' one of them calls back.

A grass-beaten path continues to climb, giving way, as the land levels out, to a wooden boardwalk across the obviously sometimes boggy ground. The fingerposts are well placed and easy to spot. It's a wonderful walk around the slopes of the mountain, before the path drops back down sharply to meet a wide stony track that descends on gently. As it does so, eight runners puff towards me on their Sunday morning workout, about to start the hard part.

I walk on a while; then take a break. I'm sitting on a log and writing notes when, 15 minutes later, the group of runners pound back down towards me. I try to photograph them, but I'm not quick enough and mess up.

'Did you get me?' the lead runner shouts, but he's well past me before I can react. I just manage to take a photograph of them disappearing – several straggler ladies struggling to keep up. Normally I'd be on a run too on a Sunday morning so I feel some empathy with them – but these days I'd be behind the ladies bringing up the rear. I've been a runner (latterly a jogger) for over 30 years, my running diaries record I've covered over 22,000 miles. But walking is something completely different – there's time to stop, look around and appreciate the views. Here they are fine: forested foreground slopes enveloping aloof purple tinged mountains.

Now I start to enter St Kevin country. Last night, while trying to plan this day's walk I asked Polly about St Kevin's bus service. She laughed, thinking that Kevin was a recently derived name that couldn't possibly be associated with a saint. She was wrong.

Below me through the trees lies a rectangular lake called Upper Lake, and tucked into the cliff above it (I read from my Wicklow Way guide book) is a two-metre-long cave known as St Kevin's Bed. Named after the legendary saint (a descendant of a Leinster king, who reportedly was born in 498 and lived to the ripe old age of 120), St Kevin's Bed is a tomb actually thought to be of man-made Bronze Age origin – circ. 2000 BC.

At the Poulanass Waterfall the Glendalough Sunday day-trippers appear in their throngs. A plaque affirms this place is part of Glendalough Woods Nature Reserve. It explains that over the centuries rock and silt had washed down Lugduff Brook and caused a delta to form which divided the lake into two: Upper and Lower Lakes, so giving Glendalough its name 'glen of two lakes'. I reach Lower Lake via flights of steps, encountering on the way American, German, Dutch, Spanish and a smattering of Irish tongues. On a bench seat here I consume the delightful deli baguette, watching families trek to and from the lake. Then continuing along the busy track I come to the Monastic 'City', founded it's said by St Kevin.

The 7th century became known as the Irish Golden Age, of which the valley of Glendalough was a part. It was a time when schools of art and learning sprang up throughout Ireland. Under the influence of missionaries, and in monasteries, Irish craftsmen produced elaborate decorated manuscripts and artefacts. It was at this time that St Kevin came to this then remote valley and set up his hermitage near the Upper Lake.

Everything about St Kevin is the stuff of legends. It started when he was a baby and was about to be baptised. It's said that an angel appeared and instructed his parents that he should be given the name Kevin, which in Latin means 'fair-begotten', or 'he of blessed birth'.

As a young man Kevin was apparently a good looking chap and, although wishing to remain celibate to pursue a priestly sort of life, he was nonetheless pursued by an attractive young lady called Kathleen. According to the writer Thomas Moore she had 'eyes of a most unholy blue'. Moore's poem: 'Glendalough – By That Lake Whose Gloomy Shore', tells the no doubt fictional tale of how the relationship ended. The call of the flesh was indeed quite strong it seems for Kevin, and the only way he could curtail his passions was to toss off all his clothes and jump naked into a bed of nettles. Kathleen either thought he'd been stung by the love bug or was playing hard to get. Either way she was actually quite impressed by Kevin's foolhardy act and continued to pursue him to St Kevin's Bed – the cave in the cliff above Upper Lake. They must both have been pretty good climbers because there have been several recorded accidents in recent times of people trying to reach the cave. But Kevin wouldn't give in to the desires of that floozy Kathy and unsportingly threw her to a watery grave below (he could, I think, just have told her to push off). It was about this time that he submitted his CV to become a saint – and surprisingly got the job.

Seamus Heaney also gave a symbolic account of another of St Kevin's legendary exploits in his poem 'St Kevin and the Blackbird'. It seems Kev was aiming to enter 'the Guinness book of fifth century records' by breaking the 'extending your turned-up palm out of your window for the longest time' record. Unquestionably he entered the famed mythical book because a blackbird made a nest in his palm and laid its eggs there, such that he was then obliged to spend weeks with his hand stuck out the window waiting for the eggs to hatch, and then waited some more for the fledglings to fly away.

I stroll around the grounds of the Monastic 'City' with the other tourists (as I now am). Everything here has the feel about it of St Kevin. I wander in and out of St Kevin's kitchen (church) and climb the grassy embankment to view the graveyard and the most impressive 30-metre-high cone-topped round tower which could well have been used as a watchtower to give warning of an oncoming Viking attack. In normal use though hand bells were rung from it to call the monks to prayer.

The track continues along the floor of the valley to a huge car and coach park crammed with vehicles before it reaches the Glendalough Hotel. Here I finally escape the crowds by climbing high above it on a footpath, back into blissful solitude.

From this point on, until I reach Marlay Park on the outskirts of Dublin, I shall be walking on ground I've trodden before. It was 17 years ago and for three days, but in the opposite direction, I walked it with my wife Anne, who's since died of breast cancer. She didn't walk the last day though, retiring at Roundwood with a painful knee; instead she caught a bus to Laragh where we met up. Apart from the walk, most memorable for its wind and rain, it was the death of Princess Diana that sticks in my mind. After the walk we stayed a night in a bed and breakfast in Bray and learned of her fate over breakfast from a group of lads. I can remember where I was on only two other such occasions: the deaths of President Kennedy and of John Lennon. Death sometimes has an unexpected way about it.

In a while I catch a final far-off view through trees of the two lakes, nestling like minute pools between the predominant dark-green tree slopes. There's still 12 kilometres of walking left to do today and now it's the middle of the afternoon.

Unexpectedly I reach a school and realise I've gone wrong yet again (first time today though) because I'm almost in Laragh. I double back to the cross-tracks and take a right fork. There's no fingerpost that I can find here. But after five minutes I check the compass; I'm walking north-west and should be going north-east. As I double back to the cross-tracks for a second time I'm tempted by a path off to the left and take it for a short while until it shoots off downhill. This is all I need. There was no trouble 17 years ago; but then most people start the Wicklow Way at Marlay Park, so the fingerposts tend to reflect this. On the fourth attempt I find the correct route, but I've lost three quarters of an hour in the process.

The Way climbs up Paddock Hill and down again. I'm beginning to feel weary. The track passes alongside a forest and narrows alarmingly; ferns increasingly engulf it. I expect it to turn right, but instead it swings left. Surely I can't have gone wrong again? What remains of the track begins to push uphill and now is no more than 20cm wide. Now it's down to 10cm and then there's no track at all – and I'm sweating considerably, ploughing through a sea of ferns. Reluctantly I pull out the compass and confirm what I know already: I'm on a westerly course and should be walking north-east. I've come so far I don't want to go back, but the field is fenced, preventing me going north-east and forcing me to continue westerly. Now there's no option but to wild-romp diagonally back down, through the suffocating ferns that hide dangerous ruts beneath, heading for the corner of a forest, where I was 15 minutes before.

I walk back along the widening path searching for my last mistake. A young woman is walking towards me.

'Are you walking the Wicklow Way?' I ask.

'No,' she says, 'I'm just out for a day walk.' But she has a 1:25 scale map which is twice as good as mine, and together we figure out where I've missed the sign. It's apparently at a place called Brusher Gate. But there's no signpost there, just three young lads lying about, taking a break. One tells me they've just come from my destination – Roundwood, and confirms I have to take a left turn. I take it and pass a water tap at the side of a house that rings a distant bell in my aging brain from 17 years past.

Now I'm on an undulating and, at this time of day, boring road until I reach a crossroads where I turn off the Way and head towards the caravan park. I make it at 6.45. The walk has taken nine hours.

I drive back to Drumgoff to collect the bike. There's no time for a shower, and only just time to pop into The Coach House in Roundwood for some grub.

Monday 30th June – Roundwood to Glencree

At 8.15am I leave the campsite and retrace my steps back to the Way. A man with short white hair leaves his bed and breakfast and walks ahead of me in the same direction. I dawdle to keep a respectable distance. At nine o'clock I reach the turnoff to the Wicklow Way. The white-haired man has paused before starting on it, and as I approach I see he's actually a she. I walk on past the young woman and, looking back after a little while, see she's now behind me by about the same distance as I was behind her.

I take great care not to get lost this morning, but a strangely 'plated over' fingerpost immediately has me scratching my head again. Luckily I manage to stay on the correct path this time. It climbs up through a forest and runs past a reservoir, with good views down to it and the hazy line of St George's Channel beyond, 15 kilometres away – as the crow flies.

It's another wonderful day, with blue skies dotted with the odd fluffy cumulus cloud. I've been very lucky with the weather.

The terrain is varied: from the forest track, there's a short uphill climb on a road, then another on a boardwalk laid in a tree lined hollow followed by a track that zigzags its way across moorland to a view over the placid cobalt blue of Lough Tay.

The weather is not always this glorious; it was raining when I was here in August 17 years ago.

It was horrendous weather on 12th August almost 68 years ago; in fact a fierce storm was battering the coastline and White Hill, which I reach just along from Lough Tay, was blanketed by thick black cloud. Meadow Pipits, snuggling down in heather to keep dry, broke cover and took to the air in fright as the engine drone drowned out the howling wind. Then suddenly the sound intensified to became a shattering roar, followed moments later by a second roar as the airplane bounced and skidded across the slope, ripping off its undercarriage and three of its propeller engines. There followed an eerie silence – apart from the ever whining wind.

It happened in 1946 on the shallow slopes just below the path on which I'm walking (as shown on my Wicklow Way map – though there seems to be some doubt about the actual spot). The plane, carrying a troop of French Girl Guides for a holiday, had been blown off its planned course to Dublin and had lost radio contact. When they broke cloud cover the pilot of the Junkers transport plane had somewhat of a shock to see a mountain in front of him. He tried desperately, but in vain, to prevent the inevitable and but for the strength of the corrugated airframe many of the 26 occupants on board would have lost their lives. As it was, nobody died, but, as none of the Guides were wearing seat belts at the time, there *were* serious injuries. The Guides' campsite was not now to be in tents as they'd anticipated but in the fuselage of the aircraft – along with turf and mud thrown in from the crash, and petrol and oil spilled out from ruptured tanks. It took five hours to raise the alarm and another six hours for rescuers to grope their way through the ever denser fog to the crash site. They got there at around midnight.

The Wicklow Way that follows the boggy ground around the slopes of Djouce Mountain has been laid with a boardwalk of hobnail-stapled (for grip) railway sleepers. It's designed not only to prevent wet feet, but also soil erosion – but it doesn't feel like a real walk – instead it seems rather synthetic. It's dry today and, where possible always the rebel, I deviate to the side of the sleepers; the trampled grass suggests I'm not the first.

The views across to the sea are uplifting. Past the petite breast-like peak of Great Sugar Loaf and the flat-chested Little Sugar Loaf I can just see my destination for the day – Bray. A couple are ahead of me. I see them in the distance for some time. They take a break and we say 'hello'. From their accents they are American (or perhaps Canadian).

For a late lunch I make the steep and rocky descent down and over the wooden footbridge to the banks of the Dargle River. It's as busy as Bondi Beach at Christmas. A party of youths and their leader clump behind me and head downstream to picnic and paddle. Two blonde girls with heavy looking backpacks, who I guess are maybe German or Dutch, labour slowly up the slope in the direction of Roundwood – taking frequent breaks to turn around and look back down. The American couple overtake me whilst I take my lunch.

Now I tackle the steep rocky path back up from the river. A little further on there's a good view down the glen to the impressive 250-metre-high Powerscourt Waterfall that the Dargle dashes madly down. I encounter the American couple here again, take the lead – and this time lose them.

The path runs through Crone woods, crosses the little Glencree River, and snakes its way to follow it pleasantly upstream before continuing on a grassy path bordered by ferns where it meets a lane and parking area.

I start the climb up from the lane on a narrow rocky path. The idea is to make it around Knockree Hill to the next lane. But it's hard work and after a few minutes I double back down – mindful that I have to catch the St Kevin bus back to the campsite and it's a long road walk via Enniskerry to the bus stop at Bray. I turn right at a lane junction and, when I see a man trimming a hedge, suspect I may have again screwed up. I tell him I'm aiming to get to Bray.

'Yes,' he confirms, 'you're in Oonagh – you need to go back up the road and take a right. I have to go into Bray a bit later to pick up my wife,' he says, 'if it was five o'clock I'd take you.'

'Thanks,' I say.

The time is only 3.45, but to be honest (as it wouldn't be breaking any of my walking rules) I'm tempted to tell him that I'll hang around. But instead, I'm off on the foot-slog. It takes until 5.30 to reach Bray where I wait by the Tudor style late 19th century Market House and Town Hall for St Kevin to collect me (his timetable tells me) at 6.40. This is not strictly true; I actually nip into a pub on Main Street for a pint.

Tuesday 1st July – Glencree to Dublin

The alarm on the mobile phone goes off at 6am. This time last year I was around 250 kilometres south-west of here in Mallow, County Cork. I know this because today's my 69th birthday. I'd originally planned to finish the walk in Dublin today as an appropriate celebration, but now it doesn't seem likely.

I need to start the walk as close as possible to where I finished yesterday, but yesterday I saw that the lanes out of Glencree were car-width, and I'm very nervous about driving the camper there; better, I think, to park on a wider road somewhere just to the west of Enniskerry and walk from there.

Then there's the question of today's finish. The end of the Wicklow Way at Marlay Park is the obvious target – but then what? I've ruled out using the bike because of the uncertainty of where to park for the drop off, and anyway I don't fancy taking the camper into the city. St Kevin's bus stops at a suburb called Mount Merrion and to catch it I'd have to walk about 6km from Marlay Park. But the closest I can get off the bus to where I'm starting the walk is at Bray, which means another lengthy plod back to the camper. This anyway is my rough plan.

I park the camper in a lay-by by a field of cows and, as I kit out for the walk, check my sad feet. I pierce with a penknife a blister on my right big toe and another on my left little toe, and squeeze out the fluid. But I decide the one on my right big toe isn't quite ripe enough, so wrap a plaster around it. Then I gently pull on the usual two layers of woolly socks – it should do the trick.

I leave the camper at 7.30 and, as I pass the youth hostel at Lacken House on the way to the start of the walk, catch sight of the white-haired girl I'd last seen near Roundwood; she's chattering with a group of young people congregated outside around a picnic table. She'll be following along behind me somewhere today for sure.

For a second time I pick my way up the narrow rocky path I'd started on yesterday. It turns out to be a fairly short section that then emerges onto a level track to skirt Knocktree and meet a lane. At a parking area I join another track that gradually winds its way up through forested land. There's blue skies and sunshine again today, but it brings out the flies as the day begins to warm up. Three women pass me, going in the opposite direction, with three dogs – all returning to their cars after their early morning workout.

The track continues to gradually climb, but then a fingerpost points to a mere ribbon of a path that picks its way up steeply on rocks around boulders, the stumps of sawn-off trees and vibrant spruce trees, where the walk turns into an interesting scramble – and the fun is to spot the next black and yellow fingerpost.

Reaching some trees at the top, I rest and look back down over the forest. I'm sure this must have been the spot of which, ingrained in my dim memory bank from some 17 years past, I've retained the image of us struggling to unfold a map in the frenzied wind that almost tore it out of our hands. I harboured then only a brief thought that I might one day complete the whole of the Wicklow Way – but had no thought that one of us would be dead within a decade. I remember that we stood looking in questioning disbelief at the prospect that we actually had to climb down this rubbled route.

By contrast the Way now becomes a flat, almost cinder-like track. I think I'm totally alone here, but then I count in the distance six deer, all of which disappear as I approach, like pebbles thrown into sand. I cross moorland around the slopes of a hill known as Prince William's Seat, possibly named after a royal visit made here by the Prince in 1821 – though the actual origin of the name may date back earlier. The Way then drops down through a forest before views appear of the village of Glencullen. Plaques on the Boranaralty Bridge across the river here record that it was rebuilt in 1905 after the previous bridge had been destroyed by a flood. I then have to follow the R116 road for a kilometre or so before climbing up onto the last bit of moorland before Dublin. I stop here for lunch – and take time out to laze in the sun. There's a view across to the distant Sugar Loafs that can still just be seen peeking out over a closer hillside.

There is a decision to be made at a junction of paths – do I add an extra kilometre or so and take a detour to see the Fairy Castle? Curiosity gets the better of me. But it's just a disappointing pile of rocks – a cairn to mark the summit of Two Rock Mountain.

Below the cairn, however, is the remains of a passage tomb, one of a series that apparently stretches across the Dublin and West Wicklow Mountains. The entrance to the tomb is somewhere below the cairn and archaeologists think that inside the tomb is a small burial chamber. Nobody has ever taken a look inside the tomb though possibly for fear of the fairies, or 'The Good Folk' as they're sometimes known, inflicting upon them a curse.

Curses it seems can be liberally applied if the fairy world is disturbed. Just like the legendary Pharaoh's Curse that's supposed to have taken the form of a mosquito and bitten the cheek of Lord

Carnarvon who sponsored the excavation of the tomb of King Tutankhamun and, who shortly after receiving the bite, himself bit the dust. Fairy castles are of the same ilk as fairy forts and were, and perhaps still are, thought to be the entrances to the world of the fairies.

One species of fairy is of course the green-coated leprechaun; an impish little rascal who's said to help Irish housewives mend shoes – he's probably getting 'jobseekers' allowance' right now. But in the past if a husband returning home from work had gone down to the cellar for a bottle and had found a little man wearing a green jacket lying drunk there, his wife could plausibly say that the leprechaun had rewarded himself with a drink or two after a hard day of shoe repairing – right! This was possibly a load of old cobblers! But leprechauns were once very rich little chaps and hid their pots of gold in fairy forts and, in the same way that the Pharaohs' curses protected tombs, so anyone interfering with fairy forts or even so much as cutting brush nearby would soon face death.

An example of fairies' wrath was heard and recorded by Thomas Johnson Westropp, an antiquarian, folklorist and archaeologist, in 1907. The story, that's thought to have occurred around 1839, concerned a man responsible for organising workmen to level a fairy fort who suddenly fell down dead. Luckily for him his wife knew a thing or two about magic and rushed to the 'fairy spot' where she did a deal with the fairies by offering to exchange her husband's walking stick for his life; perhaps not a fair exchange if you were a fairy, you might think. Nevertheless the fairies thought this was very fair(y) as they were secret ambulists (collectors of walking sticks). Before her eyes then, and that of a sizeable crowd who'd gathered, the man's walking stick disappeared from this world into the fairy collectors' coffers and the 'dead man' returned to life from his brief trip into fairyland.

From Fairy Castle the expanse of Dublin city spreads out below me. I walk back to the junction of paths and pick up the Wicklow Way again. I'm at a height of 490 metres – so now the walk is all downhill. From the moorland around Kilmashogue Mountain the Way slips down between a forest to pass a golf course and arrive at a car park where day-walkers park to explore the mountains.

Now I'm on the last stretch to Marlay Park, walking along a country lane that could have been anywhere on the long walk from Dursey Island; the only difference is that now it's very close to the city. Soon the hum of traffic on the M50 intensifies to rudely permeate the solitude and silence. I walk under the motorway and turn right to follow it towards the park. To relieve my sore feet I walk on the grass verge close to the motorway.

Ahead, on the verge a woman wearing a huge pink floppy hat is also heading for Marlay Park. We arrive there together at a large information board and map of the park. She asks me for directions, but I don't even know where I'm going let alone being able to help her.

'Sorry, I've not been here before,' I lie.

'As it's a nice day,' she says, 'I decided to hand deliver some post – and now I'm lost.'

'So am I,' I say.

She wanders off into a Portakabin to enquire there.

Looking around, I find a Wicklow Way sign that directs me through the park where I dodder alongside the river of the same name that flows through the park, and eventually into the River Liffey. The 300-acre park is crowded with pushchairs (it seems) and families enjoying the fine weather. It's a pleasant enough stroll past ponds and over little bridges to where Paddy Dillon says I'll find a car park near Marlay House and a map of part of the Wicklow Way route that signifies I've reached the end of the trail.

It's not to be. A notice reads 'THIS PART OF THE PARK IS CLOSED – PLEASE FIND AN ALTERNATIVE ROUTE'. It seems there's some sort of event about to go on, and the area has been fenced off. But it's not a particularly helpful notice – and I fumble around like a blind man in a maze and end up in the Regency walled gardens. Now I just want to get out of the park – but how? With difficulty is the answer and, after some time trying, I have to resort to the indignity of asking somebody.

On a grass verge by the main road outside the park I sit, spread out the Discovery map and a Collins Dublin street map, drink the remainder of my water, and try to figure out where to go. Marlay Park is not quite on the street map, but a brown sign by the roadside points the way to Dundrum, which is, and this is also in the general direction of Mount Merrion, where I'm hoping St Kevin will pick me up.

I follow the signs along roads and urban pathways until, when I reach a main road, the signs appear no more. This is not good. I take a right, arrive at a roundabout and take a left – which should lead me, I think, somewhere near to Dundrum. But now the road swings right, heading back south and entirely in the wrong direction.

Towards me walks a man (of about my age, I think) so I ask him how to get to Dundrum.

'You're walking the wrong way,' he confirms. 'Come with me, I'm going somewhere near there,' he says – so I do. We walk back to the roundabout whilst I tell him of my travels. I notice his shoelaces are shambling along untied and that he's carrying a pair of walking boots.

'I've just been up to Fairy Castle,' he explains. 'I do a bit of walking too.'

'I was OK,' I say, 'following the brown signs, but then they suddenly stopped.'

'Sure, that's typical in Ireland,' he says. 'We can't organise anything.'

He introduces himself as Jack and we shake hands. He's a night-time taxi driver in the city.

'It's all gone to pot these days,' he moans. 'There are 15,000 taxi drivers in Dublin, a lot of them blacks. There are only 9,000 in New York! It's been feckin shit since they deregulated.'

'So what does deregulation mean exactly?' I ask.

'Basically it means that as long as you can drive and you've got a vehicle, you can set up to drive a taxi.'

We turn right at another roundabout and pass a row of neat semi-detached houses.

'When we had the 'Celtic Tiger' the price of these houses rose from 100 to 250,000 euros. It's wrong,' Jack laments, 'somebody earning 500 euros a week can't afford a property around here.'

'Do you fancy a cup of tea at my house?' he asks. 'I live just a little way off your route.' My sore feet reply for me and we turn off the main road.

He lets us in his house and whilst the brew's on explains that his wife is out collecting their two grandsons. He also offers me a

Jameson's, which I of course accept, telling him (although he may not have believed me) that it's my birthday today. Jack tells me he became teetotal 35 years ago, having previously been an alcoholic. I hear the front door opening and his grandsons run to him, followed by his wife with a naturally puzzled look on her face at finding an old tramp-like person sitting in her kitchen sipping whisky. Jack explains quickly that I was a lost Englishman he'd found along the way, which she seems to accept.

This is a pleasant enough break but I still have to decide from where I'm going to catch a bus. Jack suggests that, although it's quite a trek, I could walk on into the city and he says I can catch a number 44 bus from St Stephen's Green that will take me right back to Enniskerry and a short walk from the camper. This decides it.

It's 6pm when I leave Jack's hospitality and trudge the eight urban kilometres into the centre of Dublin via Dundrum, Dundrum Road and Milltown Road – two kilometres east of Paddy Dillon's recommended route. By the time I reach Sandford Road in Ranelagh though it's time for another break. I take it in McSorley's, which is of course a pub, and order a lager. On the TV, Argentina is playing Switzerland in a World Cup football match. The score is nil-nil and it's nearly full-time. When it goes to extra time I decide to watch the outcome and order a cheeseburger. The match is in the second period of extra time before the meal arrives, and it looks very much like progressing to a dreaded penalty shootout. But then, three minutes from the final whistle, Lionel Messi wriggles his way through the Swiss defence and sweeps in a cross that Di Maria converts. Argentina is through – and so am I. Relieved that I won't have to watch the penalties I pick up my rucksack and wander on along Sandford Road.

I'm still thinking about the match and the possibility of those penalties as I walk under a railway bridge and hear:

'...PENALTY!' shouted by a long-haired, middle-aged man with facial stubble who suddenly appears beside me. I smile, thinking he's going to make some comment about the match, but then, as he repeats it, I hear this time *all* of what he'd actually said:

'Bring back the death penalty!' he shouts again. My immediate thoughts are that he's either drunk, on drugs or going to ask me for money. He props a pushbike up under the bridge and engages me full-on:

'My son got hit on the back of the head and killed by a bottle,' he says, 'in Grafton Street – you know Grafton Street?'

'Yes,' I say, 'I've heard of it.'

'Yes, and he'd done the same in Leeds and got away with it – the cunt,' he says. I can see by his eyes that he's not making it up. 'And the Gardai said it could have been anybody,' he says emotionally.

'I'm sorry,' I say, touching his arm, and feeling quite emotional myself. But there seems to be little more I can do or say, so I smile faintly and begin to walk on.

'Bring back the death penalty,' he shouts again. I turn around – he has hold of his bike now and is by the roadside.

'Keep smiling,' he shouts. 'Keep smiling!' Perhaps he misinterpreted my initial smile as something else. I walk along Charlemont Street and turn the corner into Harcourt Street, but I can't get him out of my mind. Maybe I could have helped him in some way – maybe I could have listened longer. Good or bad fortune can be around the corner for any of us – it's sometimes bloody frightening.

I catch the number 44 bus at St Stephen's Green without a problem. At each church we pass the man sitting next to me quickly crosses himself – there are quite a few churches.

On display at the front of the bus is a clever and amusing advertisement encouraging a visit to Dublin's Glasnevin Cemetery by taking a 'Magical History Tour' to discover if your family name is to be found there. Around this central message are grouped couplets of names; for example there are apparently 14 Stars, 7 Moons, but only one Sun; 125 Barbers and 11 Beards; 8 Guinness and 21 Stout; 1 Sane and 1 Madder; 1 Sand and 38 Castles; 687 Sherlocks and 486 Watsons. But what initially catches my eye, displayed large and bold at the top is:

27 BIGGS. 18 FELLOWS.
ONE MICHAEL COLLINS

A lady who's stood up ready to get off, looks quizzically at me as I take a photograph, probably having never even noticed the advertisement (which I think is 'dead good') before, and trying to understand what I'm up to, she stares intently at it.

It's a sad sign of the times that another woman in the seat opposite me has a mobile phone clamped to her ear for the entire journey; it's still there, like a limpet, when I get off the bus at Enniskerry.

There's now a two-kilometre uphill walk back to the lay-by and camper, where I shall wild-camp the night – but first for a pint and some more football in the local. It *has* been a happy birthday.

Wednesday 2nd July – St Stephen's Green to the sea

I perhaps have some sort of a morbid fixation with the name Kevin because instead of walking north from St Stephen's Green next morning (and true to form) I somehow contrive to walk west and finish up in Upper Kevin Street before I realise my error.

I've driven back early this morning into Enniskerry, parked on a steep hill with handbrake firmly applied, and caught the 44 bus back into the city. I've exchanged my walking boots this morning for shoes.

By the time I finally catch sight of the Liffey at Merchants Quay, and walk alongside the river to cross O'Connell Bridge, half the morning has vanished. The bridge, its plaque tells me, was originally built in 1794 and was named Carlisle Bridge, but was rebuilt and renamed in 1880. It's an interesting enough walk from there towards the sea following the Liffey. I pass the stark, spindly, forlorn bronze sculptures of the famine memorial, remembering victims of the Great Famine and of their descendants, who, a plaque inlaid within cobbles records, 'did so much to build Canada'. It was from the Customs House here that one of the first ships of the famine period sailed. Just along the way is a replica of the three-mast barque *Jeanie Johnson*. The original ship made 16 trips to North America carrying emigrants and then brought back timber. The replica ship is now a history museum; I would have liked to have gone on her, but the price and more especially the lack of time, mean that I walk on by. The impressive Samuel Beckett cable-stayed bridge, designed by the celebrated Spanish architect Calatrava, is the last I pass on the final few steps I take along North Wall Quay to the end of my walk across Ireland.

I finish at the roundabout and bridge adjacent to the ferry port's number 3 terminal; it's the closest I can get to the sea without entering the port itself. Sailings to Liverpool, the city in England where I'll rejoin the E8 next year, leave from here. From the bridge

I take a photograph of my Irish journey's end – looking out past the two little green and white tug boats to the cranes and a container ship being loaded. The expanse of the Irish Sea is beyond.

I check that the wool I picked up on Dursey Island last year is still with me in the side pocket of the rucksack. Then I pull out my logbook. It tells me the walk itself took just over 28 days. I've also been keeping a cumulative distance record: I've walked 625km on the route and a further 180km off it (getting to and from it – *and* getting lost); in old money that's a total of 500 miles. I've also biked a further 386km (240 miles) between the camper and the start and finish of each section of walk.

There are dual emotions at the end of a long distance walk. The elation at the achievement is always tempered with a kind of sadness that it's finally over. I glance once more out to sea from the bridge and slowly turn and saunter along East Wall Road. Then almost reluctantly I turn left and head back into the centre of Dublin.

Seventeen
Raise a Glass

'Some Guinness was spilt on the barroom floor
When the pub was shut for the night.
When out of his hole crept a wee brown mouse
And stood in the pale moonlight.'

'He lapped up the frothy foam from the floor
Then back on his haunches he sat.
And all night long, you could hear the mouse roar
Bring on the goddamn cat!'

Old Irish Tale – author unknown

Wednesday 2nd July – Dublin

Even though I have a street map of Dublin I've still managed to lose my way. Eventually The Dublin Writers' Museum reveals its whereabouts after half an hour's circular walkabout induced by the dreaded brown signpost's confused guidance.

The museum is on my itinerary because I feel my literary education has been sadly neglected. Maybe at my age it's too late to address this, but there are so many Irish writers I haven't read.

The museum is arranged in chronological fashion, so that Jonathan Swift (born 1667 and best known for writing *Gulliver's Travels*) I meet early on. Famous others I've heard of, but whose pages I've not turned include: Oliver Goldsmith, Edmund Burke, Bram Stoker, Oscar Wilde, George Bernard Shaw, W.B. Yeats, Samuel Beckett, Patrick Kavanagh and Iris Murdoch; many more names ring a distant bell somewhere, but that's all. I missed out on the classics.

My lack of an education in literary classics goes back to my school days – when the only Shakespeare play I was introduced to was *The*

Merchant of Venice, this alone being stored in my memory bank because I was somehow selected by the teacher to read the lines of the heroine Portia and was praised for my rendition.

A semi-literary and perhaps unconventional awakening came to me at the age of 15, when the engineering craft apprenticeship I'd embarked upon included weekly college day-release for the hopeful purpose of obtaining some qualifications – having left school with none. One of the lessons on the course was entitled 'general studies', which was intended to broaden the horizons of perceived dullard youths like us. It was the only subject for which we faced no final examination, so was thought of as a doddle and therefore we all looked forward to the 'lesson'. During one such session we were introduced to Dylan Thomas through a crackly radio recording of *Under Milk Wood*. It got me instantly hooked, and I took to reading and collecting the poetry of Thomas and of others – not a very macho thing for an aspiring engine fitter to admit to in those days.

Dylan Thomas was not only an amazing poet but was also an amazing drinker. He died in the Chelsea Hotel in New York having bragged on his return to the hotel in the early hours: 'I've had 18 straight whiskies... I think that's the record.' It was thought for many years that it was his excessive drinking that had killed him, but some doubt has recently been thrown upon this. Whatever the truth may be, Thomas was certainly a drinker who died prematurely at the young age of just 39.

The strange thing is that Thomas, one of several authors who most influenced me in my early years, was a heavy drinker. Ernest Hemmingway, Jack Kerouac and Brendan Behan were others. The question I struggle to answer is whether it is the drink that helped to free their creative spirit or the spirit that made them creative. At any rate I imbibed their books, figuratively speaking.

Hemmingway's routine was to work in the morning and booze the rest of the day. His favourite drink was a dry martini and not a mojito as is commonly believed. His alcoholism increased towards the end of his life, when he was treated for liver disease amongst other ills. But rather than die slowly from an illness Hemmingway selected his favourite shotgun, loaded it, put the barrel in his mouth and blew his brains out. He was aged 61.

Jack Kerouac's most renowned work was *On the Road*; it's still the best travel writing book I've read. He infamously appeared drunk in 1968 on the American TV show *Firing Line*. A year later, Jack was drinking whisky and malt liquor the very morning before he died from internal bleeding due to alcohol abuse. He was aged 47.

The first Irish writer I encountered in my youth was Dublin born Brendan Behan – also a celebrated boozer. His autobiography *Borstal Boy* first made me aware of the existence of the organisation known as the IRA, years before they became front page news in the 1970s.

Behan joined the IRA aged 16. His whole family were involved in their activities; his grandmother and two of his aunts were convicted of terrorist activities in Birmingham – they claimed in their defence that sticks of dynamite found up their blouses were sticks of rock – from Blackpool, aye! There had been IRA activity in Britain, and particularly in Liverpool, throughout the spring and summer of 1939 with the organisation's object of gaining the withdrawal of British troops from Ireland; electricity pylons were blown up, bombs were planted on Tubes and teargas attacks were carried out in cinemas. In August five people were killed in Coventry by a bomb, for which IRA men were hanged. The chief organisers of the Liverpool campaign were also caught in that month, which effectively put an end to official IRA activities in the city. But in October the young Behan was arrested when he was found in possession of explosives during an unsponsored attempt to blow up Liverpool docks. He naively told the CID detectives who arrested him that he'd come 'to reorganise further operations in Liverpool.' In court he declared his motives for the intended attack: 'It is my proud privilege and honour to stand in an English court to testify to the unyielding determination of the Irish people to regain every inch of our national territory.' They gave him three years in a borstal – which was to spawn his successful autobiography *Borstal Boy*. But Behan wasn't rehabilitated by borstal; two years later he was tried for the attempted murder of two Gardai detectives and was sentenced to 14 years in prison, but served only five years, being released in a general amnesty given to IRA prisoners.

When Behan found fame as a writer he also did so as a drinker, describing himself as 'a drinker with a writing problem'. In a similar work pattern to Hemmingway he would typically get up at seven o'clock in the morning and work until midday, when the pubs opened. There's a lovely story that he once offered to write a slogan for Guinness if they'd send him a few crates to 'sample'. When Guinness officials checked up how he was getting on, they found him lying on the floor between empty crates and lots of crumpled notepaper. Behan raised a bloodshot eye to them and said:

'I've got it... Guinness makes you drunk.'

He later developed diabetes, but didn't let this condition deter him from his drinking hobby. He once joked that he only drank on two occasions – when he was thirsty and when he wasn't. But the drinking finally got him, as he must have known it would. He collapsed in the Harbour Lights bar in Dublin and was taken to hospital where he died of sclerosis of the liver aged 41.

I recently discovered a link between Behan and another author I was hooked on in the early 1960s – J.P. Donleavy. He was the first of my literary heroes not to be a known alcoholic. JP was born in New York in April 1926 to Irish parents who'd emigrated. At the age of 20 he moved to Ireland and began studying at Trinity College – from which he later dropped out. Brendan was apparently the first to read the manuscript of Donleavy's book *The Ginger Man* when he came across it by chance while he lived for a time with JP in his cottage in Greystones.

'That book will go around the world,' Behan had said, and he was right (eventually). Donleavy had initially titled the book *Sebastian Dangerfield* after its rogue protagonist, and it had been rejected by 30 publishers (I know the feeling!). Brendan suggested that JP ought to contact someone he knew in Olympia Press in Paris, which led to the book's publication. Olympia bought the novel for £250 and – what JP didn't know at the time – they included it in their pornographic genre along with titles such as *School of Sin*, *The Whip Angels and Rape* and *White Thighs*. It was banned straight away in Ireland and copies were burned – always a good sign of future success! Even the way in which Donleavy received his payment was sleazy – he was paid in cash by a middleman who met him in a London Soho bookshop. The book went on to sell 45 million copies worldwide and has never been out of print, but Olympia and JP got into a legal dispute over an alleged breach of contract, which was only resolved after a 20-year battle.

I bought *The Ginger Man* in 1963 and read it in my lunch breaks (dinner-hours we called them then) in the oily engine rooms of several of Her Majesty's ships, in Portsmouth dockyard. I still have the book, covered in oil and grease as it is, and with certain pages thumbed more than others. As a 17-year-old apprentice I endeavoured to ape Donleavy's work, particularly his stream-of-consciousness narrative (which was undoubtedly influenced by James Joyce). I wrote an essay copying his writing style and entered an essay competition on the subject of 'safety at work'. Obviously the judges had not managed to obtain a copy of *The Ginger Man* (or had even read Joyce) because I won the competition and was told that they were impressed with my unorthodox style. Unfortunately I missed my 15 minutes of fame that Andy Warhol predicted everyone will receive. The prize for the competition was £50 (which was the equivalent of about two months' wages for me at the time) and I should have received the cheque at a presentation held at the Guildhall which was covered by the local newspaper; instead, the Admiralty bureaucracy somehow managed to misappropriate the letter, so that by the time I heard of my win the presentation had passed. The ironical sequel to this little endeavour in the furtherance of safety at work, happened four years later when I sliced the tip of my left index finger off in a vertical milling machine and joined the elite Dave Allen club of those so afflicted. Unlike the comedian though I was no good at telling jokes but instead developed a somewhat perverted party piece that consisted of shoving the digit up my left nostril so that it appeared to have disappeared into the depths of my nose.

These days (at least at the time of writing in June 2015) Donleavy is aged 88. He has lived in a large country house called Levington Park since 1972 – at which it's rumoured James Joyce once slept while on business in nearby Mullingar in the Irish Midlands. There's no doubt that JP was influenced by Joyce's writing style, as was Hemmingway – who hailed Joyce's *Ulysses* as a work of genius.

Joyce and Guinness are the two main attractions reported by the *Chicago Tribune* for encouraging Americans to visit Dublin.

The museum rooms in Dublin Writers' Museum are busy, as I progress through them; I sometimes have to wait patiently to see items of interest in the glass cabinets. James Joyce is of course featured prominently. But I'm disappointed that I can't find Donleavy – maybe it's because of his American birth, though he settled in Ireland many years ago and for tax purposes became an Irish citizen in 1967. Perhaps though there's still some pornographic stigma associated to his seminal and most profitable work – *The Ginger Man*.

From the museum I walk around two corners to the restored Georgian townhouse that is the James Joyce Centre.

There are three floors to explore. I first watch a documentary film of his life and works then make my way around. In the terrace is preserved the door to number 7 Eccles Street, and an informative wall plaque gives some explanation: Joyce's major work *Ulysses* is a lengthy novel that drew its framework from Homer's *The Odyssey*. It is set in Dublin, and the action occurs during a single day – 16th June 1904. Joyce visited Eccles Street (not too far from here) in 1909 to see a friend, and he decided that it would be a good place to become the fictional home of a major character in the book – Leopold Bloom. To ensure that he wasn't going to upset anyone, he checked out Dublin's *Thom's* street directory for 1904 and found to his delight that the property was at that time vacant.

On the top floor I spend a long time looking at a touch-screen history of the trials and tribulations Joyce endured in order to get his 'work of genius' *Ulysses* published.

I'd read *Dubliners*, an early work by Joyce, just before I came over to Ireland this year in order to get a flavour of his stuff. He'd had a good foretaste of the troubles he was to have with *Ulysses* while trying to get this little collection of short stories to press – it was submitted to 18 publishers and finally made it only after a nine-year battle. In the meantime Joyce got bloody fed up with the revisions he was obliged to make to his original manuscript because one of the bloody adjectives he used, particularly *that* bloody adjective was found to be objectionable to printers and publishers alike, who feared prosecution. There were also certain sections that, for the early 20th century, were considered to be far too risqué.

Ulysses followed a similarly torturous publication road. Joyce had begun writing it in 1914 and didn't complete it until 1921. But in 1918 an American journal began serialising it, whereupon it soon ran into trouble. It seems that a young lady complained to the Manhattan District Attorney about a description of one of the characters, Leopold Bloom, who was stimulated by a viewing of Gerty MacDowell's ankles to pocket-masturbate – how times have changed – or perhaps not! A court case then ensued that resulted in a conviction for the publication of obscenity. The book being banned in the United States, and Britain followed suit. Throughout the 1920s copies found in the post were burned by the US Post Office. In 1922, however, a friend of Joyce, Sylvia Beach, published the first edition of the book in its entirety in Paris. In 1923, 500 copies were burned by the English Customs at Folkestone. Ernest Hemmingway evaded this sort of action by mailing copies to a publishing friend in Canada who persuaded a reporter, commuting regularly by ferry between Windsor, Ontario and Chicago, to smuggle them into the United States. In 1933 the publisher, Random House, manoeuvred for a French edition of *Ulysses* to be seized by US Customs, in order to precipitate a court case. The contention of the United States was that the book was obscene, but the judge ruled that, when read in its entirety, it was not pornographic – and that nowhere in it was the 'leer of the sensualist'. It was first legally published in the United States in January 1934 and in Britain in 1936. Joyce thought that it would take about a thousand years before Ireland would follow suit – but he was wrong.

So was all the effort worth it? It was certainly a triumph for the principle that an artist or author should be able to work with the world as he sees it – but even Joyce recognised that *Ulysses* might not be everybody's cup of tea. In his final novel, *Finnegans Wake* (in the title of which he forgot to insert an apostrophe) he speaks of *Ulysses* as his 'usylessly unreadable Blue Book of Eccles...'

The contemporary author Robert Harris in his book *101 Things NOT to Do Before You Die* includes the reading of *Ulysses* as one of them; he remembers, as I do, the basic and loud Welsh Sergeant Major Williams snatching a book from the well-educated la-de-dah Gunner Graham, saying: 'What's this you're reading, Useless?' Graham of course corrects him. I would like to tell Mr Harris that I've already done 16 of his things 'not to do' and disagree with him about many of them (including reading Hemmingway's *For whom the Bell Tolls*, and running a marathon – of which I've completed 13). I do, however, have to agree with him about *Ulysses*; I did have a good go at it, but put it aside (temporarily) at page 172 – which is a bit like giving up in a marathon after completing six and a half miles. Even if you have an intimate knowledge of Ireland and Dublin of the period and have read Homer's *Odyssey*, *Ulysses* would be difficult in places. Harris records that his English teacher at school had said he knew of nobody who'd managed to finish the book – so I don't feel too bad.

The afternoon is drawing on as I leave the James Joyce Centre. I head back across the Liffey for one of Dublin's other major attractions – the Guinness Storehouse. But first, I divert down Grafton Street and find McDaids, a bar on the corner Harry Street and William Street.

The bar dates from around 1780. I order a pint of lager, sit on a stool at the bar and look around at the wood-panelled walls and the display of old cigar boxes. I study the clientele; most of today's patrons look and sound like tourists, it seems unlikely there are any writers amongst them. But McDaids is known to have been frequented by many of them, including James Joyce, J.P. Donleavy and Brendan Behan, so a brief visit was a must for me. It was Behan's regular hangout, and it's more than likely that many of the characters in his novels were fashioned from the patrons of the place. Donleavy is also thought to have based his 'Ginger Man' – Sebastian Dangerfield – upon a regular patron of the place.

I drink up swiftly because I'm anxious to get to the Guinness Storehouse in good time. I weave a way back up busy Grafton Street; then head west. It's about a two-kilometre walk, but when I'm close to the Storehouse I check my street map and find Echlin Street. There's nothing of significance there now, but on the corner of this street once stood the Harbour Lights bar where Brendan Behan took his last drink.

I find the entrance to the Guinness Storehouse Visitor Centre. For some reason I was expecting to tour the brewery itself, but I'm over 40 years late for that. Outside are several tourist coaches and horse-and-trap jaunting cars similar to those in Killarney. The Guinness brewery itself is located at St James's Gate just north of here on the banks of the River Liffey, but between 1903 and 1988 the building I'm about to enter was the storehouse which housed the largest beer fermentation vessel in the world, holding a million and a half pints of the black liquidation.

St James's Gate was once the western entrance to the city of Dublin. It was so named because it was the point at which Irish pilgrims left on their long trek to the shrine of St James, at Santiago de Compostela in Galicia, north-west Spain. St James, the patron saint of that country, lost his head in Jerusalem, and legend has it his body minus his head was assisted to its final resting place by angels who placed it in a rudderless, captain-less boat that sailed from Haifa to Spain. The gate itself was pulled down in 1734.

The site at St James's Gate has been associated with brewing as far back as 1670, and in 1759 it was leased to 34-year-old Arthur Guinness for a down payment of £100 and £45 a year for a period of 9,000 years. As Guinness point out in their latest cinema advert, they're only just over 250 years into the lease and have a lot of brewing yet to do. They have of course got the original lease locked away safely in a vault.

Arthur Guinness was born a Protestant in 1725 at Celbridge, County Kildare. His great-grandfather was a shepherd, but his immediate family on both sides were essentially tenant-farmers – a big step up from mere agricultural labourers. Arthur's grandparents supplemented their income by a spot of beer selling, so beer was, so to speak, already in Arthur's blood. Arthur's father Richard worked his way up the ladder, becoming the household agent for Dr Arthur Price, the Protestant Dean of Kildare, who himself progressed to become a bishop and then an archbishop. Richard's fortunes increased with each of Price's promotions and young Arthur's upbringing was not exactly underprivileged.

In his early 20s Arthur became his father's understudy and learnt the business skills that he'd later employ; he too spent eight years in the service of Dr Price, who was in fact his godfather. Price died in 1752 and bequeathed £200 to be shared by Richard and Arthur – a relatively modest sum at little more than 2% of his total will. Arthur's mother had died when he was 17 and Richard, now aged 62, remarried a widow who ran the White Hart Inn in Celbridge. This is where Arthur, for three years from the age of 27, first practised his brewing skills. He already had some background knowledge, acquired from his mother's family's dabbling in the art – for an art is what it then was – relying to a large extent upon a good sense of smell to sample the barley, hops, malt and the beer itself.

At the age of 30 Arthur made his move into the trade on his own account taking on the lease of a brewery in Leixlip, County Kildare. Almost five years later he moved to Dublin, leaving the Leixlip brewery to be run by his brother and leasing the site at St James's Gate. Legend has it that the lease was purchased with the £100 bequeathed to him by Dr Price.

For me the tour of the storehouse begins logically on the first floor with the brewing process – although illogical, very thirsty or alcoholic patrons have been known to go straight up to the Gravity Bar on the seventh floor and immediately claim their free pint that's part of the entrance ticket.

There are four ingredients to a pint of Guinness: barley, hops, water and yeast.

A wall plaque tells me that 100,000 tonnes of Irish grown barley is used every year in the making of Guinness. The Mesopotamians, who first discovered beer, soon cottoned on that barley was the best stuff to use. The grains first take a bath in water which makes them germinate, before they get to be dried in a kiln and become malt. The malt is then roasted, giving Guinness its dark colour, before it's flash cooled, milled together with unmalted grain into a grist, mixed with hot water and finally mashed, during which the enzymes convert the barley's starch into sugar.

The next ingredient is water; a huge and impressive artificial waterfall streams down into a lagoon behind me as I read a plaque that confirms that the water used comes not from the Liffey, as some would hold, but from the Wicklow Mountains. Fifteen years after Arthur Guinness took over at St James's Gate a Dublin Corporation committee and sheriff came along and attempted to cut off and fill in the water course that supplied the brewery. Arthur barred their way and threatened the party with a pickaxe – if he'd not done so it would perhaps still be Guinness (Jim) but not as we know it!

Hops, the third component, are added to the liquid that's been filtered off from the mash and has become sweet wort. Hops are what give Guinness its tang of bitterness. The wort is boiled and cooled. Then yeast is added before the mixture is allowed to ferment for a number of days. The yeast converts the sugar to alcohol and carbon dioxide.

Yeast grows in the brewing process and can be skimmed off and used over and over again. It's probable that Arthur brought the yeast culture he'd produced at the White Hart Inn with him to Leixlip and then on to St James's Gate; its descendant cells are still present in the master yeast cultures that are stored in liquid nitrogen at the brewery today. A reserve supply is always kept locked away in the chief executive's safe.

Guinness produce three varieties of draught stouts: Guinness, Guinness Extra Stout and Foreign Extra Stout all of which use the same strain of top fermenting yeast species. Stout is a variant of porter which was believed to have been invented by a brewer in Shoreditch. It became popular with London's dockland porters – hence the name. The stoutest, strongest, fuller-bodied porters, around 7% to 8% in alcoholic strength became known as stouts. Today Guinness draught is 4.2%.

Arthur Guinness was not the first to brew porter in Ireland – James Farrell had done so by hiring a London brewer John Purser to come to Dublin in 1776. It became popular in Ireland at least partly because the taxation laws then meant that imported porter was cheaper than the local ale. Arthur, however, along with other Irish brewers, campaigned to change the taxation laws that then favoured beers imported from England. In 1777 he finally achieved a result when the English controlled Irish House of Commons changed the tax coding to level the playing field. This was the catalyst that prompted Arthur to brew and market his first porter in 1778; by the following year he'd developed a system for the quality production of his Guinness porter in volume. He brewed his last ale in 1799. The rest is history – and there has been a lot of it.

An escalator takes me up to the next floor of the building where I progress around the exhibits, guided by a virtual master brewer, Fergal Murray, who appears at crucial points on various screens to explain the history and development of the company and its processes. It soon becomes apparent that the art of brewing has been supplemented and changed considerably by scientific advancement.

An old black and white film of a cooper making oak barrels and securing them together with metal hoops highlights how things have changed dramatically since Arthur's time; it was bloody hard work then. Today the kegs are all of stainless steel, with no cooper in sight. In its heyday the brewery employed a large variety of trades that also included carpenters, plumbers, engineers, printers and of course brewers; the brewery was a community within itself that numbered at its peak around 5,000 employees.

By 1838 the St James's Gate brewery was the largest in Ireland. A year later control of the company was handed to Arthur's grandson, Benjamin Lee Guinness, who began the process of making Guinness a part of Irish culture and life.

For a start he chose as a logo the Brian Boru harp, named after the great high king of Ireland who died in 1014. It's a cherished antiquity of the land that's held, together with the Book of Kells, at Trinity College, Dublin. The harp logo was registered as a trademark in 1875 and, when the new Irish Republic was formed in 1922, they asked Guinness if they could use their harp logo as a national symbol. Guinness turned down their request, so they were obliged to turn their harp through 180 degrees, and today it appears in that orientation on coins, passports and official seals of the Republic. Every glass of Guinness in which a pint of Guinness is poured has (or should have) upon it the Brian Boru harp.

By 1881 the annual production at the brewery had exceeded a million barrels and in 1886 Edward Cecil Guinness, the third son of Benjamin Lee Guinness, had expanded the brewery into the largest in the world and had decided to trade it on the London Stock Exchange.

By the beginning of the First World War the annual output of Guinness was over three and a half million barrels. But the end of the war saw the world hit hard times which continued into the mid-1920s and adversely affected Guinness sales. Advertising was purported to be the new innovation that would revive sales – and so it proved. An initial campaign, commenced in Scotland in 1928, went national a year later with the slogan 'Guinness is Good for You'. At the time it was actually prescribed to post-operative patients and new mothers because of its high iron content and 'nourishing properties'. By law (the ass) Guinness is prevented from making such claims today.

Now my thirst is making me think about that promised pint that will undoubtedly be good for me – even though I'm still not yet a convinced convert. But first I have to learn how to appreciate it.

The entrance to the tasting rooms is through an illuminated infinity tunnel that leads to an area known as the fountain of truth. It seems like a magic land. Flavour fountains of vapours attack the nostrils consecutively with the smell of hops, roasted barley, malt and beer. The guide then leads a group of us through into the velvet chamber where we're each presented with a miniature glass of the black stuff. But we're not allowed to drink it until we're taught how. I quickly learn how, and am now fully prepared to put this recently acquired knowledge into full-blown practice.

So I leave the tasting rooms and climb up through the floors of this unique steel framed building, constructed in 1904. It's shaped around a giant pint of Guinness at the top of which sits its frothy head: The Gravity Bar. In my hurry to get there I miss a fourth floor highlight of the tour, where apparently the six steps necessary to pour a perfect pint are taught.

The Gravity Bar gives a 360-degree panoramic view of Dublin city and beyond. It's packed with tourists (perhaps not many Irish) from all around the world. There's no chance of me gaining a coveted seat on the periphery, so I walk slowly clockwise around the bar. To the north the brewery complex rises dominantly in the foreground, its upper reaches rising above me here even at this height and encroaching above the otherwise flat (but actually of course curved) horizon line. To the east the whole of Dublin is spread out below us. I think I can just catch sight of the sea, where my journey ended this year and from where east, across the Irish Sea in Bootle, Liverpool, it will hopefully restart next year. To the south are the Wicklow Mountains from whence I've slowly trekked – I try to pick out my route.

But now it's time for the pint. Plenty of black attired young bar staff are serving behind the circular glass topped bar, and I hand in my complimentary voucher to a young girl, who's simultaneously processing several other customers. She takes the Brian Boru harp labelled Guinness glass (which is curved so that it will eventually properly display the beer's foamy top) and holds it at the prescribed 45-degree angle. She pulls the handle horizontal so that the Guinness flows until it's within three quarters of an inch from the top of the glass (if you're an American or an old English bloke like me) or about 20mm if you're neither of these. Then, in accordance with the recommended step four of the pouring procedure, she waits for the surge to settle; the bubbles rise to create an amber sub-head that slowly melts into and forms a frothy white head above it – it seems to take an absolute age – meanwhile she's away serving other customers...

What I don't know at this point is the work that Guinness had put in to produce the perfect pint – how the guarantee of a lovely creamy head is always achieved. Bill Yenne's wonderful book: *Guinness – The 250-year quest for the perfect pint* later explains for me how it's achieved.

In 1945 Sir Hugh Beaver joined the company, a year later becoming its managing director. He was the chap who, in 1951, got into an argument with a mate whilst on a hunting trip in County Wexford over what was the fastest game bird in Europe. No book could be found to solve the dispute and Beaver thought there should be one – almost by accident then the famous *Guinness Book of Records* was spawned.

Five years later, however, a more serious problem worried Beaver; lager had become more popular, at the expense of draught stout – and sales were down. Obtaining a consistently good pint of Guinness in those days was difficult; it relied upon beer being poured, by a skilful bar person in a pub, from two separate casks – one above the bar and one below it. Beaver gave the task of finding a solution to the problem of inconsistency to Michael Ash, a mathematician. Ash found that the secret of always achieving a good creamy head was in maintaining the correct mixture of nitrogen and carbon dioxide found within the beer. His first successful application that incorporated this principle was named 'Easy Serve'. It was a single keg system containing two sections, one of stout and the other a mixture of carbon dioxide and nitrogen under pressure; it employed the principle of 'nitrogenation' and was test-marketed in 1959. Further refinement resulted in a restrictor plate employed at the point of service to stimulate the nitrogen bubbles.

...I don't know any of that stuff now. All I know is that my thirst tells me the average 119.5 seconds that the Guinness Storehouse factsheet say should be left for the surge to be completed has been far exceeded – in fact I think the girl has forgotten me. I'm just about to jog her memory when she picks up my glass again and, completing step five of pouring the perfect pint, fills it until the head brims the glass. She then skims the head with a wooden spatula to level it (a step not recommended by the factsheet, I later find out). Finally she smiles and hands me my 'free' pint. She has the steady hand that the factsheet says she should have (for the last and final step) and spills none of the precious stuff, although mine's a little shaky – I'm about to taste only my third pint of Guinness, at the age of 69.

But before I take my first sip I turn away from the bar, walk to face the Wicklow Mountains and think about all the people I'd met along the way and all those from Ireland's history who'd enriched my knowledge of the place. I raise my glass to them (hoping nobody is actually watching me and wondering if I'm sane). I think I may have actually discovered the craic.

If I make it all the way to Istanbul by the age of 84 perhaps I might also make it into the *Guinness Book of Records* as the oldest man to walk the E8 across Europe. But maybe not; maybe to achieve an entry in that famous book I really would have do something outrageous like walk from Istanbul *backwards* – and then on across the Irish Sea and Ireland to Dursey Island. By this time I will definitely be somewhere close to Spike.

I've waited long enough. The Guinness waits. I look to the horizon and sip from beneath the froth – now at last I am your convert, Arthur. This may only be my third pint of Guinness but as sure as heaven it won't be my last.

Notes and References

General: In addition to research undertaken at The British Library and literature listed in the bibliography and below, the following websites were found useful:

The Catholic Encyclopaedia.
Internet Archive, an American digital library.
Irish History Live.
JSTOR.
Library Ireland.
Wikipedia.

Chapter One **A Dream not yet Spiked**

p7 The song 'I'm walking backwards for Christmas' was written by Spike Milligan and Tony Carbone and was sung by the former together with Peter Sellers and HarrySecombe. It was released in the UK in June 1956 and reached number four in the singles chart.

p9 Distance information taken from Traildino.com website.

Chapter Two **The Beara Way**

p13 The poem *The Lament of the Old Woman of Beare* was translated by Gerald Murphy in his book entitled *Early Irish Lyrics: Eighth to Twelfth Century*, published by Oxford University Press, 1956. I'm grateful to poet Leanne O'Sullivan for supplying this information.

Mythology has it that the old woman had seven consecutive periods of youth during which the men she lived with came to die of old age. She is said to have been turned to stone and that the rock that was once her now lies beside the coast road from Eyeries to Ardgroom – I must have cycled past it without realising it.

p14 Information from the Beara Historical Society website.

p15 Geocaching website – Dursey Sound and cable car.

p17 O'Sullivan Clan – Beara Tourism.

p17 It's just as well I didn't have the foresight to suspect that the results of the cablecar inspection would highlight a potentially serious problem with the steel tensioning cables. This prompted the Council to close the service with immediate effect – a fact I later learn on the Internet. It was also extremely lucky that I'd decided to start the walk when I did.

p24 Bogosphere: the strangest things pulled out of peat bogs.

Chapter Three **The White House**

p33 The song has been recorded by Mary Black and the Fureys. Jimmy McCarthy is a singer/songwriter who was born in Macroom, County Cork.

p37 Quotation from: *The Collective Works of Sir William Petty*. Pub: London 1899, p.xl, included in *Sir William Petty: Critical Responses* edited by Terence Wilmot Hutchison.

p39 Of interest is a website: homepages. Rootsweb.ancestry.com: The Mayburys of County Kerry Ireland. It records that three Maybury hammermen: Thomas, Francis and John were all employed at Petty's ironworks.

p42 The Gunpowder Plot, in which Guy Fawkes took part, was headed by Robert Catesby. It was a failed attempt to assassinate King James I.

p43 Orpen's report: *An Exact Relation...* Ref: *A Kerry Pastoral in Imitation of the First Eclogue of Virgil*, by Murroghoh O'Connor, London: 1892, edited by T. Crofton Crocker.

pp44-45 Ibid.

Chapter Four **The Kerry Way to Australia**

p48 This poem, of 18 verses, was first published in The County Magazine, Volume 1, page 176 in November 1786.

pp50-51 Information taken from *Griffiths Valuation – County of Kerry, Barony of Magunity*, for 1852, P141 and 1853, p99.

p51 '...but forty-five miles and one furlong from Killarney' taken from *The Dublin Penny Journal Volume 3, No. 114 (Sep 6 1834 – p73)*.

p52 Information on Harmon Blennerhasset taken from *West Virginia Historical Society Quarterly – Volume XIII, No.1; January 1999 titled: A Chronicle of the Life of Harman Blennerhassett*, by Michael Burke.

pp54-55 In an (perhaps foolish) attempt to establish the validity of Patrick O'Donoghoe's suggestion that there was a plaque in a house in which Edward Eagar had supposedly lived, I emailed Peacock Farm Hostel (which I almost approached in my search for Gortdromakiery). They gave me a few leads and a name of a local resident, which I followed up as best I could without having an actual address. I posted a letter addressed to the name given at Gortdromakiery, sticking to the envelope a photocopy of the most likely of the three houses I'd seen. With the letter I enclosed a five euro note for return postage. I saw neither a letter nor the five euro note again.

p59 Ref: *Mr Justice Day: The Diaries and the Addresses to Grand Juries (1793–1829)*, edited by Gerald O'Carroll, p167.

pp61-62 Quotations from: *A Stranger in Ireland*, by Sir John Carr, pp210 & 259–260.

p62 Prison routine: Summer timetable, Cork Gaol was gleaned from the visit.

p63 I found an interesting website concerning Gallows Green: WINDSONG. Rihla (Journey 13): The Gallows' Green, Cork and Ghosts of Women Burnt for 'Petit

Treason', posted on de worde.blog spot.com on Friday 14 May 2010 by Roger Dereham.

pp64-65 Quotations: 'a new creature' and 'I think there was a remarkable...' are from *Colonial Litigant Extraordinaire*, p20.

p65 *Providence* information was obtained from website: www.providenceconvictship.com.

p67 Prior to 1783, when the American colonies became the United States, transportation to the West Indies and America was also an enforceable punishment, so the idea of transportation was not exactly new.

p67 Ibid.

p69 'peaceful quietude blended with sub-tropical air', advertises Norfolk Island on the website: www.norfolkisland.com.au.

Chapter Five **The Blackwater Way**

p73 Thomas Davis was born in Mallow, County Cork in 1814. He was a philosopher and advocate of a united Irish nation that would push for independence through the study of its history and revival of the Gaelic language. Associated with the Young Ireland movement and a writer of nationalistic ballads, he died of scarlet fever at the age of 30.

p75 A timeline of the Black and Tans was found at http://militaryhistorynow. com/2015/11/09/the-black-and-tans-war-nine-fascinating-facts-about-the-bloody-fight-for-irish-independence.

p75-77 Website: www.cairogang.com gives a good account of the Headford Junction Ambush on 21st March 1921, which includes references to *The Times* report on 23rd March 1921 and to the *Nenagh Guardian* report on 26th March. 'Tommy surrender' and 'No surrender, Paddy' appeared in *Kerryman* 18th March 1977. *The Times* report was from Wednesday 23rd March 1921.

p78 The website: www.womenofbrighton.co.uk titled: Katherine Parnell – Women of Brighton gives a good account of the Parnells.

p89 A *Feis* is a traditional Gaelic arts and culture festival.

p89 The Bureau of Military History (BMH) 1913–1921 held by Military Archives was set up to 'co-ordinate material to form the basis for the compilation of the history of the movement for Independence from the formation of the Irish Volunteers on 25th November 1913 to 11th July 1921.' It includes 1,773 witness statements.
Witness statement taken from the BMH:
WS 1375 – Mathew Murphey.

p90 Witness statement taken from the BMH:
WS 1351 – Humphrey O'Donoghue.

p92 The castle document can be viewed on www.liveauctioneerd.com. Lot 200:1916 (15th April): The Famous 'Castle Document'.

p93 Witness statement taken from the BMH:
WS 64 – Cornelius Meany.

Chapter Six **More Bog Country**

p94 Originally from Claraghatlea, Millstreet, Francis Duggan has lived for the past 23 years in Victoria, Australia.

p94 The survey by Dublin University was reported on website: wwwthejournal.ie, in an article entitled *Revealed: British to blame for Ireland's drink problem*, 18th June 2013.

Other websites consulted were: www.mytravelcost.com, www.economist.com, epianalysis.worldpress.com and alcoholireland.ie.

p100 Keying in 'Murphy's bar in Ballynamona' on Google in early 2014, 'The Railway bar' came up. So maybe it has changed its name since I was there in June 2013?

p103 The Gardai are the Irish police force.

Chapter Seven **Starlings and Rooks**

p105 William Butler Yeats was born in 1865 of Anglo-Irish descent. He is considered by many to be one of the greatest poets of the 20th century. His earlier works incorporated Celtic mythology in a romantic nationalistic literary style. The poem 'Easter 1916' was an artistic breakthrough that saw him for the first time engaging in the political present.

pp106-107 Information on the Gaelic Athletic Association was found on the websites of the National Library of Ireland: www.nli.ie – *The 1916 Rising: Personalities & Perspectives*, and of the National Geographical News: news. nationalgeographic.com – *Gaelic Football, Hurling are Irish Passions* from article dated 28th October 2010.

p108 The Defence of the Realm Act is discussed by Eric Chester in New Politics, winter 2013, Volume XIV-2, whole #54, found on website: Newpol.org – New Politics – Traitors, Spies and Military Tribunals: The Assault on Civil Liberties During World War I.

p108 Details of the executions at Kilmainham Gaol were given by the guide at the prison during my visit.

p109 The camp at Frongoch is described on website: www.hiraeth.org.uk – North Wales's University of Revolution, posted 9/6/2–13 by Paul Dicken.

p110 Witness statements taken from the BMH:
WS 33 – Daniel Hegarty.
WS 873 – Charles Browne.

p116 & p121 Witness statement taken from the BMH:
WS 1,133 – Miss Annie Barrett.

p119 Witness statement taken from the BMH:
WS 687 – Right Rev. Monsignor M. Curran.

p120 Witness statement taken from the BMH:
WS 1,269 – John Ronayne.

Notes and References

Chapter Eight **Ferment in Fermoy**

p128 Lionel Johnson was an English poet, essayist and critic who was born in 1867 and who died 35 years later of alcohol abuse. He spent his life in London, where at the age of 24 he became a Catholic convert.

p128 Useful information on Fermoy was obtained from website: www.blackwater.ie – Fermoy – Blackwater Valley.

p132 Witness statements taken from the BMH:
WS 978 – Leo O'Callaghan.
WS 1003 – Patrick Ahern.
WS 1030 – John Joseph Hogan.
WS 859 – Laurence Condon.

pp132-133 Extracts quoted from the inquest of Private Jones's death were obtained on website: www.cairogang.com, from 9th September 1919 *Irish Independent*.

p133 Blackwater Sub Aqua Club recovered pocket watches from the river near Fermoy Bridge in 2009. Ref: blackwatersubaqua.ie.

p134 '*Mairfidh a chlú*' literally translated from Gaelic is 'his reputation will survive'.

p134 The quotation is from a speech delivered by John Redmond to a group of 500 Irish Volunteers at Woodenbridge, County Wicklow on Sunday 20th September 1914 as reported in the *Irish Independent* on 21st September 1914.

pp136-142 Accounts of General Lucas's capture, its repercussions and his escape are from newspaper reports: *The Irish Times* – Monday 28th June, 29th June, 30th June and 31st July 1920; also from the *Clare Courier* as found on www.clarecaurier.ie.

p136 Balfour's quotation: 'they would not permit justice...' was found in Michael Biggs Oslo paper, referenced to Costello 1995, p165.

p139 Witness statements taken from the BMH:
WS 388 – Joseph Good.
WS 845 – Tom Malone (alias Sean Forde).

p141 Witness statement taken from the Bureau of Military History:
WS 656 – Richard O'Connell.

p142 Lucas's statement that he was treated 'as a gentleman by gentlemen' was widely reported; it was a view he maintained despite the possibility of his being court-martialled.

Chapter Nine **It's a Long Way to go**

p145 Witness statements taken from the BMH:
WS 1030 – John Hogan.
WS 1003 – Patrick Ahern.

p145 A 'decade' is a group of ten beads that form part of a rosary, used by Catholics to assist in prayer.

p145 An account of the hunger strikes in Mountjoy Gaol can be found on website nla.gov.au/nlanews – *The Mercury*, Hobart Tasmania reported on Wednesday 14th April 1920 and Monday 19th April 1920.

p146 The House of Commons debate is recorded in Hansard: HC Deb 19th October 1920 volume 133 cc 769–71. Hamar Greenwood's statement that 'There was evidence of the most decisive nature against this man' is contained within this.

p147 The graves of Liam Lynch and Michael Fitzgerald were in Kilcrumper Old Cemetery. I still don't know how I missed finding them.

p148 Information on Kilworth rifle range is on website:fermoyireland.50megs.com/KilworthRifleRange.htm.

pp155-158 Witness statement taken from the Bureau of Military History (BMH): WS 783 – Thomas Ryan.

p158 Croke Park information is at www.crokepark.ie – Famous Matches: Bloody Sunday 1920. Also at www.gaelicweb.com/irishampost: Irish American Post – September 2002/Vol3. Issue 3: An Eyewitness Account, Croke Park, 1920. Another Bloody Sunday Brings Back More Terrible Memories by Elaine Larkin – Phat Traffic International Features Agency: An excerpt from Fr Diarmuid Ó Péicín CI's private archive of tape-recorded interviews with Frank Burke in the late 1960s and early 1970s.

Chapter Ten Tipperary Tribulations

p160 The Galtee Mountain Boy was Paddy Davern who survived both the War of Independence and the Irish Civil War. Little seems to have been recorded about Patsy Halloran who wrote the song. The folk singer Christy Moore added a fourth verse.

p163 The extract from de Valera's letter of 30th August 1921 to Lloyd George; 'ready at once to appoint plenipotentiaries' was taken from website: www.ucc.ie/celt/online – Official Correspondence relating to the Peace Negotiations, June–September, 1921 (p17).

p163 Extract from Lloyd George's letter of 7th September 1921 to de Valera: 'You will agree that this correspondence has lasted long enough' – Ibid (p18).

p164 Extract from letter sent from Liam Lynch to his brother Tom on 26th September 1921:'You may rest assured that our Government as well as the army is out for the Republic and nothing less' from website: www.nli.ie – National Library of Ireland – Collection List No. 109 – Letters of Liam Lynch (1917, 1920–1923) (MS 36,251/20) (Accession No. 5760).

pp164-165 Information from website: research.dho.ie – Research at the Digital Humanities – documents on Irish Foreign Policy – The Anglo-Irish Treaty. December 1920–December 1921.

p165 The IRB's statement: 'Members of the organisation...' from *Irish political documents, 1916–1949*, by Arthur Mitchell and Pádraig Ó Snodaigh: National Library of Ireland, MS.17, 525 (2) McGarrity Papers.

p165 Extract from letter sent from Liam Lynch to his brother Tom on 12th January 1922: 'My attitude is now as always...' from website: www.nli.ie – National Library of Ireland – Collection List No. 109 – Letters of Liam Lynch (1917, 1920–1923) (MS 36,251/20) (Accession No. 5760).

p167 The Irish language is not Gaelic (the Irish refer to it as Irish but others generally refer to it as Gaelic). Irish is stated as one of the 24 languages of the member states of the EU.

p168 Extract from letter sent from Liam Lynch to his brother Tom on 16th January 1922: 'You can rest satisfied...' from website: www.nli.ie – National Library of Ireland – Collection List No. 109.

p168 Extract from letter sent from Liam Lynch to his brother Tom on 6th March 1922: 'If we can force...' Ibid.

pp170-171 Accounts of the death of Liam Lynch were also researched from reports given in *The Irish Times* on 11th April 1923.

p171 Liam Lynch: 'My God I'm hit, lads' from *No Other Law* by Florence O'Donoghue, p305.

p173 I couldn't find a translation from Irish for 'jennet and realthan' but assume it was a donkey and cart.

p173 Frank Aiken's instruction to 'dump their arms' taken from website: www.theirishstory.com : *Frank Aiken: Nationalist and Internationalist.*

Chapter Eleven Sally Power's Honey Meadow

p176 Information on Edmund Power from website: archives.rootsweb.ancestry.com and blog posted by Janet Crawford on Friday 2nd May 2008.

p180 'happiness consists...' Quotation reference is from website: http://www.brainyquote.com/quotes/quotes/m/marguerite381598.html, by Marguerite Gardiner. (n.d.), Retrieved 14th May 2015.

Chapter Twelve Folk of the East Munster Way

p182 Thomas MacDonagh was executed for his part in the Easter Rising at the age of 38.

p183 The quotation: 'talking through her fanny' from website: www.todayfm.com 'David Norris Accuses Meath TD of 'Talking Through Her Fanny' – by Aingeala Flannery, 15th July 2013.

p184 Rhododendrons: article from *Irish Daily Mail*, Wednesday 2nd July 2014: 'National park under threat from invasive rhododendron', by Anne Lucey.

p185 Quotation: 'no objections had been lodged...' from: oireachtasdebates. oireachtas.ie Houses of the Oireachtas (Amendment) Regulations 2013: Motion (Continued).

p186 Salmon information from website: adventure.howstuffworks.com. 'How the salmon spawn works' by Chris Marlowe.

p186 The Old Bridge at Carrick from website: www.buildingsofireland.ie. – National Inventory of Architectural Heritage.

pp191-192 A good account of The Clancy Brothers and Tommy Makem's rise to fame in America is at website: irishamerica.com. – The History of the Clancy Brothers/Irish America, by Tom Deignan, contributor, April/May 2009.

p193 Tom Butler, Elizabeth's 'Black Husband' is by Valerie Christie, from website: www.theanneboleynfiles.com

Chapter Thirteen **The South Leinster Way**

p195 J.K. Casey (1846–1890) was a Fenian from Mullinger.

p197 Website: www.kilkennypeople.ie gives some interesting history about Tybroughney: 'Tybroughney Castle – Bastion of Romans and saints and now restored by Dowleys'. Unfortunately I did not have time to explore the castle.

p197 St Modomnoc information was taken from website: www.irishcultureandcustoms.com, featuring an article: 'The Bees Who would not be left Behind', by Bridget Haggerty.

p199 Bee information from website: pollinators.biodiversityireland.ie; a paper by U. Fitzpatrick, T.E. Murray, R.J. Paxton & M.J.F. Brown (2006), titled: The State of Ireland's Bees. Also from: www.ycbk.org/beetrivia.html. Honey Bee Trivia – York County Beekeepers' Association, and from www.soilassociation.org. Soil Association – Keep Britain Buzzing.

p201 Lumberjacks information from website: Careercast.com. 'The worst jobs of 2015: No. 199 Lumberjack/Careercast'. Also from website: Listverse.com. 'Top 10 Most Fatal Occupations – Listverse.

pp201-202 Irish Forests from website: www.agriculture.gov.ie. 'Irish Forests – A Brief History – Department of Agriculture, food and the Marine' produced by Forestry Service, Department of Agriculture, Fisheries and Food, 2008. Also website: www.forestry.ie. Directory & Portal – 'Irish Forest & Timber Industry', link to 'Information', then link to 'Facts and Figures'.

p205 Quotation: 'the morning star of liberty to Ireland', taken from website: www.libraryireland.com. – *A History of Ireland and Her People*, by Eleanor Hull – Volume 2. Chap. XV – 'Revolution and Rebellion'.

p205 Quotation: 'In my anger I made something like a vow…' from: *The life of Theobald Tone*, by himself, p27.

p210 Peg Washington's Lane, being: 'the width of herself' was supplied to me by the Graiguenamanagh Historical Society. According to website: commons.wikimedia. org it is: '…really only a passage and there is probably a narrower one in places such as Staithes in Yorkshire'.

p211 Information on the abductions from website: www.naomiclifford.com, 16th October 2013: 'Glimpses of Life, Love and Death in the Georgian era', taken from John Edward Walsh, *Ireland Sixty Years Ago*, by James Mglashan, 1847.

p212 Henry Hammond is featured on website: www.irishidentity.com – The Heroic Blacksmiths of 1798.

p213 Quotation: 'louder and more peremptory in their demands' from *General Thomas Cloney – Wexford Rebel of 1798*, by John Joyce, p6.

p215 Information on Anthony Perry from website: www.byrneperry.com.

p220 Quotation: 'being a General, Colonel, Major, or Captain in the rebel army' Ibid, p38.

P220 Quotation: 'for being present at the murder of John Gill...' Ibid: p38.

Chapter Fourteen **The Gate of Tears**

p223 John O'Hagan, born in Newry, County Down (1822–1890) was a lawyer, writer and Young Irelander.

p227 William Deane Butler information from website: www.dia.ie. – Dictionary of Irish Architects 1720–1940, from the Irish Architectural Archive 2015.

pp230-236 Good overviews of the famine period can be found on websites: www.irishhistorian.com – Timeline of the Irish Famine, and website: www.deskeenan.com – Des Keenan's Books on Irish History (online version): Chapter Nineteen – The Famine Years II and Chapter twenty – Lord John Russell; these cover the period from June 1846 to December 1850.

p232 The Corn Laws from website: www.britainexpress.com – The Corn Laws in Victorian England.

p234 Workhouses from website: irishworkhousecentrc.ie/the- workhouse-story. The Workhouse Story: The Irish Workhouse – An Overview, taken from: *The Workhouses of Ireland*, by John O'Connor.

Chapter Fifteen **The Wicklow Way to America**

p237 John F. Poole was born in Gloucester, Massachusetts in 1856. The song was performed by Tony Pastor, a vaudeville and variety show performer who was born in Manhattan in 1832. (Information from website: 'Exploring the Irish in America through Found Poetry' herb.ashp.cuny.edu/items/show/1632.)

p238 Shillelagh information from website: www.irishcultureandcustoms.com – 'Shillelagh Blackthorn Walking Sticks', by Bridget Haggerty.

p239 Faction fighting from website: www.museum.ie – 19th Century Faction Fighting – National Museum of Ireland.

p239 The discussion on the erection of pylons from website: www.eirgridprojects.com – 'Grid Link Project', and website: www.thejournal.ie – Phil Prendergast: '8 reasons why pylons should not go ahead', January 2014.

p244 www.rootsweb.ancestry.com: 'Cambro Norman Invasion of Ireland' records that Phillipe Le Hore (Wexford) came over to Ireland with Strongbow.

p247 There is some interesting snippets of information about Tinahely on website: www.boards.ie – Tinahely History – boards.ie.

p248 The campaign to keep the local studies section of the library open attracted 886 supporters over the following weeks and it reopened on 6th January 2015.

Chapter Sixteen **The Rocky Road to Dublin**

p249 D.K. Gavan (sometimes known as the Galway poet) is credited with writing the song 'The Rocky Road to Dublin' for Harry Clifton, a music hall singer and songwriter, who popularised the song.

p249 Much useful information was gleaned from *The Wicklow Way Guide Book*, published 1995 by EastWest Mapping of Ballyredmond, Clonegal.

p255 Glenmalure information from: www.heritagecouncil.ie – Exploring the mineral heritage of County Wicklow.

p258 'Ireland in the Golden Age' information was taken from www.museum.ie.

p258 Website: www.glendalough.connect.ie – Monastic Chapters –1 proffered much useful information concerning the legends of St Kevin.

p261 Details of the French plane crash on Djouce Mountain taken from Wicklowway.com, www.billnelson.ie and from djouce-boards.ie www.boards.ie – Pat O'Brien (posted by Barry D, EastWest Mapping); a book: *When Our Plane Hit the Mountain* has also been written by Suzanne Barnes, published 2005 by New Island.

p266 An article about leprechauns – 'Leprechauns: Facts about the Irish Trickster Fairy', by Benjamin Radford can be found on website: www.livescience.com.

p266 Reference: *The Men Who Eat Ringforts*, an article by Tony Lowes was found on www.friendsoftheirishenvironment.org.

p266 The story recorded by Thomas Johnson Westropp was taken from *A Folklore Survey of County Clare* and was found on website www.clarelibrary.ie –'Fairies and Fairy Forts and Mounds'.

p267 Part of Marlay Park was closed because The Kings of Leon were due to appear there three days later.

p268 In 1978 taxi drivers won a court case to restrict their numbers; this was good for the taxi drivers but not so good for customers. During the period of the 'Celtic Tiger' an increased taxi demand could not be met. Taxi plates changed hands for amazing sums of money, many drivers borrowing to pay for the plates. Plates were also rented or passed within families.

In 1998 a Competition Authority report demanded changes, and in 2000 a law was passed that made taxi licences available to anyone who could drive, had a roadworthy vehicle and could rustle up 5,000 euros. There was outrage and protests from the cabbies. Some existing taxi drivers saw their investment disappear overnight and there were suicides and marriage break-ups as a result. The desired effect was however achieved in that during the next decade national taxi numbers increased five fold. But solving the supply problem caused many other problems: there have been reports that taxi drivers with criminal records have been violent and abusive to passengers; part-time drivers flood the market at weekends, forcing regular drivers to work excessively dangerous hours to make a living; there are not enough legal parking spaces for taxis and many of Dublin's 13,500 taxis are actually illegal.

The above information was sourced from website: www.irishexaminer.com – 'Political push behind deregulation' by Scott Millar.

p271 The *Jeanie Johnson* information was found on website: www.jeaniejohnson.ie.

Notes and References

Chapter Seventeen Raise a Glass

p274 The fact that Ernest Hemmingway's favourite drink was a dry martini and not a mojito was taken from website: www.foodrepublic.com – '7 Things you didn't know about Ernest Hemmingway's drinking'.

p275 The Behan family's and the IRA's bombing campaign in Birmingham and Liverpool was taken from website: www.academia.edu – 'Fear and Loathing in Liverpool: Popular Reaction to the IRA's 1939 Bombing Campaign in Liverpool', by Phil Scraton, and from *Brendan Behan*, by Ulick O'Connor.

p275 Information on Brendan Behan's life was taken from website: www.ricorso.net – 'Brendan Behan 1923–64'.

p275 Behan's quotation: '...a drinker with a writing problem' was taken from website: www.brainyquote.com.

p276 The quotation: 'That book will go around the world' was reported during an interview with Donleavy published in *The Independent* on Thursday 5th August 2010, found on website: www.independent.co.uk 'A Singular Man: J.P. Donleavy on his fascinating life since The Ginger Man'.

p277 There is some interesting articles about Donleavy's present and past life on websites: tmagazine.blogs.nytimes.com/2014/03/07 – 'J.P. Donleavy is Still Standing' and www.theguardian.com – 'Profile: James Patrick Donleavy'.

p278 The tribulations concerning the publication of *The Dubliners* were found on website: mentalfloss.com.

p278 Information on the publication of *Ulysses* was also from website: mentalfloss. com – 'The Long and Difficult Publication History of James Joyce's Dubliners'.

p279 The interplay between Leopold Bloom and Gerty MacDowell is described on website: sparknotes.com – 'Ulysses – Episode thirteen 'Nausicaa'.

p279 The James Joyce Centre informed me that *Ulysses* was never banned in Ireland, and that Lilliput Press first published it there.

p280 McDaids information drawn from website: www.chibarproject.com – 'The Chicago Bar Project'.

pp280-287 Good summaries of the history of Guinness are to be seen on websites: www.heavemedia.com – 'The man who Invented beer: All about Guinness, by Adam Cowden, and on www.guinness-storehouse.com/en/History.aspx.

p283 A useful Guinness website is: www.craftbrewingbusiness.com – 'What's the difference between porter and stout?' by Keith Gribbins.

p285 Website: bompasandparr.com/projects/view/the-guinness-tasting-rooms, gives a good flavour of what can be expected from a visit to the Guinness tasting rooms.

p285 The six steps to pour the perfect pint of Guinness can be found on website: www.guinness-storehouse, pdf No. 11. 'Political push behind deregulation' by Scott Millar.

Bibliographical Sources

Aubrey, John, *Brief Lives Vol. 2 – A Brief Life of William Petty, 1623–87*, The Clarendon Press, 1898.

Ballyn, Sue, *Lives in Migration: Rupture and Continuity – The British Invasion of Australia. Convicts: Exile and Dislocation*, Australian Studies Centre Publications, 2010.

Barnard, T.C., *Sir William Petty as Kerry Ironmaster*, Royal Irish Academy, 1982.

Bartlett, Thomas, Dawson, Kevin & Keogh, Dáire *Rebellion: A Television History of 1798*, Gill & Macmillan, 1998.

Barton, Brian, *From behind a closed door: Secret Court Martial Records of the Easter Rising*, Blackstaff Press Ltd, 2002.

Bateson, Charles, *The Convict ships, 1787-1868*. Brown, Son & Ferguson, 1985.

Behan, Brendon, *Borstal Boy*, Hutchinson and Co. Ltd, 1958.

Biggs, Michael, *Hunger Strikes by Irish Republicans 1916-1922*, Workshop on Techniques of Violence in Civil War, Centre for the study of civil war, Oslo, August 2004.

Borgonovo, John, *The Battle for Cork, July-August 1922*, Mercier Press, 2011.

Bourke, Edward J, *The Guinness Story*, The O'Brien Press Ltd, 2009.

Bowker, Gordan, *James Joyce*, Phoenix, 2012.

Butler, Charles, *Easy Introduction to Mathematics, Volume 1*, Bartlett and Newman, 1814.

Byrne, Seán, *A Report for the Health Service Executive Costs to Society of Problem Alcohol Use in Ireland*, Health Service Executive, Kildare, 2010.

Carr, Sir John, *The Stranger in Ireland*, 1806

Carrol, Aiden, *Seán Moylan, Rebel Leader*, Mercier Press, 2010.

Carroll, Francis M, *American Opinion and the Irish Question 1910-23*, St Martin's Press, Inc, 1978.

Chamberlain, Austen, *The Austen Chamberlain Diary letters: The Correspondence of Sir Austen Chamberlain with his Sisters Hilda and Ida*, Cambridge University Press, 1995.

Clancy, Liam, *Memoirs of an Irish troubadour*, Virgin Book Ltd, 2002.

Cloney, Thomas, *A Personal Narrative of Those Transactions in the County Wexford, in which the Author was engaged in the awful period of 1798*, Printed for the author by James M Mullen, 1832.

Bibliographical Sources

Collins, Kenneth J (ed) & Tyson, John H, *Conversion in the Weslian Tradition*, Abingdon Press, 2001.

Coogan, Tim Pat, *De Valera Long Fellow, Long Shadow*, Hutchinson, 1993.

Coogan, Tim Pat, *Michael Collins*. Hutchinson, 1990.

Coogan, Tim Pat, *Ireland in the Twentieth Century*, Arrow Books, 2004.

Cottrell, Peter, *The Anglo-Irish War, The Troubles of 1913-1922*, Oxford: Osprey Publications, 2006.

Cottrell, Peter, *The Irish Civil War, 1922-23*, Osprey Publications, 2008.

Crofton, Ian (ed), *Turncoats and Traitors*, Quercus books, 2009.

Cronin, Jim, *A Millstreet Miscellany, Millstreet's Green and Gold*, Aubane Historical Society, 1984.

Crosby, Travis L, *The Unknown Lloyd George: A Statesman in Conflict*, I.B. Tauris, 2014.

Cross, Colin, *The Fall of the British Empire, 1918-1968*, Hodder & Stoughton, 1968.

Curtis, Edmund, *A History of Ireland from earliest Times to 1922*, Methuen and Co Ltd, 1936.

Cusack, Margaret Anne, *An Illustrated History of Ireland*, Longmans, Green and Company, 1868.

Dickson, Charles, *The Wexford Rising of 1798: Its Causes and its Course*, The Kerryman Ltd, 1955.

Dillon, Paddy, *The Irish Coast to Coast Walk*, Cicerone, 1996.

Dixon Hardy P. A, *Guide to Killarney and Glengariff*, Dublin Penny Journal, 1834.

Dorney, John, *Peace After the Final Battle*, New Island Books, 2014.

Dunn, *A Description of Killarney, 1776*, Printed for J. Dodsley, 1776.

Eagar, Lieutenant Colonel Edward Frank. F, *The Eagar Family*, Aylesbury and Slough: Privately printed by Hazell Watson and Viney, 1958.

Eagar, Frederick John, *A genealogical history of the Eagar Family, and their maternal connections in the county of Kerry*, Dublin, 1861.

Elliott, Marianne, *Wolfe Tone Prophet of Irish Independence*, Yale University Press, 1989.

Fanning, Ronan, *Fatal Path*, Faber and Faber, 2013.

Fieldman, Paula R (ed), *British Women Poets of the Romantic Era: An Anthology*, JHU Press, 2000.

Forristal, D., *Irish Martyr, Jesuit Brother, 1566-1602*, Messenger Publications, 2002.

Foster, Allen, *Fosters Irish Oddities*, New Island Books, 2006.

Foster, R.F, *Modern Ireland 1600-1972*, Penguin, 1988.

Gahon, Daniel J, *The Peoples Rising: The Great Wexford Rebellion of 1798*, Gill & Macmillan, 1995.

Gahon, Daniel J, *Rebellion! Ireland in 1798*, The O'Brien Press Ltd, 1997.

Gibbons, Verna Hale, *Jack Judge, The Tipperary Man: A Biography*, Sandwell Community Library Service, 1998.

Guinness, Patrick, *Arthur's Round*, Peter Owen, 2008.

Hague, William, *William Pitt The Younger*, Harper Collins, 2004.

Harris, Robert, *Can't Be Arsed: 101 Things NOT to Do Before You Die*, Anova Books, 2008.

Harris, Tim, *Restoration: Charles II and His kingdoms 1660–1685*, Allen Lane, an imprint of Penguin books, 2005.

Howard, John, *A State of Prisons in Britain 1775-1905*, Routledge/Thoemmes, 2000.

Hughes, Robert, *The Fatal Shore*, Collins Harvell, 1987

Hull, Eleanor, *A History of Ireland and Her People*, The Phoenix Publishing company Ltd, 1926.

Jeffares, Alexander Norman, and Bolger, Muriel, *A Short History of Ireland's Writers*, O'Brien Press Ltd, 2014.

Jordan, Thomas E, *A Copper Farthing, Sir William Petty and his Times, 1623-1687*, The University of Sunderland Press, 2007.

Joyce, John, *Graiguenamanagh: A Varied Heritage*, Graiguenamanagh Historical Society, 2009.

Joyce, John, *General Thomas Cloney: Wexford Rebel of 1798*, Geography Publications, 1988.

Joyce, P.W, *A Concise History of Ireland*, Longmans, Green and Co, 1903.

Judd, Denis, *The Life and Times of George V*, George Weiden-Field and Nicolson Ltd, 1973.

Keating, Geoffrey, *The History of Ireland*, Translated into English by Edward Comyn and Patrick S Dinnen; published by the Ex-classics Project, 2009.

Kelly, John, *The Graves are Walking, The History of the Great Irish Famine*, Henry Holt & Company, LLC, 2012.

Laycock, Stuart, *All the Countries We've Ever Invaded*, The History Press, 2012.

Leeson, David, *The Black and Tans: British Police in the First Irish War, 1920-21*, McMaster University, 2003

Macilwee, Michael, *The Liverpool Underworld – Crime in the City 1750-1900*, Liverpool University Press, 2011.

Madden, Richard Robert, *The Literary Life and Correspondence of the Countess of Blessington*, T.C. Newby, 1855.

McBride, Ian, *History and Memory in Ireland*, Cambridge University Press, 2001.

McCarthy, Cal, *Cumann Na mBan and the Irish Revolution*, The Collins Press, 2007.

McCarthy, John, *A Ghost Upon Your Path*, Bantam Press, 2002.

McCavitt, Dr John, *The Flight of the Earls*, Gill and Macmillan, 2002.

McCracken, Eileen, *Charcoal-burning Ironworks in Seventeenth and Eighteenth Century Ireland*, Ulster Archaeological Society, 1957.

Bibliographical Sources

McDougall, Walter A, *Let the Sea Make a Noise: A History of the North Pacific from Magellan to MacArthur*, Harper Perennial, 1993.

McGuffin, John, *Internment*, Anvil Books Ltd, 1973.

McLachlan, N.D, *Edward Eagar (1787-1866), Australian Dictionary of Biography*, Melbourne University Press, 1966.

Mitchell Arthur and Ó Snodaigh Pádraigh, *Irish political documents, 1916-1949*, Irish Academic Press, 1985.

Murphy, Seán J, *Studies in Irish Genealogy and Heraldry: The Gardiner Family, Dublin, and Mountjoy, County Tyrone*, Centre for Irish Genealogy and Heraldry, 2010.

Murphy, William, *Political Imprisonment and the Irish 1912-1921*, Oxford University Press, 2014.

O'Carroll, Gerald (ed) *Mr Justice Day: The Diaries and the Addresses to Grand Juries (1793-1829)*, Polymaths Press, 2004.

O'Conhubhair, Brian (ed), *Rebel Cork's Fighting Story 1916-21*, Mercier Press, 2009.

O'Connor, Ulick, *Brendan Behan*, H. Hamilton, 1970.

O'Donoghue, Florence, *No Other Law*, Irish Press, 1954.

O'Farrell, John, *An Utterly Impartial History of Britain*, Doubleday, 2007.

O'Ferrall, Fergus, *Daniel O'Connell*, Gill & Macmillan, 1981.

Ó'Gráda, Cormac, *The Great Irish Famine*, Cambridge University Press, 1995.

Oman, Charles, *History of England*, Henry Holt, 1900.

Orejan, Jaime, *The History of Gaelic Football and the Gaelic Athletic Association*, The Sport Management and Related Topics Journal, Volume 2, Issue 2, 2006.

Orpen, G.H, *The Orpen Family*, Privately printed, 1930.

Pakenam, Thomas, *The Year of Liberty, The Great Irish Rebellion of 1798*, Weidenfield & Nicolson, 1997.

Prendergast, John, *The Cromwellian Settlement of Ireland*, Longman, Green, Longman, Roberts and Green, 1865.

Prendergast, Phil, *8 reasons why pylons should not go ahead*, The Journal. i.e. 2014

Read, Charles A (ed), *The Cabinet of Irish Literature: Selections from the Works of the Chief Poets, Orators, and prose writers in Ireland*, Nubu Press, 2010.

Read, Stuart, *Armies of the Irish Rebellion 1798*, Osprey Publishing, 2013.

Reece, Bob (ed), *Exiles from Erin*, Macmillan Academic and Professional Ltd, 1991.

Rees, Jim, *Surplus People, from Wicklow to Canada*, Collins Press, 2014.

Rees, Jim, A *Farewell to Famine*, Dee-Jay Publications, 1994.

Rigge, Simon, *The British Empire No 58: Ireland The Tortured Colony*, Time-Life International, 1973.

Ryan, Meda, *The Real Chief*, Mercier Press, 1986.

Ryle Dwyer, Thomas, *De Valera*, Poolbeg Press, 1991.

Ryle Dwyer, Thomas, *Tans, Terrors and Troubles, Kerry's Real Fighting Story, 1913-21*, Mercier Press, 2001.

Sadlier, Michael, *Blessington d' Orsay*, Constable & Co, 1933.

Schmuhl, Robert, *All Changed, changed utterly: Easter 1916 and America*, UCD Sholarcast, Series 6. The UCD/Notre Dame Lectures, 2012.

Sheenan, William, *British Voices: From the Irish War of Independence*, The Collins Press, 2005.

Smith, Charles, *The Ancient and Present State of Kerry*, published by W. Cater, J Robson, T Payne, Dr Wilson, G. Nicol, T. Evans (and 4 others), 1774.

Smith E.A, *Whig Principles in Party Politics, Earl Fitzwilliam and the Whig Party, 1748-1833*, Manchester University Press, 1975.

Smith, G.N., *Killarney and Surrounding Scenery: Being a Complete Itinerary of the Lakes*, Johnson & Deas, 1822.

Smith, Kevin Lewis, *Colonial Litigant Extraordinaire*, K.L. Smith, 1996.

Smyth, Jim (ed), *Revolution, Counter-revolution and Union: Ireland in the 1790s*, Cambridge University Press, 2000.

Sullivan, C.W, *Reconsidering the convict ships*, New Hibernia Review/Iris Éireannach Nua. Vol. 12, No. 4, University of St Thomas (Centre for Irish Studies), 2008.

Taylor, A.J.P, *English History, 1914-1945*, Oxford University Press, 1965.

Temple, Sir John, *The Irish Rebellion*, John Temple, 1641.

Tone, Theobald Wolfe, *The life of Theobald Tone*, Edited by William Theobald Wolfe Tone, Whittaker, Treacher and Arnot, 1831.

Walsh, Paul V, *Irish Civil War 1922-1923, A Military Study of The Conventional Phase, 28 June- 11 August, 1922*, A paper delivered to NYMAS at the CUNY Graduate Center, New York, NY on 11th December 1998.

Ward, John, *The Lives of the Professors of Gresham College*, John Moore, 1740

Westropp, Thomas Johnson, *Folklore of Clare: A folklore survey of County Clare and County Clare folk-tales and myths*, Clasp Press, 2000.

Wood, Herbert, *Sir William Petty and his Kerry Estate*, Royal Society of Antiquaries of Ireland: The Seventh Series, Vol. 4, No.1, June 1934.

Woodham-Smith, Cecil, *The Great Hunger*, Hamish Hamilton Ltd, 1962.

Yeadon, David, *At the Edge of Ireland*, Harper Perennial, 2009.

Yenne, Bill, *The 200-Year quest for the Perfect Pint*, John Wiley & Sons, 2007.

Index

Appendix
Journey Record

Sunday 16th June – Dursey Island to Allihies

Walking				Cycling	
On Route		Off Route			
Miles	Km	Miles	Km	Miles	Km
11.0	17.7	5.5	8.8	6.0	9.7

Monday 17th June – Allihies to Eyeries

Walking				Cycling	
On Route		Off Route			
Miles	Km	Miles	Km	Miles	Km
10.0	16.1	0	0	11.0	17.7

Tuesday 18th June – Eyeries to Lauragh

Walking				Cycling	
On Route		Off Route			
Miles	Km	Miles	Km	Miles	Km
16.5	26.5	0.5	0.8	13.2	21.2

Wednesday 19th June – Lauragh to Kenmare

Walking				Cycling	
On Route		Off Route			
Miles	Km	Miles	Km	Miles	Km
15.5	24.9	1.0	1.6	16	25.7

Saturday June 22nd – Afternoon – Killarney

Walking			
On Route		Off Route	
Miles	Km	Miles	Km
0	0	7.5	12.1

Sunday June 23rd – Kenmare to Muckross (campsite)

Walking			
On Route		Off Route	
Miles	Km	Miles	Km
12.7	20.5	8.8	14.2

Tuesday June 25th – Muckross (campsite) to Guitane Lough to Shrone (and Rathmore)

Walking			
On Route		Off Route	
Miles	Km	Miles	Km
14.0	22.5	6.0	9.7

Wednesday June 26th – Rathmore to Millstreet

Walking			
On Route		Off Route	
Miles	Km	Miles	Km
12.5	20.1	10.0	16.1

Friday June 28th – Millstreet to Boggeragh

Walking				Cycling	
On Route		Off Route			
Miles	Km	Miles	Km	Miles	Km
17.4	28.0	6.8	10.9	8	12.9

Saturday June 29th – Boggeragh to Ballynamona

Walking				Cycling	
On Route		Off Route		Lost and Not lost	
Miles	Km	Miles	Km	Miles	Km
19.3	31.0	10.5	16.9	24.5	39.4

Monday July 1st – Ballynamona to Killavullen

Walking				Cycling	
On Route		Off Route			
Miles	Km	Miles	Km	Miles	Km
10.6	17.1	1.5	2.4	5.0	8.0

Tuesday July 2nd – Killavullen to Fermoy

Walking				Cycling	
On Route		Off Route			
Miles	Km	Miles	Km	Miles	Km
16.0	25.7	0	0	13.2	21.2

Thursday July 4th – Fermoy to Araglin

Walking				Cycling	
On Route		Off Route			
Miles	Km	Miles	Km	Miles	Km
17.0	27.4	2.3	3.7	10.5	16.9

Friday July 5th – Araglin to Clogheen

Walking				Cycling	
On Route		Off Route			
Miles	Km	Miles	Km	Miles	Km
12.5	20.1	3.1	5.0	17.5	28.2

Saturday July 6th – Clogheen to Newcastle

Walking				Cycling	
On Route		Off Route			
Miles	Km	Miles	Km	Miles	Km
13.5	21.7	2.8	4.5	10.7	17.2

Sunday July 7th – Newcastle to Clonmel

Walking				Cycling	
On Route		Off Route			
Miles	Km	Miles	Km	Miles	Km
13.0	20.9	1.3	2.1	11.5	18.5

Monday June 16th – the following year – Clonmel to Carrick-on-Suir

Walking			
On Route		Off Route	
Miles	Km	Miles	Km
18.5	30.0	2.0	3.2

Wednesday June 18th – Carrick-on-Suir to Mullinavat

Walking			
On Route		Off Route	
Miles	Km	Miles	Km
14.3	23.0	4.0	6.4

Thursday June 19th – Mullinavat to Mount Alto

Walking				Cycling	
On Route		Off Route			
Miles	Km	Miles	Km	Miles	Km
14.8	23.8	6.8	10.9	5.9	9.5

Friday June 20th – Mount Alto to Graiguenamanagh

Walking				Cycling			
On Route		Off Route		Not Lost		Lost	
Miles	Km	Miles	Km	Miles	Km	Miles	Km
13.8	22.2	0	0	6.7	10.8	7.5	12.0

Sunday June 22nd – Graiguenamanagh to Tomduff

Walking				Cycling	
On Route		Off Route			
Miles	Km	Miles	Km	Miles	Km
12.0	19.0	0.2	0.4	15.5	24.8

Monday June 23rd – Tomduff to Kildavin

Walking				Cycling	
On Route		Off Route			
Miles	Km	Miles	Km	Miles	Km
8.8	14.2	0.5	0.8	9.0	14.5

Tuesday June 24th – Kildavin to Shillelagh

Walking				Cycling	
On Route		Off Route			
Miles	Km	Miles	Km	Miles	Km
13.7	22.0	4.5	7.2	15.0	24.2

Wednesday June 25th – Shillelagh to Tinahely

Walking				Cycling	
On Route		Off Route			
Miles	Km	Miles	Km	Miles	Km
10.0	16.1	3.5	5.6	5.2	8.4

Friday June 27th – Tinahely to Iron Bridge

Walking				Cycling	
On Route		Off Route			
Miles	Km	Miles	Km	Miles	Km
12.4	20.0	1.5	2.4	10.8	17.4

Saturday June 28th – Iron Bridge to Drumgoff

Walking				Cycling	
On Route		Off Route			
Miles	Km	Miles	Km	Miles	Km
10.0	16.0	1.5	2.4	6.0	9.6

Sunday June 29th – Drumgoff to Roundwood

Walking				Cycling	
On Route		Off Route			
Miles	Km	Miles	Km	Miles	Km
16.8	27.0	4.9	7.9	11.2	18.1

Monday June 30th – Roundwood to Glencree

Walking			
On Route		Off Route	
Miles	Km	Miles	Km
10.6	17.0	8.8	14.2

Tuesday July 1st – Glencree to Dublin

Walking			
On Route		Off Route	
Miles	Km	Miles	Km
18.6	29.9	5.1	8.2

Wednesday July 2nd – St. Stephen's Green to the sea

Walking			
On Route		Off Route	
Miles	Km	Miles	Km
2.1	3.4	1.0	1.6